EXPAT EVERTONIAN

The diary of a football fan working abroad

CLIFF GREEN
EXPAT EVERTONIAN
The diary of a football fan working abroad

First published in Great Britain in 2012 by The Derby Books Publishing Company Limited, 3 The Parker Centre, Derby, DE21 4SZ.

ISBN 978-1-78091-012-3
Printed and bound by CPI Antony Rowe, Chippenham

Contents

PART 1
World Service
Wilderness

Chapter 1
My world restored

9 September 1989: Everton 3 Manchester United 2

Douglas Wakiihuri. Not a name that trips off the tongue and a name unfamiliar to me before 23 April 1989 and pretty much forgotten from that day forth. If any of you readers know who he is, then you must be a blinding pain in the arse at the local pub quizzes. Douglas actually won the London marathon on that Sunday morning in spring 22 years ago. As to what happened to the rest of his career, I have little knowledge. His feat resonated with me at the time though, because it followed the day when I made a decision that was to literally change the whole direction of the rest of my life. Early on that Saturday, I had received a phone call from the unfortunately named Ralph Diaper, headmaster of a school in Kenya, offering me a post as a teacher of mathematics in a secondary school situated in the north of Nairobi. I had somewhat plumped for the location in a similar way to how the fictional character, Dr Garrigan in *The Last King of Scotland* had chosen Uganda to practise medicine by spinning the globe in his bedroom and jamming his finger against it; his digit determining that his destination would be the tiny landlocked country cushioned against Lake Victoria; a country that I was also to become very familiar with in the not too distant future. For me, all those years ago in my late 20s, I didn't use a spinning globe as my life's roulette wheel but rather the *Times Educational Supplement*. For those not familiar with the education profession, I should explain that this is the teachers' bible that provides a directory of job vacancies on a weekly basis. Before the days of the internet version, thousands of disillusioned or desperate teachers could be found scouring the pages of this publication every Friday looking for that dream job in an exotic location with an exotic salary, where unruly children have been outlawed and job satisfaction is a guarantee.

Despite having landed a dream job already in Shrewsbury Sixth Form College as my first full-time classroom assignment, I was young, single and not quite prepared to disappear into a vortex of self-satisfaction and comfort in 'The Graveyard of Ambition' as Shrewsbury is affectionately known. I figured, though, that the only way was down if I sought another post within the UK, so my fingers began their random path through the *TES* stopping at every overseas post that I was remotely qualified for. I had interviews for teaching appointments in the Middle East, Hong Kong and New York, all of which failed to convert into a contract and I had too many rejections and plain silence in response to other applications, for me to list here. By the time Braeburn High School came up with the offer in late April, I had just about given up and was preparing for a third year of teaching in Shrewsbury which was, I should stress, by no means a poor consolation prize. I had even written off the Braeburn post before the phone call from Mr Diaper, having decided, after the interview a week earlier, that, no matter how low the cost of living in East Africa might be, I could, under no circumstances, live on a salary of £420 per year net. When Mr Diaper clarified that he had been quoting a monthly salary and not an annual one, somewhat disorientated by the fact that my pay had instantly increased twelvefold, I gratefully accepted the job. I then reached for the atlas to find out where the hell Kenya was. When Mr Wakiihuri romped (or staggered, I really don't remember) home in the London marathon just over 24 hours later, I saw this as a sign. I'm not sure what the sign was and, given that a Kenyan winning a long distance running event is about as surprising as an American baseball team winning the World Series, I was obviously attaching much too much significance to his achievement. But here was a Kenyan making a name for himself in England; could I be about to reverse the roles in his country? Well, I was young, and evidently still a little idealistic.

About three months later I was standing in the carpeted staffroom of Shrewsbury Sixth Form College delivering my leaving speech to a packed house of around 70 teachers of mainly middle age and beyond. I was a rare symbol of youth in the establishment. Well, within the confines of the staffroom at least. With their jumpers, corduroys and tweeds they hung on to my every word as it was not common for someone below the age of 30 to be departing. I didn't actually have much to say that was worth hanging on to. I do remember one snippet, though, which stated how I would definitely miss England for three reasons: English pubs, *Coronation Street* and Everton Football Club. They sighed with polite murmurs of amusement but, no doubt, they felt inside what a shallow guy they had had in their midst. I thanked all the staff then and there for their support and companionship and, looking back, I genuinely do think that they were extremely tolerant of one so lacking in worldly knowledge and sophistication. I knew my mathematics and football and who Gail Tyldesley was shagging at the time but I knew little else. I sure needed to travel.

I had been to around 300 Everton matches in the '80s; a decade that began with the first big move of my life when I transferred from Hampshire to Liverpool to watch my beloved Blues first-hand; oh yes, and to study for a degree in mathematics at the University of Liverpool. After graduating in 1983 I skirted through the career of accountancy before moving into teaching. I had moved around a lot in that decade but always tried to ensure that I was living within a 50 miles radius of the hallowed turf of Goodison Park. My life revolved around Saturday afternoons. I was genuinely concerned about how I would cope with the withdrawal from this drug living on another continent. Commuting to Goodison from Nairobi was not an option.

At the start of the following season I tried to eke out every last moment of my relationship with Everton. It was like saying goodbye to a girlfriend who I wouldn't see for a long time. Every last second had to be savoured. The plan was that we would be apart for just two years but I had to let the team know that I still cared for them, still loved them and that they would always be in my heart. I went to Coventry for the first game of the 1989–90 season. It was a new era. The glorious team of the middle of the eighties was just about dismantled. Norman Whiteside, who had provided one of the only bad days of 1985 when he denied us the double with his Wembley winner for Manchester United, was now making his debut for us. His and the team's performance were forgettable, though, as we went down 2–0. I then went to two home games, as we nullified the threat of the precocious Gazza to beat Spurs 2–1 and then swept away Southampton 3–0. I now had five days left in the UK and I was counting down the minutes and hours: I was getting nervous. Each programme I watched on TV, each radio programme, each place I visited, I mentally noted was to be the last for me to experience for at least two years. This included, of course, the last *Coronation Street* that I watched on the Wednesday evening. That coincided with the last Everton match that was to take place on common soil to myself for two years; a 1–1 draw away to Sheffield Wednesday which I couldn't possibly attend as I was too preoccupied at my parents' house in Andover in Hampshire packing for the big day on 1 September 1989. Emotional goodbyes were limited by traffic congestion on the way to Heathrow on that Friday evening meaning I had to rush for the Air France flight, destination Jomo Kenyatta International Airport, Nairobi.

As if to soften the blow and ease me off my addiction, I arrived in East Africa at the beginning of a weekend known in the football world as an international break; no meaningful football for another eight days as far as I was concerned as it is a weekend set aside in the football calendar from time to time for the national teams around the world to fulfil various fixtures and, therefore, prevent any fixtures taking place for clubs in the major leagues. The school's promised purpose-built staff apartments were not quite finished. In an attempt to appease the new staff, we were dispatched on safari to the Maasai Mara for three days. We camped yards from where we had earlier seen lions roaming around and at the very spot where the British woman, Julie Ward, had mysteriously died 12 months before (and whose demise no one has explained to this day). This was exciting stuff. This was living on the edge. This was a different world.

On our return to the Kenyan capital, we moved into our barely completed one-bedroomed pads. The next day was a chance to go shopping in the big grimy city of Nairobi and six of the new teachers including me were given a driver for the day to take us around to various places in a clapped out Land Cruiser. A few of the young male recruits wanted to buy a car of their own. I was skint; still trying to sell my jalopy in the UK to gather sufficient funds. I was also becoming irritated with the company of these new unselected 'friends'. I chose to go for a walk alone while the others perused a dodgy second-hand car dealers. It was possibly the least secure street in the whole of Nairobi that I chose to walk down, especially for a naïve white guy. It was two o'clock in the afternoon but the lack of cover of darkness was no protection. Six hoodlums jumped from nowhere. At least I think it was six but, lying on the floor having my jacket ripped from my back, I didn't have the awareness to clock details. If

I had shouted out 'Thieves', I might have had a chance of getting some things back; mob rule is popular in sub-Saharan Africa, and the public announcement of a mugging taking place can result in an instant lynching of the perpetrators. I was new, lacking in worldliness; I knew of no such response (lynchings in Shrewsbury town centre are rare). I just got up, dusted myself down and felt stunned and sorry for myself. I would have at least managed a vague description for the police except the assailants had nicked my glasses from my nose. Nairobi was a blurred as well as a rather scary place at that particular moment.

Apart from the glasses and jacket, virtually everything else of value on my person that day had also gone except, thankfully, the rest of my clothes (and I was lucky in that respect I was told). Undeveloped photos of my first African safari, my settling in allowance from Braeburn of the equivalent of about £100 and, most gnawing of all, my address book, all disappeared in that swift back street assault. Virtually every contact I had in the world had gone from my possession with the loss of my address book. That night I started the long process of trying to resurrect it by writing to people at those addresses that I had committed to memory and asking them to send me all other addresses that they might have that were relevant to me. There was no email in those days and the process would be long; I could remember almost no phone numbers and, anyway, telephone communication to Europe could best be described as a hit and miss process. I was not in a state of sufficient emotional stability to engage in any further frustration at that point.

Braeburn kindly reimbursed my lost settling in allowance, presumably on the basis that I hadn't yet settled in, but otherwise I entered the second Saturday on the dark continent, with poor vision and low morale. I felt isolated and alone and I was seriously questioning this big decision of mine. At around 5 o'clock that afternoon I searched my solitary case of luggage (virtually all my other belongings were in freight somewhere in a Jomo Kenyatta Airport warehouse awaiting clearance) and found my treasured transistor radio. Already I had learnt where the clearest signal of World Service was to be found. I twiddled the tuner and caught a familiar voice from BBC2 Sport and glued my ear to first half latest scores. Strangely I cannot recall which match was chosen for the second half commentary but I do recall hearing that Everton held on to a 3–2 home win against Manchester United to go second. Suddenly the mugging, the loneliness, the fact that it was already dark outside at just

7 o'clock in the evening didn't matter. This was a new life and an Everton win now allowed me to face it with confidence and optimism. I had a great night out with my new friends that evening. Forget the fact that I was over 4,000 miles from home for the foreseeable future; Nevin, Newell and Sharpie had ensured that my world was restored.

Chapter 2
End of an era

23 September 1989: Everton 1 Liverpool 3

When was the last time Everton were top of the League approaching the last week of September? I think you will find the auspicious (perhaps, inauspicious given the time elapsed since then) date is the one above.

We'd had a hesitant start at Coventry but then a run of five wins and a draw had put Colin Harvey's team at the summit as we faced the 'derby' at Goodison.

My world was well detached from the Merseyside fervour. I was just establishing a routine of life in Nairobi. Almost a month had passed since my dramatic debut in the southern hemisphere. An entrance that had included camping with lions in the Maasai Mara and being mauled by muggers in the backstreets of the Kenyan capital. Mental adjustment was stabilising and I was actually beginning to enjoy the wall-to-wall sunshine, the warm hospitality and the whole adventure of entering a brand new world and culture. New experiences were being thrust into my face almost daily, testing my adaptability and my resolve. A nucleus of new colleagues and friends, many of whom were going through the same metamorphosis, aided the slide into this parallel universe to the one that I had experienced for almost three decades since my birth. Friends in the UK were long-established, proven over time; these new ones were less substantive, more transient, probably because my state of mind at that time dictated that this whole transmogrification was to be only temporary. However, comparisons were becoming less harsh as I settled in and one or two 'sound' friends were beginning to emerge from the bewildering mass of new faces that I was encountering.

Have you ever heard of a pedal kart? I hadn't until September 1989. A pedal kart is basically an unwieldy version of a go-kart with no engine. The driver sits in a seat about six inches from the floor with legs in front to position the feet on pedals that are attached to the front axle of the machine. By pushing the pedals the front axle revolves and a bicycle chain over the front axle and connected to a chain wheel on the rear axle helps rotate the back wheels. There are no gears and it requires a massive initial effort to gather forward momentum. Once moving, though, significant speed can be reached and reliable brakes are essential. Steering is by bike handlebars positioned for easy grip at about neck height in front of the seat. In summary a pedal-kart is like a four wheeled push-bike, flattened. I tell you all this because on the penultimate Saturday of September in 1989, Braeburn High School, my employers, had entered three pedal-karts for the Round Table 24 hour pedal-kart race at the Moi National Stadium in Nairobi. It was a fundraising event involving institutions and businesses throughout the city and, since the beginning of the term, students at the school where I now taught had been flapping sponsorship forms in the faces of every teacher and fellow student they came in contact with, trying to raise as many pledges as possible for the big occasion. It was an annual fixture in the Nairobi calendar and everyone seemed very familiar with what it was all about. For me and the other rookie British teachers at Braeburn it was one of those new experiences that I referred to above. The profile of the typical Braeburn teacher, determined largely by the ungenerous salaries paid and the school's far-flung location, was one of relative youth, fitness and 'have a go' spirit. It was not difficult, therefore, to put together a 12 person squad of staff to keep one kart going for a whole day. The other two karts were occupied by student teams. The whole dazzling spectacle was to start in a blaze of fanfare at 3 o'clock on the Saturday afternoon and end at 3 o'clock Sunday afternoon. I headed up to the Moi National Stadium straight after lunch on Saturday 23 September with a group of teachers to sample some of the atmosphere before the knee-grinding action began.

Three friends and I managed to find a football from somewhere (we may have even taken it from school with us, I don't remember) and, with no sign of security guards anywhere, went through an open gate straight onto the pitch of the national stadium. So there we were, four British teachers having a kick-around in the goal at one end of

Kenya's equivalent of Wembley. The most distinct memory I have of this bizarre escapade was thinking how hard and bumpy the surface was considering this was supposed to be the best pitch in the country. The stadium was immense with the perimeter of a concrete bowl curving up to the sky all around us and, as with so many ambitious sub-Saharan building projects, it seemed somehow unfinished and had extremely noxious smelling toilets.

Our mini-football adventure ended after about 20 minutes when an official looking gentleman came striding across the field to usher us back through the open gate from where we had emerged. He didn't appear too perturbed, though, as he chatted about English football teams and then waved us goodbye cheerily before locking the gate with a padlock. No further entry into the stadium was now permitted or required as the big 'race' was to take place on the tarmac around the outside of the stadium. Tension was building as last minute adjustments were made to the 50 or so contraptions assembled in the make-shift 'pits' and gradually all the karts were manoeuvred to the starting line or as close as they could get as it was only wide enough to take about 15 karts cheek by jowl. There was a speech made by some dignitary and then a loud hooter launched the whole show amidst a carnival atmosphere of cheering and ululating. Each circuit took about 4 minutes to complete and we had people in our camp timing each lap. We initially all took it in turns to do a lap but, as we entered the night, we went into shifts so that we each had a four hour break to sleep. Not that much sleeping could be done in that time. Tiredness determined that a rest was necessary but surging adrenalin meant that resting the brain would be impossible. All I remember is that when I had to get back into that seat at 7am after my four hours off, I felt quite unsure whether I would make it all the way round for a single lap. But strangely some unforeseen energy materialised and I embarked on some of my fastest times of the whole race during that breakfast period as the sun emerged. Physiologists could probably explain this unexpected phenomenon. I also remember a great sigh of something close to delirium when major welding work was required to repair a sheared axle and our team were out of action for two hours as we approached midday on Sunday. Most of all I remember smiles, sunshine, excitement and a massive sense of camaraderie and achievement as the final, sinew stretching lap was completed as the sun was at its hottest on that final Sunday of September 1989.

Of course, I had taken my precious transistor radio with me as it was a virtual bodily appendix during every Saturday afternoon to catch the latest football scores. It was too bulky to carry with me in the kart, though; the angle of my pumping thighs (steady!) would have probably meant the radio would have slipped from my pocket and shattered on the track halfway round. But others kept their ears to the action as I did my lap about 20 minutes into the match on the Saturday afternoon. I was elated on my return as I heard that Mike Newell had put us one up against the enemy, so elated that I offered to do another lap soon afterwards in place of a colleague who was already feeling the strain. I remember enormous deflation as I extricated myself from the red machine on this occasion to be greeted by a gloating Liverpool fan telling me that his team had equalised while I'd been rattling my bollocks off around Moi Stadium. By the time I was settled in the kart again, we were 3–1 down. I swore like mad all the way round and had expended a huge amount of emotional as well as physical energy by the time I came screeching into the pits as darkness was closing in on that Saturday evening. The anger and hatred and all the rest of the bile that accumulates in me when Everton lose to Liverpool was still there, especially as we had been knocked off the top of the table, but somehow the gloom did not cling for so long. Goodison Park literally was a different world to the one that I now inhabited. It was the first time I had not been at a home derby since October 1980 (when I had failed to get a ticket because I'd only just arrived in Liverpool to begin my university course). I had wondered how I would cope; what would the cold turkey taste like? Thanks to an immensely invigorating charity event involving thousands of people pedalling self-made leg-powered contrivances around a huge sports stadium on the outskirts of the hub city of East Africa, it wasn't half as bad as I thought it might be. Just as my beloved Blues signalled a farewell to the higher reaches of English football on that weekend, I was also finally coming to terms with the end of an era.

Chapter 3
If paradise is half as nice

21 October 1989: Everton 3 Arsenal 0

My fortunes in Kenya were oscillating like the massif of the Ngong Hills that rise in beautiful ripples to the south west of Nairobi. I had not yet completed two months in my new life on the equator but had already experienced the highs of camping in the Maasai Mara and viewing the snow-capped wonder of Kilimanjaro as a backdrop to herds of elephant and other wildlife during a weekend trip to Amboseli National Park, while also encountering the lows of a mugging in the Kenyan capital and the slightly embarrassing incident of having my birthday cake stolen from my own party. People are poor and hungry in this part of the world and they will exploit any opportunity.

My job was also fluctuating considerably. Having never taught any child below the age of 16 before, I was struggling with the psyche and behaviour of the year 9s and year 10s (or the third and fourth forms as they were still referred to at Braeburn High School in 1989). Fortunately, the underlying disposition of the children of an international school in Africa, is one of great tolerance and gentleness. If I had been having my baptism with 13 and 14-year-olds in an inner city comp in the heart of, well, Liverpool, I would surely have been eaten alive. Already I had participated in the unique and rather quaint activities of a 24 hour charity pedal kart race and a school version of *It's a Knockout* organised by the Braeburn PTA. Pillow fights across the swimming pool and seven-legged sprints among other bizarre events. Health and safety would never allow such things in the UK.

The plethora of cheap but high quality restaurants as well as our down at heel local pub, The Castle, meant the lack of a TV was not an issue of concern. None of the new young recruits at the school had the luxury of a television. Financial constraints dictated this but, the fact was, we were having one big party. It was like being back at Uni at the age of 28. Quite apart from the fact that, with the absence of satellite TV, the local Kenyan programme output was worth watching only for its crass *Crossroads* type comic value, there simply weren't enough hours in an evening to eat out, drink to oblivion and watch TV. Television was the obvious and convenient casualty when it came to prioritising.

So much hard work and hard play was taking its toll, though, and I was groping my way towards a much needed half term holiday as we entered the second half of October 1989. On the Wednesday afternoon school ended for a four day recess and, as soon as the last school bus full of children had left the compound, a group of ten of us boarded a school minibus to get a lift to Nairobi station. It was the regular bunch of new staff plus a couple of 'old hands'. The deputy headmaster, Dave Anderson (who sadly passed away in 2009 after suffering a stroke) made his own way down to the station with his four children who all attended the school. Dave was a great guy who had lived in East Africa since escaping the perils of teaching in East London in the early '60s. He had recently divorced from his Ugandan wife. She took his house in England and he took their four delightful children. It was a deal that appeared to have suited all parties down to the ground.

The train journey was a throwback to some colonial days with a silver service restaurant and old fashioned wooden carriages. The train barely moved above 50mph, making nodding off in the four bunk sleepers an effortless process. Having breakfast while seeing the wildlife of Tsavo National Park rush by the window, was exhilarating. I reflected on what the corresponding half term a year earlier in Shrewsbury had been like; cold, dark and a trip to Villa Park to see us lose 2–0. I had to pinch myself.

The 14-hour journey to Mombasa came to a slow grinding halt at 8am. On alighting, the immediate effect of the humidity and heat enveloped us like a warm, damp blanket. We managed to commandeer a minibus driver to take us to Tiwi Beach on the south coast. It was a 30 minute journey involving a short ride on a dilapidated ferry and a final five minutes driving into the undergrowth that eventually ended with the sandy car park of the Tiwi Villas resort. This consisted of a scattering of straw covered rondavels and a spacious, open wooden bar that was perched on the edge of the white sands of the Kenyan coastline.

For the next two and a half days I just caught my breath. We swam in the warm Indian Ocean, played football in the sand until the sun melted us and walked from bar to bar along the deserted unbroken beach that literally stretches for hundreds and hundreds of miles. With each intake of cheap lager, the pounding sun dimmed our senses a little more making the feeling of unreality come a step closer. This really was a dream. The evenings became a further detachment from the real world as a hearty meal of curried prawns or the like was washed down with lashings of Tusker beer amid vacuous conversation about who knows what. In fact most of the talk was probably along the lines of: 'I can't believe this is true'.

On the Saturday, a slight tension was building. Just for me, not anyone else. As I trudged back from the beach at around 6.30pm I knew that the Everton game was reaching its final stages. I had no idea of the score and, to my horror, I had discovered as soon as I had arrived in Mombasa two days before that my little trannie didn't seem to have the power to pick up a World Service signal on the Indian Ocean coastline. Amid all the bonhomie and sheer joy of the environment I had been immersed in, there had been this nagging problem occupying my mind. How was I going to find out the result of our game at home to Arsenal?

I made one last desperate attempt to seek out World Service in my banda before giving up and going to the bar for the usual evening's entertainment of alcohol fuelled chat. Just past the first half pint and, as I was starting to accept that I may well have to remain ignorant of how Everton had fared until at least I returned to Nairobi, Dave Anderson came strolling in with his four kids in tow. Dave was a larger than life character in many ways, always laughing and jovial. He evidently also had a more powerful radio than I possessed. Already knowing that I was the most fanatical football fan on the staff and that my fanaticism revolved around the blue half of Merseyside, he was very pleased to announce that Everton had beaten Arsenal 3–0 and that Liverpool had lost 4–1 at Southampton. I had spent much of the previous three days pinching myself, now I was in total disbelief. Our season had been going slightly off the rails made worse by the fact that Liverpool were swanning it at the top. But Dave had been too precise and sure-footed in his statement for it to be a wind-up. He even told me the scorers I think (Neil McDonald and two from Pat Nevin). The word paradise had swirled around my head many times during my first adventure on the East African coast but there is only so much joy one man can take. I took more than my fill that Saturday evening and, while everyone else was loving the warm moist Mombasa air and the sound of the waves and the chirping of the cicadas, I had just a little bit more joy to savour than any of them; I had the double ecstasy of a six goal swing for Everton over the Dark Side and against formidable opposition at that. Mombasa may have been paradise but it was still only half as nice as the combination of those two, oh so sweet, football results.

Chapter 4
Hippos, whores and hopelessness

5 November 1989: Aston Villa 6 Everton 2

'Yes,' I said, 'I'll come,' I said. 'Where is Baringo, anyway?' I asked.

That was the spirit of adventure that now engulfed me in late October 1989. The club captain of Railway Wanderers, the long established expat football team in Nairobi, was soliciting for interest in a trip to a central region of Kenya on the first weekend of November. We had just played a match against KBS (Kenya Broadcasting Station) and I had scored twice in a 4–2 win. Drinks were now flowing in the Railway clubhouse and my cup was overflowing in every sense. By the end of that Tuesday evening my head was swirling and my name was on a list of about 20 other expat footballers to go for a Saturday jaunt to Lake Baringo Lodge, returning on Guy Fawkes Day.

A guy called Dave Powell drove me there on the Saturday morning with another couple of players. It was a journey of over four hours and covered some almost desert terrain. In the middle of this 'desert' we had a blowout. I remember being astonished by the fact that, at the time we pulled to a halt to attend to the offending tyre, there was no one in sight. Within two minutes a crowd of around a dozen villagers had congregated to watch this spectacle of four *muzungus* (white men) changing a wheel.

I say villagers in a loose sense, as there appeared to be no sign of a village or, indeed, any form of human habitat anywhere within the visible horizon. These people just seemed to emerge from the tumbleweed, anthills and cacti. They muttered to each other in gentle voices as we put on our show of changing a wheel and giggled here and there at our struggles and ungainliness. At the end they requested to be given the damaged tyre and pointed to their improvised Firestone sandals on their feet to demonstrate exactly what they would use the rubber tread for. We were unwilling to part with the replaced wheel but did hand out a few coins and pens as consolation.

We arrived at the lodge mid-afternoon having stopped for lunch on the way. Having had a quick walk round the luxury accommodation including an alluring sun-kissed swimming pool and observed Lake Baringo nearby, we all assembled in the open plan lobby to head into the bush in a selection of vehicles for the focus of the trip; a match against the staff of Baringo Lodge. The spectacle was to take place on a nearby pitch which consisted of a bare patch of ground amidst the wasteland with metal tubing bent into the shape of a goal post at each end. There were no markings on the pitch; the edge of the playing area being determined by where the tufts of coarse grass sprouted up. As was often the case in these rural games, the superior level of organisation and accoutrements (the Kenyans all played bare footed) of the Europeans proved too much for the superior skill levels and sheer enthusiasm of the indigenous players and we won 3–0. A report in the Railway Wanderers' newsletter for November 1989 records that 'Cliff Green ran through a preoccupied defence and faced the undernourished keeper and was about to score. Unfortunately he seems to be a perfectionist and, while he had his tape measure out calculating the angle of optimum trajectory, he was tackled.' I'm sure that that is an exaggeration of my 'Jermaine Beckford moment' but I do recall being quite a crowd pleaser that afternoon and, just as with the tyre changing spectacle earlier in the day, there was a significant crowd to see my comical antics; a vast congregation that had gathered to watch this match in the searing afternoon sun seemingly having materialised from the sand clouds.

The after match celebrations began instantly with beers produced from some cool boxes at the side of the pitch as the final whistle blew. And so the après-match activities continued with more drinks and food at the lodge and a darts tournament. At around 11.00pm, I was thinking of bed. I had not realised what hardy souls some of these expat footballers were, though. Not wishing to appear a feckless lightweight from the backwaters of Shropshire, I joined about 10 other Wanderers as we headed into the nearby village to sample the nightlife. An extremely smelly, sweaty and crowded mud construction provided the local nightclub. Some 70s disco vibrated the unstable shack as a bunch of white footballers piled in through the front door paying a toothless doorkeeper a few Kenya shillings for the privilege. Some fairly cramped dancing and plenty more beer drinking took place for a couple of hours. The local women were, let's say, wanting in decorum and subtlety and, in many cases, a full set of teeth. I had never found it so easy to 'pull' even though I most definitely didn't want to. I was quite relieved when Dave offered me a lift back to the lodge at around three o'clock in the morning. Some didn't make it back so soon and the Railway clubhouse back in Nairobi was rife with gossip of AIDS tests and some very scared footballers over the next few months.

I had been told that Baringo was famous for its hippopotami and that these large cumbersome creatures come to graze in the evenings before spending the day in the water to cool down. I was now about to witness some of these lumbering night time manoeuvres first-hand. I was drunk, I know, but it was absolutely true that to get to our rooms in the lodge that night, we had to skirt past hippos gently waddling around the lodge including some that were grunting happily right next to the swimming pool. Hippos are the greatest killers of humans on the African continent even though they are vegetarian. The problem is that, if they perceive that their route to their beloved water is being cut off, they will panic and run directly towards their bath trampling to death anything that happens to be in the way. As I was now being given this basic lesson of 'don't get between a hippo and his water' by more seasoned operators such as Dave Powell, I was desperately sidling along the sides of the chalets smelling the breath of the hippos less than a couple of metres away as I went. If anyone tells you that a dose of caffeine is a good way of sobering up, let me suggest a confrontation with a yawning hippo at three o'clock in the morning as an even more effective method of fending off a potential hangover.

Next morning a weary group of footballers took their buffet breakfast in the main dining room recalling some of the detail from the previous 'very interesting' day. The hippos were nowhere to be seen; they had lolloped back to the lake for another day's loafing.

The journey back was quicker than the reverse journey the day before with no punctures and no stopping off for a bite. Around 2 o'clock I was back at the staff compound of Braeburn High School in Nairobi where I had now been employed as a teacher for two months. All that remained now was to do a little preparation for the week's work ahead and wait for the Everton result.

Everton, under Colin Harvey were having one of those 'symmetrical seasons' where our home form was almost the mirror image of our away record. Apart from a defeat to Liverpool in September, Goodison was a fortress. Apart from a streaky 1–0 win at Charlton, we had been terrible away from home. Still, a win at Villa would put us in the top four. As always I was optimistic; this was still the Everton that had become accustomed to League Championships and FA Cup Finals in recent seasons. It hadn't yet dawned on Evertonians like me that those halcyon days were actually receding inexorably. There was no satellite TV or mobile phone or internet to link me more closely with my spiritual home on such occasions and I had to wait for the very unclear transmission of the sports bulletin on the BBC World Service to discover the fate of the Blues. As always a sense of nervousness and helplessness began to envelope me. Impatience and trepidation got the better of me. I knew it was the live game on television in the UK and the friend I used to go to the matches with before I left for my African adventure, Chris Grundy, would be glued to it unless he had actually decided to travel down to Villa Park, but he didn't tend to go to away games. I gave Chris a call on my unreliable land line. Connection tended to be random but, on this occasion, I got through at the first attempt. I had miscalculated the time, though. Forgetting that the clocks had been put back an hour in the UK the weekend before, I phoned when I thought the match would have concluded; it, in fact, had 20 minutes to go. The crackles and the fuzz from the precarious phone line could not hide the truth, the terrible truth. 'We're 5–0 down' intoned the voice of Chris. 'Hang on…make that 6–0.' He gave me some details but I wasn't really listening. This was tantamount to receiving the news of the death of a loved one. I couldn't take it in, 6–0. Six, fuckin' nil. We never let in six. Everton never got hammered by anyone. What had gone wrong? I felt desolate, depressed and so completely and utterly helpless. If I'd been at Villa Park, would it have been the same score? Surely I could have made a difference.

Just for the record, a goal from Tony Cottee and an own-goal, brought a semblance of respectability to the scoreline, but it was still a devastating blow. For all the excitement of playing football in the bush and the Baringo nightlife of whores and hippos making up yet another amazing weekend in my new existence, Everton had still managed to bring me right down to earth with a display of staggering ineptitude. And, if the truth be told, that First Division football result from Birmingham on 5 November 1989 had managed to overshadow everything else that had transpired that weekend. Perhaps I needed therapy. Or perhaps I should have just done something more final like go with one of those Baringo tarts with a gob like Stonehenge!

Chapter 5
A fading feeling

26 and 30 December 1989: Derby County 0 Everton 1, QPR 1 Everton 0

So Christmas came early. The Christmas holiday at Braeburn High School began at lunch time on 1 December. I was discovering another pleasant deviation from life in cold, congested Britain as a result of working on the international teaching circuit. In England my former colleagues still had three whole weeks of dragging themselves out of bed to wipe the frost from their cars and negotiate their way through the traffic and street lights to their heated classrooms and staffroom. Only then with three days left until Christmas could they make use of those town centre stampedes commonly referred to as Christmas shopping days. For me I had five weeks of sun drenched Kenyan leisure time to fill, with just the odd glimpse of incongruous tinsel in the shops to remind me that this was actually the festive season.

This was my 29th Christmas on the planet. I may not have been able to recall the early ones in a fragile world gripped by the Cuban Missile Crisis and the assassination of JFK but, within the limits of my cognitive capacity, this was to be a Christmas different to any that I had ever experienced before. For a start it was the first time that I was to spend 25 December away from the UK and away from my family. It was a thought that was filling me with a little trepidation. I could not afford to be alone or bored during that period or the tsunami of melancholy would swamp me. No morning sherry with the neighbours, no devouring of the succulent roast turkey lunch with the family followed by the Queen's Speech and the inevitable James Bond re-run and then the anticipation of the most exciting part of the whole overindulgent, crapulent excess; the football programme on Boxing Day. How could I combat the nostalgic sense of homesickness that was bound to envelope me at this time? Several of the expats didn't even try to 'tough it out' and, during the first two weeks of that endless Christmas break, I accompanied quite a few teachers to Jomo Kenyatta Airport to see them off for their festive holiday in the snow. Others invited their family to Nairobi. I accompanied one teacher, an acerbic but extremely amusing Scottish teacher of Computer Studies as it was then known, on an entertaining four day safari to Amboseli with his parents. During the first night in our bandas amidst the cicadas, mosquitos and gas lamps, I learnt on World Service that Howard Kendall's return to English club management had resulted in his Manchester City team clawing a 0–0 draw out of Goodison Park. In the same bulletin I learnt that Nick Faldo had been named the Sports Personality of the Year; surely a contradiction in terms!

When that safari ended there was just one week until the celebration of Christ's birth. I was running out of ideas of what to do for Christmas and people to do it with. In an act of desperation, I linked up with Victor Soskin. If ever you need an example of the eccentricity that the expat world seems to attract; the odd-balls, misfits and weirdos that just can't hack it in the restrictive routine of life in old Blighty, then Victor is right up there as archetypal. Having not given him the most flattering introduction, I should also say that Victor was personable, sociable and completely harmless. Not the kind of person I would have befriended in Shrewsbury, though (or been able to find in Shrewsbury!), but options were running thin for me as Christmas approached in 1989.

Let me make this absolutely clear; I am not a mountaineer, but when you are in East Africa, there are two mountains very close by that you simply cannot ignore. Kilimanjaro which I had just viewed again from Amboseli National Park; majestic and snow covered but much too high for a novice like me to contemplate climbing (although two years later I was to prove myself wrong on that theory) and Mount Kenya with its three jagged peaks. Two of these summits needed ropes and harnesses and courage to conquer none of which I possessed. The third and lowest peak was called Point Lenana and, by all accounts, could be ascended by amateurs like Victor Soskin and me. At 16,355ft it was still nose-bleed territory but it didn't require any expertise or experience of hillwalking let alone mountain climbing. As a way of taking my mind off the home comforts of the British fireside, an expedition to climb Mount Kenya with a loon ticked all the right boxes. Victor, not surprisingly at a loose end and without prospects of human company or things to do for the Yuletide, snapped my hand off at the idea of the two of us reaching Point Lenana on Christmas Day.

Preparations for the big climb were unconventional. The first, and indeed only, planning meeting taking place in Buffalo Bills, a notorious magnet for scantily clad prostitutes on the south side of Nairobi. By the end of the evening we had produced a four day food supply shopping list of mainly pasta and hot dog sausages, decided a route from bottom to top and received several offers of a bed for the night with a lithe black female body for company. Victor, as I recall, accepted at least one such offer. I drove home alone questioning my sanity in embarking on such an ambitious project with someone who apparently preferred the risks of climbing the local women more than climbing the local mountains. Actually, he had a point!

The expedition began at 2.15pm on 23 December. Victor and I had completed the shopping in Nairobi that morning and now got into the back of a Land Cruiser pick-up driven by a guy called Terry who had decided to accompany us at the last minute along with his girlfriend, Alison who taught at Braeburn Primary School, hence the connection. Terry was an ex-army super hero type character who now operated his own logistics business evacuating people from war zones across the African continent. He claimed to have no knowledge or experience of climbing mountains, although he clearly had a lot more idea than the clueless couple of Braeburn mathematics teachers that now huddled under the canopy of the back of his pick-up with a pile of camping gear, rucksacks and packets of spaghetti. It was a rough four hour drive to the relative comfort of Naro Moru Lodge where the four of us had a pleasant evening getting to know each other while contemplating the challenge ahead. The next night was much less civilised. We were supposed to have climbed approximately halfway up on the Western route ready to make the final ascent on Christmas morning. Persistent heavy rain meant that manoeuvring the Land Cruiser even to a point from where we could start walking was a hazardous task. It actually took virtually the whole day and we had to settle for staying in a very basic wooden hut at what was called the Met Station at the foot of the mountain. Our Christmas Eve was spent trying to stay warm with whisky, soup and the singing of a variety of songs with a group of German tourists. As we finally tried to force ourselves to sleep in damp, cold sleeping bags on damp, cold wooden floorboards, the luxury of previous Christmases kept fighting its way into my consciousness.

The next day was a battle with what is quaintly referred to as the Vertical Bog; hundreds of metres of marshland at an angle of approximately 45 degrees elevation. Each step was a guessing game as to how far into the squelching mud your foot would sink. My record was a two footed lunge up to my groin. As we emerged from this five hour ordeal, the icy air blew through our sopping wet clothes and the mud began to form a hard crust on my jeans, socks and training shoes; yes, I had actually decided to climb the second highest mountain on the African continent in a pair of Reeboks! There was no room in Makinder's Hut when we arrived so it was a night of sub-zero temperatures in a two man tent with the maverick Mr Soskin. A shivering game of Charades had bizarrely provided the post pasta and hotdog entertainment. Sleep was obviously not forthcoming on that Christmas night and Victor and I were happy to end the façade at around 4am as we packed up the tent, leaving Alison and Terry behind in theirs, to make the final ascent to the top of Point Lenana.

It was during those last few hundred feet that I discovered that I actually had a fear of heights. As we clambered around the rock face, Victor kept commenting on the fantastic view. I couldn't bear to look anywhere other than the next nook or cranny where I was going to lodge my foot or grab with my hand. When we finally crawled over the last rock to sit on the summit in a space no bigger than your average bathroom, I simply sat shaking with cold and fear, clutching my knees up to my chin wondering how the hell I was going to get back down, while Victor proudly balanced on the highest peak with arms wide open like Kate Winslet on the bow of the *Titanic*. Getting back down actually proved easier than expected. Victor had a cunning plan. Whether it was devised for my benefit or to satisfy his manic desire for the ultimate thrill, I don't know, but, after he had surveyed what was probably an exhilarating scene (I never found out) for 20 minutes or so, we began our descent. Victor went first. I closed my eyes and went second. As I clung rigid to the rock face not wanting to move up or down, I heard the crazed tones of Victor. 'Let's take the short cut' he suggested. I glanced to my right and saw him turn round and push himself off of the rocks with a jut of his bum and there he went, sliding down the glacier on his backside. I did an instantaneous weighing up in my head and decided a quick death crashing into a crater lake at 50mph was preferable to the slow agony of being frozen into the rock face over a period of days (and with the progress I was currently making that seemed quite possible). In an instant I repeated Victor's swivel and launched myself on a fantastic sled ride without a sled. It was fast, it was awe inspiring, it was face freezing, it was tearing a massive hole in the seat of my pants and, halfway down, it dawned on me that it was actually bloody dangerous. The drop into the glacier lake was approaching fast. Brakes were needed urgently. I dug my heels into the icy snow. The friction did its job, my feet slowed down quickly. The rest of my body maintained its original speed, though, and soon I was doing somersaults down the side of the glacier. As the slope arced out towards horizontal, my rolling motion slowed down and finally I was dumped on my front in the white stuff about 20 metres from the lip of the glacier lake. Victor came trudging over to me overcome with excitement. It was the first real emotion I had seen from him as he tended to accept madness and unpredictability as the norm. This act of death defying stupidity had brought even Victor Soskin out of his comfort zone, though. Even he had found sliding down the side of Mount Kenya with his arse as a toboggan, something to laugh out loud at. The two of us staggered back to the safety of the Austrian Hut viewing post about 400 metres away where a crowd was assembled considering their final ascent. Alison and Terry were among them. 'So, you've been up already?' asked Alison. 'Yes', we replied and were about to regale our spectacular descent but Alison spoke first. 'We've just been watching. There were a couple of idiots sliding down the glacier just now, doing somersaults and handstands and all kinds of things. Absolutely ridiculous. They could have killed themselves. In fact they deserved to kill themselves. Just stupid.'

Victor and I kept quiet.

So that was the story of my first and somewhat unconventional attempt at mountaineering. By the end of that day we were back at Mackinder's and this time we found space inside. I had a blinding headache but I couldn't ascertain whether it was due to altitude sickness, the fact that we had run out of food supplies or the severe bumps on my head that I had received from my ice gymnastics.

The festive season, of course, comes in two parts. I had negotiated my first Christmas away from England but what about New Year? All the Braeburn staff had arranged various safaris and events to see in 1990. I wasn't invited to any of them. Did I want to be alone? Who else would be left on the shelf on 31 December?

It was 6.45pm on 28 December 1989 when Victor Soskin and I boarded the 7 o'clock overnight train from Nairobi to Mombasa. During the rickety ride back from Mount Kenya in the back of Terry's Land Cruiser, Victor had noted in the *Daily Nation* newspaper a story of travellers using cargo dhows to reach Zanzibar. It had an element of risk but it was cheap and exciting. Emboldened by our antics on the glacier of Point Lenana, I agreed to Victor's cock-eyed plan to sail the Indian Ocean for the equivalent of about £5 to see in the New Year on the exotic spice island 50 miles off the coast of Tanzania. We were on our own, though. Alison and Terry, who had possibly sussed that we had been the two lunatics doing cartwheels on the west face of Lenana, had decided to keep a safe distance from us from now on. They were electing to have a more sedate and romantic end to the year.

On arriving in Mombasa, Victor took on the defiant persona of a man on a mission. I followed behind as we headed for the docks. Before we could buy our tickets we had to report to the Ministry for Immigration; a tiny dishevelled office upstairs in a white tenement building. A wiry man in ministry garb and with a glint in his eye gave us forms to fill in. After completing these forms to his satisfaction, we then signed a disclaimer. Unfortunately we were to lose our copies of these scrappy pieces of paper in the midst of a storm, but from what I remember the words were not too ambiguous, something along the lines of: 'Should the dhow sink, you and your nearest and dearest agree not to blame anyone'. We literally were signing our lives away. What the hell? We had rewritten the record books on the fastest descent of a mountain, what fear did riding a dodgy boat in shark infested waters hold for us?

So, armed with our premature death certificates we headed to the place where the dhows departed. We showed our passports with the various bits of paper just acquired to the immigration officer seated in a shed and then waited on the dockside watching a dhow being loaded with plastic water containers, bowls, buckets, barrels and boxes of Omo. Without wishing to lose our desired demeanour of hardened seafarers too much, we asked a few questions to people in the vicinity like: 'Is this the boat to Zanzibar?' and 'When does it leave?' Answers, even to the first question, were vague and not to be relied upon, but we paid our 200 Kenyan shillings and boarded anyway.

It was 4.30pm and we sat among the plastic containers for a full three hours before the boat finally set sail. So we were already sun baked and terminally bored before we even began. It was just about dark as we headed out into the Indian Ocean. Save for a

40 watt light bulb swinging from the ceiling of the one man cabin that lit up the crazed facial features of the guy responsible for steering the dhow, there was no other light to be seen in or out of the vessel. It was becoming scary. I peered through the window into the cabin and gained little solace from the fact that this half-brained pilot was looking at a map of the west coast of India. Was that where he was heading or was he simply aware that that is where he often ended up? As it approached midnight, I was in desperate need of a distraction to take me away from the discomfort and boredom. Victor's off the wall conversation provided a distraction that I could do without. So Mother Nature intervened. For the next four hours we endured the most ferocious of tropical storms. The dhow started to lurch from side to side violently until we had to literally hang on to anything fixed on deck just to prevent ourselves being washed overboard. The plastic containers, loosely tied together began to swing and slide around crazily. At one point, as the eye of the storm began to blow such a wind that it tested my white knuckles to the limit, I surveyed the scene and felt as if I had been thrust into a movie. The sea would rise up as the boat tilted and another cascade of water, as if thrown deliberately from the film set, would drench me. It couldn't be real. I pinched myself, regrettably it was. Meanwhile Victor was clinging to the railings at the bow, throwing up violently. And that 40 watt light bulb continued to swing inexorably almost hitting the ceiling at the furthest points of its pendulum arc. For the second time in a matter of days I was sharing a death defying experience with Victor Soskin.

Needless to say, we survived. As the storm moved away to batter other unfortunates in the waters to the east of the African continent that black night, I and most of the other 17 people on board (yes, I counted them), used blankets to try to alleviate the uncontrollable shivering that took over as we waited for the sun to rise again. Victor and I were the only two *muzungus* on board and we were treated with a combination of curiosity, deference and sympathy by the rest of the roughly hewn crew. We were served several plates of *ugali*, the thick white maize staple of Kenya, in a watery gravy. From near watery grave to watery gravy in a matter of a few hours, I hated its gritty tastelessness and never ate the stuff again after that horrendous voyage. Peeing was over the side of the boat. If you needed a crap, I don't know what the solution was. There were no women on board and, presumably never women on board, as there was no squatting facility.

Victor's conversation was starting to torment me as much as the sun and boredom by midday of the next day but when you are crammed onto 22ft of planks with a pile of plastic and 16 other people you cannot converse with, it's pretty hard to get away from your travelling partner. All reading material had been swept into the ocean in the early hours along with that doom-laden disclaimer. You can imagine my sheer joy when land was spotted around lunchtime on that Saturday 30 December. You can, therefore, also imagine my utter dejection when the pilot, with the same intractable grin that had gripped his face from the moment we had left terra firma, started to turn his wheel to the left away from the aforementioned land. Evidently his map had proved useless, as I had suspected it would, and his way of finding the required destination had been to head south down the Kenyan and then Tanzanian coastline until he came to a familiar piece of headland at which point he knew he had to redirect his pile of timber directly east until he 'hit' Zanzibar. Sure enough, seven further mind-numbing hours after sighting land, we finally 'hit' Zanzibar just before I hit Victor. Incredibly we were detained on that boat another hour as they set up an immigration and customs point which we had to negotiate before we could finally have the freedom of finding a hotel. So it had been a full 29 hours from the time we boarded to the time we disembarked. I made one decision that night and I did not care whether Victor was with me or not. After exploring Zanzibar I was going to return to Mombasa by aeroplane. Victor disagreed. Sadly he got his way. All flights for the first week of 1990 were fully booked. On the evening of 2 January we boarded a passenger dhow crammed with 138 people (no, I didn't count them but I saw the captain's list!). Again we were the only two *muzungus* and again there was a midnight storm but mercifully the whole journey took a mere 17 hours this time. I guess the east coast of the continent of Africa is easier to locate than a dot like Zanzibar.

So what has all this to do with Everton Football Club? On the day that my boyhood heroes were winning 1–0 at the Baseball Ground with a Stuart McCall goal, I had almost died a spectacular, icy death on the slopes of Mount Kenya. On the day that the Blues were losing 1–0 on the Loftus Road plastic, I was on the verge of being swept into the jaws of sharks in an African tempest. As I caught up with the festive First Division soccer scene with English newspapers that arrived in the Kenyan capital five days after publication in the UK, I felt joy at the result against Derby and despair about the result against QPR, but it was just a twinge in either direction, not an uplifting elation or a mind-wrenching anguish that Everton results usually inflicted on me. I had exciting tales of mountains and oceans to retell. I had scrapes with death to recount. I was living a somewhat exciting life; one goal in two matches against mediocre opposition with a team including Ray Atteveld couldn't really compare (although I later learnt that we had beaten Luton 2–1 on New Year's Day with Whiteside and Sharp on target). For the first time in two decades since my love affair with Everton had begun, the feeling was fading.

Chapter 6

Love lost through a dodgy mechanic and a newspaper typo

17 February 1990: Oldham Athletic 2 Everton 2

And there I was, sitting in my newly acquired orange Ford Capri not moving very much at all while a lava flow of traffic was manoeuvring around me on the busiest roundabout in Nairobi at the busiest possible time; 5.30 on a Friday afternoon. And why was my flame coloured piece of retro metal not moving in time with the morass of fume belching, horn blasting traffic? Because I had the Capri's stubby little gear stick in my hand. And what's wrong with that? I hear you ask. Well, I was standing *outside* the car at the time. Standing outside the car simultaneously trying to seek assistance whilst endeavouring to hide my embarrassment at having clogged up the most congested section of tarmac in the whole of the Kenyan capital city in the middle of rush hour. There was no sub-Saharan equivalent of the AA to call upon. Indeed there were no mobile phones to call help from anyone. In the end some guy did take pity on me and managed to tow me to the garage that had supposedly repaired the gearbox just a few hours earlier. Surjit was the name of the mechanic responsible for the bodged job and his silly grin was nearly skewed permanently by the aforementioned gear stick being inserted into his front teeth when I saw him on that forecourt to welcome me and my forlorn looking '70s icon. As he lay under the car replacing the crucial bolt that he had evidently omitted a few hours previously, he showed remarkable trust in my capacity for restraint as he said that loose gear sticks were a common fault with the Capri and that the car was worth about 30,000 Kenyan shillings, which was precisely half of what I had paid for it approximately a week earlier. He had the good sense not to charge me for his extra 10 minutes of labour as I drove off only to once again find fresh air instead of second gear just before entering the main road. As I got out of the car gesticulating wildly with gearstick once more in hand, Surjit's smile remained fixed and his cheery disposition undaunted. Finally he seemed to do the job and it was hard to hate him. This is Africa, I told myself. Keep your sense of humour. It was another story to tell the folk back home.

It was approaching half a calendar year in Kenya for me, and I was now beginning to really settle. Indeed I now had a girlfriend. Jill was her name and she was a trainee teacher from Boulder in Colorado who was carrying out her teaching practice in the International School of Kenya (ISK). It wasn't normal for teaching practice to be carried out overseas but her uncle and aunt, Bill and Kathy had pulled a few strings with their niece's school in Colorado and had wangled a one semester placement at the predominantly American High School situated in the north-west outskirts of Nairobi. Jill was being accommodated by Bill and Kathy in their luxurious house in Lower Kabete along with their three young children, Blair, Andy and Zak.

Our relationship was still in its formative stages when we decided to go for a Sunday day out to climb Mount Longonot, about 40 miles north of Nairobi in the beautiful Rift Valley. I describe it as a climb but really it amounted to a fairly gentle two hour hike. We had already spent much of the weekend together starting with a Valentine's party in a plush hotel on the Friday. The drive back to her place took a detour and we ended with a bit of a canoodle in the grounds of Nairobi University until some armed security guards curtailed our fun and we had to use a bribe to persuade them not to report us for such unacceptable behaviour in a public place, albeit in the pitch blackness of midnight in an unlit field. Saturday was spent just relaxing together around her place. Under the strict rules of her uncle and aunt (and the untimely interception of Securicor the evening before), this was still a very sugar-coated, chaste affair. Like my car, the relationship was a throw-back to some bygone age.

The prospect of a whole day out away from the city with just the two off us was, therefore, a major step and the anticipation and sap were rising; for me at least. As happens in the early stages of romance, time and life in general seem to take a vacation from the norm. Routines disappear and the mind and memory seem to be driven by a whole new set of cogs and sprockets. Having recently turned my life upside down with the move to East Africa, I was probably even more susceptible to a transition into the tangled mess that is caused by a sensually induced hormone imbalance.

As I awoke on that Sunday morning and prepared my breakfast before driving out to pick Jill from her guardians' home, there was a little nagging question in the back of my head: 'Are Everton still in the FA Cup?' All the pre-occupation with my new found love on the Saturday had meant that I had not managed to catch the football results that weekend. So, as I drove the four mile route to collect my companion for the day, I stopped by at a street vendor to purchase a copy of *The Nation* newspaper. I scanned the English football results from the previous day printed erratically on the inside back page. A jolt of anguish went through me as I saw Oldham Athletic 3 Everton 2. Oldham from the Second Division had defeated the erstwhile mighty Blues. As I completed my journey to Jill's house, romantic expectations were temporarily shoved aside by a concoction of the more familiar football related feelings. Excuses about that wretched plastic pitch, curiosity as to who scored our inadequate tally of goals and frustration at the fact that our road to Wembley was already over at round five while Liverpool's continued as they had won 3–0 at home to Southampton. No doubt I was slightly wrong-footed as I entered Jill's house to be greeted by her extended family. My composure had been restored somewhat by the time we departed with wishes of 'You guys, have a good time,' ringing in our ears. I remember that detail because it was the first time that I had heard of a girl being referred to as a guy. Another irritating Americanism that has infiltrated our language over the past two decades until it has become acceptable.

The detail of that baking February day in the Kenyan savannah is for another type of book; A Mills and Boon romantic tale where the boy is charming and gallant and the girl is sweet and demure. A picnic with fizzy drinks and gentle teasing at the top of a windswept mountain in one of our former colonies. Giggles and kisses interspersed with a bit of sweaty exertion caused by nothing more risqué than the ascent of the slopes. At mid-afternoon, the sepia tinted reel suddenly comes loose, though. The click click click of the unharnessed celluloid rattling abjectly on its spool forms the backdrop as the real world of Cliff Green in Africa re-emerges. As we reached the orange Capri, Jill requested to drive. I was now unburdened of the stifling rules of the UK such as having the correct insurance and I was in love. 'Yes,' I said immediately. Jill assured me she knew the rudiments of driving a car and she started the engine without hesitation. It purred into action seamlessly. She then engaged first gear and we started to search for a bar to quench a searing thirst brought on by a combination of dust and dehydration. As she searched for second gear a jolt went through me like the one that hit me when the newspaper had revealed that awful football result earlier in the day. Again it was a sharp injection of nauseous disappointment brought on by the sense that a familiar unwanted outcome had been realised; a feared prophesy fulfilled. As Jill's left hand struggled with the short gear stick, I noticed that it was becoming dislodged in her hand. As she pulled the rod from the rubber casing in astonishment, I told her to put her foot on the brake. So there we were on a dust ridden street in the middle of Longonot town on the Old Naivasha Road, three miles from a volcano but a long way from home in a car with little prospect of experiencing the thrill of kinetic energy. The initial reaction was laughter. 'Good', I thought, my girlfriend has come through the 'sense of humour test' but what now? I managed to jam the gear lever into second and we trundled some distance to a garage where some emergency resuscitation was carried out on Surjit's handy work. Having parted with virtually every shilling in my pocket for the service, we could afford just one beer each in the Belle Inn, a famous watering hole for Longonot hikers. Jill, more concerned about our return to Nairobi, refused point blank. She was probably being prudent and sensible but that beer had been fixated in my head for some time and I was not ready for this crushing disappointment. While waiting for the mechanic to repair the gearbox, I had glanced again at *The Nation* newspaper and seen the little footnote to the Everton result. Because of the poor typesetting it was at the end of the line so I hadn't noticed it when I had flicked through the results earlier. It read: 'replay at Goodison Park on 21st Feb'. So we had drawn. It was a misprint after all. I was elated and used this morsel of good news to get over the present trauma caused by a dodgy gearbox and enforced alcohol abstinence. The journey to Jill's home was a silent one. Every gear change filled me with trepidation and my throat felt like a rope was wedged down it. I had no idea what Jill was thinking and I was beginning not to care too much. Indeed my head was more preoccupied with whether we had drawn 2–2 or 3–3 (or indeed some other score) than where this relationship was going. Perhaps Jill could sense that my concern for her fears and thoughts had evaporated in some other mist that she was unaware of, but nothing was quite the same for us again after that fateful day on Longonot. She redeemed the situation a little when we reached her home by producing some ice cold beers and sizzling pizzas from the kitchen and then she put on a video of *Out of Africa*. How apposite that I fell asleep halfway through, exhausted by the events of the day. The romantic images conjured up on the screen with its obvious parallels with Jill and me had faded away to be replaced with thoughts of the forthcoming replay on Wednesday night. Thoughts of the young lady from Colorado replaced by the Old Lady in L4.

The relationship stumbled on for a further month or so but it was all a bit antiseptic, never again reaching the passion of that midnight romp in the University meadows. The Longonot excursion had signalled the beginning of the end of our affair. The downhill from the peak of the volcano on that Sunday afternoon, a metaphor for the direction our romance took thereafter. My mood swings on that mid-February day aroused by the loose gearstick and the cruel misrepresentation of an Everton result had sealed our fate.

The ending was written on the wall well in advance of the denouement that unfolded in a disastrous weekend at Lake Baringo in late March where thoughts of a dirty weekend were destroyed pretty early on the Saturday as Jill unleashed a clearly rehearsed lecture about how I put an intangible shield around me by setting standards for everyone including her and entrenching myself in certain aspects of my life that seemed unshakable and out of reach to those around me. What could she possibly have been referring to?

At least Cottee (2) and Sharp gave me a 3–1 win against Norwich to console myself with as we slept in separate beds in the tented lodge. Everton weren't in the FA Cup any more, though; we'd lost 2–1 in a second replay on that fucking plastic pitch at Boundary Park two weeks earlier.

Chapter 7
Italia 90: the death of the beautiful game…and my patriotism

11 June 1990: England 1 Republic of Ireland 1

The question is often asked of people seriously afflicted by a football obsession like me: 'How did it all begin?' The question is asked in a faintly sympathetic way as if there might have been an alternative if circumstances had been different; if I had just turned a different corner at the fateful moment when I caught sight of a professional football match for the first time. The fact that I can't imagine life without football now and that an 'international weekend' when Everton are not in action seems interminably long and empty, suggests that I was going to be blighted with this lifelong debilitation come what may. At school there were always the boys that had two left feet and could not tell their West Brom from their West Ham. In those days we thought of them as somehow 'girlie' or gay, while the majority who looked forward to football matches and PE lessons were 'normal'. Of those, some had more ability than knowledge while others were more into facts than showing talent on the field. I was more of the latter; in fact I was the extreme end of the spectrum; I was a 'statto' who knew every detail and every number relating to every player and team of significance. My knowledge was gleaned from newspapers and radio and TV and *Shoot*. Imagine what I'd be like as a schoolboy now with the information overload of the technological revolution. Frightening.

Even though my fanaticism was clearly in my DNA, an unavoidable genetic inevitability, there is no doubt that one team and one man pushed me headlong into the world of football more than anything else. It was Brazil and their talisman, Pele in the 1970 World Cup in Mexico. Watching those matches beamed from the other side of the world on a grainy black and white picture on our little family television set, filled me with such wonder and excitement. Pele, in my opinion is still the greatest player there ever was and will remain that way until I die. Not only his immeasurable skill and athleticism but his sheer enjoyment of the game and his desire to entertain. The recent sobriquet attached to Wayne Rooney of 'The White Pele' is not only insulting to the Brazilian but insulting to the intelligence of all of us who saw Pele in his prime. Those endlessly played video snippets of him dummying the hapless Uruguayan goalkeeper and then firing wide of the gaping goal or attempting an audacious lobbed shot from the halfway line against Czechoslovakia, were examples of football played in a new dimension. A new dimension of technical ability and also a new dimension in attitude; carefree, unfettered, unshackled by the fear of failure and confident enough to know that, if one chance was missed, another would arrive very soon afterwards. I was mesmerised and entranced and, without realising it, I had become addicted. I was in love for the first time and I was just eight years old.

From that time onwards, I looked forward to the World Cup with relish. Every four years, a month of over-indulgence like an extended Christmas in the middle of summer took hold. I looked forward to it for months in advance and then, when it began, I parked myself in the living room and watched and analysed every game on television. West Germany in 1974 with the bizarre Zairians not fully au fait with the rules, Argentina 1978 with the ticker tape and the questionable semi-final against Peru and the flowing hair of Kempes. We then moved on to Spain in 1982 and the best Brazilian team since the golden age of Pele who were thwarted by the resurrection of the phenomenal Paulo Rossi just when he seemed finished. 1986 was Mexico again and no Englishman can look beyond the 'Hand of God'. Again how people can utter the name Maradona in the same breath as Pele when considering the greatest player of all time is beyond me. Up to that point, life had been punctuated by these festivals of football, these splurges of unabated happiness as the world stopped for the beautiful game.

And so it came to pass that Italia 90 was fast approaching and I was some way from the action, teaching mathematics in an international school in the heart of East Africa. I was 28 but the childlike enthusiasm had not dimmed. As the big day of the opening ceremony and match approached, panic started to set in. Would the matches be shown live on TV here in Kenya? In fact, would they be shown at all? The FA Cup Final a month earlier had not filled us with confidence. British expats from miles around had piled into the British High Commission in Nairobi to watch a live transmission of the game but, as the match between Crystal Palace and Manchester United went into extra time, the packed room was suddenly filled with howls of disapproval and disappointment as only the 90 minutes had been booked by the Kenyan broadcasting station and we were reduced to huddling around transistor radios to hear the end of the 3–3 draw on BBC World Service.

With a week to go to the World Cup kick-off it still wasn't clear what sort of coverage, if any, the Kenyan TV stations were going to provide. We'd started to hear rumours that the French embassy was installing a special satellite dish to receive matches live but you had to be an invited guest of a French national to attend. Before I reached the stage of scouring the city for a French friend who was seriously interested in football, the heart-warming news came through; KTV were to transmit all the World Cup games live (apart from when there were games played simultaneously). The only television in the entire Braeburn High School staff compound at that time belonged to Rob Williams, a good friend who had arrived at the school the same time as me in September 1989. He had just broken up with his girlfriend and had bought a television as some sort of temporary replacement, I guess. He was (and still is) a very sociable, accommodating guy and, in line with the spirit of camaraderie that prevailed in that first year of the staff apartments, he opened his living room as a public television viewing lounge for the 4 weeks duration of the tournament, even when he was not present himself. Being a very keen football fan (Grimsby Town) he usually *was* present, though.

For that opening game on 8 June 1990 his living room was extremely well populated as there was African representation on the pitch and so several Kenyan staff also attended. It is something of a paradox that a continent that is so fragmented by tribalism on a parochial level, is so internationally united when it comes to sport. Thus the Cameroon team represented 'Africa United' on this Friday evening and the Kenyans were completely partisan. Given that the opponents for this curtain-raiser were 'those cheating Argies', the English staff were pretty well united with the Kenyans in who they were supporting. There was much noise and drinking in Rob's living room that evening as we turned a blind eye to Cameroon's appallingly violent tactics and just enjoyed the winning goal from Francois Omam-Biyick. In the drunken haze of that Friday evening we would not have detected it, but the cynicism of the Cameroonians that night was a portent of darker things to come in this tournament. The World Cup of 1990 turned out to be one of the dullest, most negative sports events of all time. As 1–0 followed 0–0 and dissent followed foul and back pass followed sideways pass, I began to clutch at straws. Seeing Cameroon's next match if only for the goal celebration of the ageless Roger Milla and the Kenyans in Rob's house became a highlight of the competition.

England, of course were a disappointment and, it is in respect of our national team that a life changing experience came over me during Italia 90. I have to confess that I lost interest in the England team. In fact, it was more extreme than that; I actually began to dislike England. In fact, I started to support their opponents. It's hard to pinpoint how this transmogrification came about but here is a rough chronology of the disintegration of my support of England. In the early days of my love affair with football, I supported England and Everton equally. As I started to watch Everton regularly through the '80s, the international scene became less relevant. When they introduced the international breaks to allow countries to prepare for their matches, I became mildly irritated by the inconvenience of not having an Everton match to go to on a Saturday. As Everton declined and their representation in the England squad diminished, I actually became indifferent to the fortunes of my home nation. As tribalism increased in me and in the game in general, I actually began to dislike aspects of the England team, notably the ubiquitous presence of Liverpool players in our national squad. This process had all been incremental and subtle, though. I had supported England fervently in their endeavours of 1986 and hated Maradona like the next Englishman for causing our exit in the manner that he did. But that England team had 4 Evertonians in it. There was not a single Liverpool player in the entire squad. Since then, without realising it, my disinterest in England had progressed to distaste.

How conscious I was in June 1990 of this 'anti-patriotism' manifesting itself inside me, I am not sure but it all came out in the arena of Rob's living room on the evening of 11 June when England opened their campaign against The Republic of Ireland in Cagliari. The room was awash with England fans baying for a trouncing of the Irish. I sat there silently, not joining in the banter, strangely subdued, inwardly digesting the fact that I had my own agenda for this match. A scared teenager on realising he's gay or that she might be pregnant probably goes through a similar self-examination. The fact was, I couldn't deny it, I wanted Ireland to win. In fact, I wanted it so badly it was hurting; this silence, this denial. It would have to come out into the open sooner or later. In fact, it came out in the 72nd minute of the match that unfolded before us. That was when an Everton hero of mine for the previous eight years scored his equaliser for the green shirts. Kevin Sheedy, Welsh by birth but with Irish ancestry, a former Liverpool reserve who saw the light and moved across Stanley Park, rifled in a trademark left foot drive to silence the English. Except for me, that is. I kind of yelped with joy as the shot sped past Peter Shilton in the England goal. And what made it so much sweeter was that it was a mistake by the biggest traitor to Everton until Rooney took his ignominious crown in 2004, Steve McMahon that had gifted Sheedy the opportunity. The Everton prodigy turned Liverpool and England midfield bulldozer had passed the ball inadvertently straight to Sheedy to score. This description of the goal may be filled with irrational bias but that's the point. The passion and feeling told me I loved that goal. It gave me the same feeling as if our Kevin had been in the blue shirt of Everton smashing the ball past a bemused goalie at the Gwladys Street End as was a more familiar scenario. Of course, I was sitting amongst members of academia, people of the professional class and of proven intellect so there was no chance of me getting my head kicked in, but it was still a fairly courageous expression of unbridled joy to have displayed in that company. The fact was, though, it was not premeditated, it was not an act planned to antagonise. It was a genuine, whole-hearted declaration of the soul. In the Club v Country argument, there was only one winner for me from now on.

So the ice was broken. I was now 'outed'. Whether I was regarded as a 'Judas', I don't know. Everyone was probably too polite to say and I really pushed them to the limit when I walked out slamming Rob's living room door in disgust when David Platt scored the 120th minute winner against a brilliant Belgian team in the first knock-out round approximately two weeks later. I was in a divided room when Cameroon self-destructed with their indiscipline against England in the quarter-finals. Suffice to say I was the only white on the side of the blacks. I came back into the fold for the semi-finals, though. Even my new found aversion to England could not transgress ingrained sensibilities against the Germans and I almost cried with Gazza as Bobby Robson's men came so close to a Final against Argentina. And there is no doubt I would have supported the Three Lions in that match as well, had England reached the Final; the Falklands, 'Hand of God' and all that, is not easy to forget.

The 1990 World Cup Finals was a watershed in many ways. Such was the mind-numbing negativity of it all, it resulted, two seasons later, in the most significant change to the rules being introduced probably since the game of football was invented. The back pass to the goalkeeper could no longer be picked up thus eliminating the game killing time-wasting that had plagued the tournament. For me, it was the time when I lost my affiliation to my own country's football team and I also fell out of love with the World Cup after 20 years.

My antipathy towards the England football team didn't lose me friends and, following that dire Final, I joined about 10 other staff mainly from 'Rob's regulars' for a great week in Mombasa as the school closed a week early because of unrest and the fear of a political coup in Nairobi. Mombasa was safe. When we arrived at our hotel and asked the receptionist about the potential for a replica of the trouble taking place on the streets of the Kenyan capital happening at the coast, he replied: 'What riots are those then? We didn't know about riots. It's too hot to riot in Mombasa'. The World Cup was over and I was immersed back into my new world in Kenya with its mix of humour and danger.

Going by my metamorphosis over the previous four weeks, I was becoming ever more distant from my homeland in more ways than one.

Chapter 8
Mixed fortunes

3 November 1990: Everton 3 Queens Park Rangers 0

Quite often I have tried to form a connection between my own personal fortunes and those of my football club, no matter how tenuous. I'm sure fellow football fanatics know what I'm talking about. It is from where all the ridiculous superstitions of footballers (and probably other sportsmen and women for that matter) are borne. Thus, a particularly good piece of luck midweek in my life could signal an Everton victory at the weekend or vice versa. Even if the correlation was weak, it did not deter me from making similar predictions again. Over time I started to observe that the relationship between my life and that of Everton Football Club was actually an inverse one. Thus the good fortune of Everton had an uncanny ability to come at time when my own life was going through a personal trough. In fact it wasn't so much fortune as form. The halcyon days of the mid-eighties when Everton swept all before them and apparently could do no wrong coincided with a period of my own life's lowest ebb with a failed accountancy career and failed 'first love' to battle with. Maybe God was just compensating me. Certainly, this 'opposite trending' of Everton FC and Cliff Green has persisted for much of my life. The start of Everton's capitulation from sixth to near relegation in the 1996–97 season could be traced almost exactly to a particular day; my wedding day!

And so it was in the autumn of 1990 that I was having an absolute ball; totally at ease with myself and my new circle of friends in my new life in Kenya, while back at home Everton were having a nightmare. With the loss of European football caused by the Heysel tragedy of 1985, Everton had suffered more than most. Possibly the most powerful club side in Europe at that time, we had no opportunity to test ourselves against the best on the continent. Most people suspect that the lack of opportunity to take Everton into the European Cup was the main factor behind Howard Kendall moving to Spain to ply his trade in Bilbao after he had won his second League title as Everton manager in 1987. The demise since then had been more rapid than any Evertonian had imagined was possible. Neville Southall, that eccentric dishevelled genius in our goal during the glory days of the 1980s saw the writing on the wall and didn't like what he was reading. He started the 1990–91 season with a bizarre half time protest in the game at home to Leeds when he refused to go into the dressing room with the rest of the players preferring to skulk around on his goal line for the 10 minute interval in front of a bemused Goodison audience. Perhaps he was pining for Howard Kendall to return. I know many Evertonians were. His outlandish show of petulance didn't help the team. That defeat was followed by two more and we were rooted to the foot of the table by the time the first victory arrived at home to Southampton on 29 September. Ironically that belated success came on the day of probably the lowest moment, or at least the most terrifying moment of my time in Kenya. In that panorama of joie de vivre at the beginning of my second year in Kenya, the one blot on the landscape came in the form of a violent break-in at the Braeburn staff compound when a gang of machete-wielding thugs stormed three of the ground floor apartments at 2 o'clock in the morning. Fortunately the occupiers of the three residences that took a direct hit were either not present or managed to escape. I was on the other side of the building to where the attack took place and, in the confusion of those sleeping hours with the sound of screaming and smashing glass waking me up, I dragged on some clothes and legged it up to the askari (night guard) at the compound gate. Armed with just a bow and arrow, he was in no mood to take on the band of thieves. Instead he made a lot of noise something like a loud whimpering which is what I was doing anyway. The combined noises of all the teachers eventually persuaded the robbers to leave but not before they had virtually emptied the three apartments completely. Seeing two rag clad guys carrying a fridge across the field into the blackness of the night is a sight that will stay with me for ever. So once again, the inverse relationship between the lives of me and my football club had raised its head.

The first bit of joy created on the football pitch by my beloved Blues all season had triggered an explosive unwanted interruption to my idyllic personal existence in sub-Saharan Africa. Several of the teachers involved in this scary experience never fully recovered from that crisis, and Braeburn High School suffered badly. Eight of the 11 teachers who had commenced their contracts at the same time as me a year earlier had left by the end of this, their fourth term; the horrors of the mass break-in had evidently broken the camel's back already weakened by the poor salaries and dramatic cultural change they were experiencing. As security on the staff compound was beefed up which didn't require much as, up to that point, it had consisted of a single string of barbed wire separating us from an open field and a flimsy gate manned by an untrained, underpaid askari with bow and arrow and torch, a few teachers went on strike in protest. The venerable Dave Anderson, the newly appointed acting headmaster was thrown into the lion's den of trying to quell the fire. He succeeded to some extent although two teachers vanished during the ensuing week never to be seen or heard of again.

In a strange way I almost enjoyed the post-invasion drama. It was another tale to write home about and, as one of the few who was determined to stick it out, I felt some sense of fortitude and resilience, even courage. Besides, as I have said, I was simply loving my time in Kenya; a slight encounter with a bunch of desperados who had actually murdered the occupants of the house they had attacked earlier in that week, was not going to detract me from my African adventure; it would just embellish it.

Everton were back near the bottom of the League by the time November arrived. That win on the day of the most unsubtle burglary in history, remained the only three point haul gained in 10 attempts. On the first weekend of November I had arranged to go on a weekend trip with the expatriate football team, Railway Wanderers. So at 10 o'clock in the morning of 3 November 1990, I set off in my faithful orange 'Bodie and Doyle-mobile' accompanied by two members of the Braeburn teaching staff who had decided to sample some time out with the football team even though they were non-members. We stopped off at Karatina, a medium sized town, for some lunch in the type of café typical of that found in rural Africa; garish formica table covers, jingly music, lethargic service and a menu limited to local fare or leathery chicken and chips. By mid-afternoon we had arrived at the Aberdare Country Club, a beautiful park set in rolling hills in central Kenya. Immediately I was greeted by a throng of Railway players asking whether I thought Colin Harvey had deserved the sack and who I thought would be Everton's next manager.

Such was my lack of contact with the UK in these times before the internet and mobile phone revolution, this was all news to me, but I felt honoured that I was regarded as the font of wise thoughts in these matters and proffered some instant analysis along the lines that Colin is a great Evertonian and a great coach but, for some reason, he could never quite adapt to the role of manager. Regarding the question of a replacement, there was only one candidate. Bring back Howard Kendall from the wilderness of Manchester City where he never really belonged in the first place. I was still young enough not to believe in the cynical, but often astute point of view that 'you should never go back'.

As was tradition in these Railway weekends, we had a fixture to fulfil against our hosts. So that afternoon on a hard, knobbly pitch that would not have passed the most elementary health and safety check, if such a thing had existed, Railway Wanderers took on the waiters, cleaners and security guards of The Aberdare Country Club in a game of football played in something approaching a gale. We won 2–0 and I scored one of the best goals I have ever scored, a dipping volley from 30 yards (although that distance tends to increase each time I recollect the moment!) I was one of the few Railway players to play the entire match and received many plaudits at the end. All in all, my star was climbing to a new galaxy. Being accepted as part of a group is a basic human need even for the most geeky misfit, or perhaps especially for the most geeky misfit. At Railway Wanderers I was very much part of the group. I had acquired from the club members the affectionate (I hope) moniker of 'Rainman' for my encyclopaedic recall of statistics relating to pop music charts and football results which had allowed me to star in several quizzes. I had also organised a number of pop music quizzes at the club and the British High Commission. It was very easy to become a big fish in the small pool of British expatriates inhabiting Nairobi at that time. I had a reputation as a sort of 'Mike Reid with football'. In these few hours in the undulating landscape of the Central Highlands of Kenya, though, I had had it proved to me and my ego that I was also received as some kind of oracle on all things related to Everton and as a fairly useful footballer to boot. I was the only Evertonian in the entire club which obviously set me apart somewhat, but the fact that my opinion was so readily sought on what, it seems, was the biggest story going around English football at that time, made me feel pretty important. Of course, as I headed back to the lodge, a nagging thought in the back of my head told me that all these warm feelings of bonhomie generated by the compliments and conversation of my teammates had to be a precursor to another Everton disappointment back home. The fortunes of Everton and me were always aligned in opposite directions after all. Imagine my pleasant surprise, therefore, when I heard through the crackle and hiss of my transistor radio that Newell, Nevin and McDonald had given us a 3–0 win at home to QPR. Even though Jimmy Gabriel had been in charge as caretaker manager, the word was that Everton had put on a great show and the players 'did it for Colin'. A strange sentiment really because, if they had 'done it for Colin' in the previous three months perhaps they would have still been 'doing it for Colin' for the rest of the season. It was an interesting paradox, though, that someone who is obviously a nice guy and popular with everyone – the fans and the players all supported Colin Harvey – could not motivate the players to win matches. His coaching skills were unquestioned and the players weren't that bad; there were still several remaining from the glorious team of the mid-eighties, and yet, somehow, Colin Harvey just could not make it work on the field. That was, until the day he left, or so it seemed from this sublime performance against QPR played out at Goodison Park on the first weekend of November 1990.

During the evening in the lodge as the events of the day were dissected among the beers and frivolity, I was once again the centre of attention as the one to explain why Everton had put on their best performance of the season when they effectively had no one at the helm. As the discussion expanded, the club chairman, Martin Barnard came round to make the draw for the golf tournament that was to take place the next morning. Despite my pleading that I had never struck a golf ball in anger in my life, I was put down to tee off with the opening threesome at 8.30am. No one was exempt from the competition.

So there I was, concentrating on that little white dimpled ball perched on its tee, giving gentle practice swings with my 3 wood as the mist rose to unveil a beautiful Sunday morning on the edge of Nyeri. And as the clocks struck half past eight, the first golf ball of the day was struck with some venom. It skewed off at something close to right-angles with the direction of my swing. A large hedge prevented it scaring or damaging the giraffes and zebras grazing on the horizon, although it certainly brought fear to one or two of the mass of onlookers who had gathered for the start of the Railway Wanderers Open, especially the handful who had ventured slightly in front of where I now stood feeling deep shame and embarrassment. I would rather not recount the details of the next two hours or so of my life that transpired at that time, my first ever nine holes of golf, or something vaguely resembling it. Suffice to say, there was a 'Hackers' Prize' for coming second from last and I didn't finish high enough to qualify. From hero to zero in the space of less than 24 hours. Everyone took it as a laugh. I also put on a front to that effect but, for several months afterwards, I experienced those bollocks tingling shots of mortification as pictures of that wild slash into the bushes flashed back into my mind.

As I drove my two Braeburn colleagues on the four hour journey back to Nairobi on that Sunday afternoon, I had to reflect on what a weekend of mixed emotions and fortunes it had been for both myself and the football club I loved. It had finished on an embarrassing sporting low for me, whereas, the players of Everton could wallow in some rare sporting success. Two days later, my good form and fortune returned as I learnt that Howard Kendall had returned as manager of Everton. And like all Evertonians, we were possibly even more delighted when we learned that Colin Harvey had returned as first-team coach just a week after his sacking as the manager. I was elated because this was all good news for Everton. But, hang on a minute, my good fortune and Everton's good fortune never coincide. What could this all mean?

Chapter 9
Derby month

27 February 1991: Everton 1 Liverpool 0

What it all meant, of course, was that the re-forming of two thirds of Everton's Holy Trinity as the Everton management team (Alan Ball never played any role at Everton after his premature departure as a player in 1971) never came close to being the dream ticket that Evertonians had all hoped for. The disintegration of the team from the magnificent, all conquering days of half a decade before had been allowed to fester for too long and gone too far; the malaise was ingrained and while English clubs were tentatively being allowed to rejoin the European competitions, Everton were nowhere near being part of that party. Some have said that Everton should have automatically been England's first representatives in the European Cup following the lifting of the ban, as we had been the champions of England when the punishment was imposed. If that had happened, I believe it would have been an extremely short-lived campaign such was the parlous state of our wonderful club at that time. There may have been some logical justice in such a decision but it may well have back-fired into an ignominious chapter in the club's history. A trouncing in the first round (there were no group matches in those days) against a mediocre team from an unfancied nation was not out of the question and would have done for Everton's credibility as an esteemed football club what my hopeless thrash into the Nyeri hedgerow had done for my credibility as a golfer, or, indeed, as a coordinated human being. So for the rest of that season, Evertonians lived in the hope that the best English player never to have won an England cap would somehow recapture as a manager those spectacular achievements of 1984 to 1987. As the impact was not instant (it took another month for Kendall to win his first game of his second reign) we began to seek solace from that word that all football fans turn to when success isn't quite as instant as we wish for; TRANSITION.

It was a word also applicable to Braeburn High School at this time. With so many teachers prematurely leaving the school during Christmas of 1990 dispirited by the poor pay and the horrific September house attack, a flow of new blood entered the staffroom. One of the new recruits was a very loud and large Australian called Neil Rickards who took over the IT department having fled Kuwait following the Iraqi invasion that had stunned the world in August. This was another aspect that made international life so raw and exciting. World events that only touched me through the television set or radio when I lived in the solitude of Shropshire, could now touch me directly with real people in my life. Neil took the trauma of his sudden unexpected upheaval with the phlegmatic nonchalance you might expect from an Aussie, but also that I have come to expect from someone who has travelled; a philosophical outlook that I would like to think I have also developed over two decades away from the UK. Having said all this, the backdrop of war taking place in Kuwait as Saddam Hussein took brinkmanship a step too far, was a chilling one for all of us during those days of Operation Desert Storm in January 1991, especially as we had some Iraqi children attending Braeburn at that time.

February 1991 was the month when I lost a good friend. We had had some exciting times together and she had provided me with many laughs and entertainment as we had survived several scrapes in each others' company but in the early hours of Saturday she passed away on the deserted Thika highway on the northern edge of Nairobi when two of the new young Braeburn teachers inadvertently parked her on her head having forced her into a number of somersaults first. Yes, my orange Capri lay there severely battered and concussed until the local constabulary towed her away to rest in peace (and pieces) at the Muthaiga police post. Dave Williams and Steve Anderson had already been saddled with the nickname of the Danger Brothers after less than a month in the Braeburn fold for their hell-raising lifestyle when I made the fatal error of lending them the flamed coloured mean machine for another of their raucous nights on the town. Exactly who was driving when the car spun out of control having hit nothing in particular on a clear dual carriageway at 1.30 in the morning, was never established. Everything was sort of rearranged after impact. All we do know is that the two of them had a miraculous escape with both of them too drunk to suffer any shock and, accordingly, probably too relaxed to suffer any structural damage save for Dave having a chipped front tooth. Neither of them even went to hospital and both of them were extremely apologetic at what they had done to my car. That was when my new found phlegmatic, 'take it in your stride' approach to life took hold. I responded to their expressions of remorse by telling them that I was just relieved that they were still alive. I didn't even harass them for any compensation, although they did pay me a token amount over the next few months. My third party insurance did not cover a write-off caused by two uninsured (and, in Dave's case, unqualified) drivers being at the wheel of the car with approximately half the contents of the Kenya Breweries inside them. At the time, I was also falling in love again and the young, blonde Braeburn art teacher that had taken my fancy, Vicky, had just acquired a new bright yellow Suzuki jeep. From an injury prone orange motor to a fighting fit lemon one that held romantic possibilities didn't seem such a bad deal. Such was the sanguine state of my mind at that time, I could turn any situation, no matter how seemingly grim, into something positive.

February 1991 was also the month of the Merseyside Derby. In fact, there were to be four of them in the space of just 18 days. With severe weather wrecking the fixture list on 9 February, just four matches were played in the whole of England, it meant that Everton's 3–1 defeat at Anfield received probably more coverage on World Service than it deserved or I desired. However, it came when I was still in the first flushes of romance with Vicky and so the pain was dulled a little. The following Sunday 17 February I was eating at The Utalii Hotel on Thika Road not far from where the spectacular demise of the Capri had occurred two weeks earlier. The company on this occasion was made up of three of the more senior members of Braeburn's teaching staff as they were entertaining a senior teacher from Lincoln School in Kampala who had brought a group of children across to Kenya on a school trip. The four of them had an agenda of school related discussion and I cannot actually recall why I had been invited along other than the fact that I tended to get on well with most of the staff from management downwards and I also liked to eat at The Utalii where the service and food were impeccable as it was a training restaurant for hospitality staff from the whole of the East African region. I do remember, however, that, from halfway through the main course onwards, what little interest I had in the conversation going on at that table at that time, dissipated completely as I noted that the fourth round FA Cup tie between Liverpool and Everton was reaching its closing stages.

If I had appeared a little distracted during the meal, thus far, I must have cut a figure of someone in a completely different universe now. I realised that I had better depart the scene before I began to draw attention to myself as someone having a severe concentration deficit. The match was live on television back in the UK. I excused myself to the bathroom. After relieving myself I looked for a waiter who could help me make an international phone call; not always a straightforward request in a public place in Nairobi at that time. Fortunately Utalii Hotel could oblige and I called through to a good friend of mine, Steve Bogie, who I knew would have watched the game. At the not insignificant cost of 385 Kenyan shillings I made a two minute call to learn that Everton had extracted a replay from Anfield in a goalless draw where Everton had probably had the better chances. I returned to the dining table with a glow on my face. Suddenly the tension was gone and, while pictures of those missed chances in front of the Kop played out in my imagination at the back of my head, I contributed eloquently and volubly to the remainder of the evening.

The replay was three days later and I had spent the intervening period thinking of little else. On the Wednesday night I again found myself in a conversation that I could not concentrate on. This time it was down at our 'local', The Castle. Vicky was part of the gathering and she drew me into a debate about whether we, as human beings, are all conditioned by society or basic innate emotions. A rather heavy topic when my mind was some 4,000 miles away at a floodlit Goodison Park trying to imagine what was going on. I explained to Vicky that it was the raw emotion of wanting to 'beat the enemy' that was controlling my behaviour at that very moment. She was clearly confused. I elaborated which just made her more mystified. How could a football match in Liverpool determine my mood and inability to communicate at a social gathering on the edge of Nairobi? I could give no sensible explanation and just wanted to go back to my apartment to glean any morsel of information I might be able to from the World Service; the tail end of news bulletins, a five minute special sports report, anything that might give me an update. But Vicky was providing my transport and so I was stuck there in the gardens of this ramshackle inn with the words of an animated discourse drifting above my head and past my ears as I anxiously checked my watch.

The agony was over at about one o'clock in the morning when I finally got my lift home. I fled from Vicky's jeep leaving a bemused and disappointed driver, to frantically scramble for my keys and rush to the phone in my living room. I got through to my Evertonian friend, Chris Grundy, immediately. He tortured me by giving Liverpool's score first: 'Liverpool 4' he announced. 'Oh, shit! We'd been hammered. At home as well'. But Chris's voice was too cheerful, too full of expectation. And sure enough the second half of the result followed: 'Everton 4'. I got the full story of how Everton had equalised four times and that it had gone to extra-time. Graeme Sharp and substitute Tony Cottee had scored two apiece. I was so elated, so joyful, I had to tell someone but there was no one to tell. Everyone had retired to bed for a working day the next day. My relationship with Vicky was still too fragile to test it with a request to share my ecstasy at this unearthly hour especially as the signs that evening had not suggested that she fully comprehended what this football madness was all about. So, I had to just content myself with keeping it all in like a kind of pleasurable constipation. I know I didn't sleep a wink that night.

I overflowed with my delight to anyone who would care to listen in the Braeburn staff room the next morning. Delight that was compounded by the news that we had won the toss for the second replay to be played at Goodison Park and that Kenny Dalglish had resigned as the Liverpool manager soon after the match had concluded. The thorn in our side for so many years, our nemesis of 1986, scared away by the mighty Blues at Goodison. The analogy of the brave Everton heroes defeating the evil red sub-class and chasing their despised leader into the turbulent waters of the River Mersey flowed from my lips with hyperbole that morning, even though we had actually only drawn the match. And fortunately there was not a single Liverpool fan on the Braeburn staff at that time to stand in the way of my vitriol. Some, like Vicky, tried to introduce some sensible logic to temper my outrageous claims, but they were not football people; they did not count.

So we move on to the final part of this emotional saga. It was played out almost exactly one week later. Having played in a staff football match against the staff of Hillcrest School on the other side of the city, I found myself getting tanked up with Tuskers in much the same company as the previous Wednesday evening. This time the debate with Vicky over football had become fractious. She was a feisty character which was part of her attraction and she refused to accept my emotional attachment to Everton Football Club as little more than some attention seeking ruse, a male need to attach himself to an identity. As a cold, logical argument, it made perfect sense especially as I wasn't even from Liverpool, but the fact was, for me it wasn't the case. My feelings were just that; feelings, uncontrollable emotions that gripped me whenever an Everton result was imminent. I couldn't help the nervousness going through my body, the near paralysis caused by the fear of receiving the news of an unsavoury outcome to the Everton match. An outcome that told me that Everton's score was less than that of the other team especially when the opposition was those hated Reds.

As a compromise Vicky tried to accept my addiction to all things Blue but refused to accept the negativity of hating all things Red. Again I had no defence, other than that's the way I feel. We then moved in to the dangerous territory of how this passion for something so distant and irrational could not be replicated with a more immediate connection with a real person in your actual world, like the person arguing with you right now, for instance. To try to tell a woman that does not share the football fever that there is no point in comparing a man's love of a football team with his love of a girlfriend or wife is like a woman trying to convince her husband or boyfriend that the other guy she went out with for a drink last night was 'just a friend'. Territorial instincts come into play and it's not easy to circumnavigate them.

Suffice to say, with my stomach churning with the realisation that the match at Goodison was over and nothing could now change the result, my mood went solemn and the altercations between Vicky and me became more monosyllabic and spiky. Once again I was dropped unceremoniously at my door at well past midnight to race to my phone to call England. This time I chose Judith as my source of information. She was a fanatical Evertonian and former neighbour of mine in Wem, near Shrewsbury. Judith informed me with joy in her tonsils that we had won 1–0 with an early goal from captain Dave Watson. This time my delight could not be suppressed. I was definitely going to share this fabulous feeling with someone. Vicky was obviously not a candidate so I turned to my faithful friend across the corridor, the one who had made his living room public property during the World Cup, the Grimsby Town supporter and one of the three survivors from the Braeburn teaching cohort of

September 1989. Rob Williams also liked his drink and I had little problem convincing him to drive me back down to The Castle again. Steve Anderson, one of the Danger Brothers, also joined us. I'm not sure where he emerged from but, I guess, 1 o'clock in the morning was much too early for him to go to bed. We persuaded an askari to open up the bar at The Castle and then act as barman. We went home at 4 o'clock, by which time I was convinced that I had converted Rob, Steve and the askari to the wonderful religion that is Evertonianism. I probably became teary eyed as I described Watson's goal which I had never actually seen (and have never seen to this day incidentally) and I probably talked of how Wembley was now a formality.

Sadly it wasn't; we lost at West Ham in the quarter-final 12 days later. All that emotional energy expended in February for what purpose? That's what supporting a football team is all about, I suppose; especially when that team is Everton.

Chapter 10
Perspective

20 August 1991: Everton 3 Arsenal 1

So my first two year contract was over. Having started up the A level Accounting course at Braeburn High School, I had made myself temporarily indispensable, especially as one member of its first cohort of five students in the class happened to be the son of Dave Anderson, the acting headmaster and good friend. With some negotiation with the managing director of Braeburn, I was given a one year contract under the normal terms of a full two year contract. It was unusual to allow a one year extension but I guess they were just grateful that I had seen out the two years which only three out of 11 had managed to do. Of those, it was just Rob Williams and I who had not even ventured back to the UK for a visit during that period. The contract did not provide for a flight back during the two years and, given my precarious financial position, spending in excess of £500 to return to my homeland did not make economic sense. Additionally, I had gone to Kenya with the attitude that I had to make it work come what may and that the only way to do this was to fully absorb myself in my new life and not take a second glance over my shoulder at what I had left behind. During the first six months when some acute homesickness took hold, it was probably to my benefit that I had adopted this approach of blinkered determination. Besides I'd had a succession of friends and family coming out to visit during that time. Indeed, as I boarded the Sabena flight to Heathrow via Brussels on 2 August 1991, I left two friends from the UK back in my apartment with a wildlife safari and a trip to Mombasa lined up for them.

It is hard to explain the feeling I had as a colleague dropped me at Jomo Kenyatta International Airport on that first Friday morning in August. I felt so confident, so excited and so, well open-minded about everything. I felt like a seasoned international traveller. I had stories to tell and adventures to relate to all those people I had left back home nearly two full years earlier. Remembering how unsure and tentative I had been when taking the flight the other way, heading into the unknown, 23 months on, I now negotiated the airports and aeroplanes with a self-assurance, even a nonchalance that comes from having truly tested oneself in another culture. I think the key word is PERSPECTIVE. When you live in one place your whole life, the view is distorted by bias and prejudice which in turn breeds insecurity and fear of the unknown. When you move away, that place that you occupied for so long is suddenly viewed from outside, as one small part of a vast panorama. All those points of view that were taken without question or debate, are now softened by the knowledge that other people see things in a different way and have very good reason for doing so.

I had plenty of time to go through this philosophical exploration during the 14 hour return to London. There were two details of that journey I particularly remember all these years on. One was the feature film showing on the small screen (no choice of what to watch, of course, in those days), *Postcards from the Edge* with Meryl Streep and Shirley MacLaine depicting two people who seemed to have lost all perspective, and the sports pages of the free copy of the *Daily Telegraph* that I had picked up on the last leg of the journey which informed me that Peter Beardsley had swapped the red of Liverpool for the blue of Everton for a mere £1 million. Even by the prices of that time, it was surely the bargain of the century. And why did the England star want to move from high flying Liverpool to stuttering Everton? Howard Kendall was weaving his magic already, it seemed. Just as appeared to be the case for one of its most ardent fans who was returning to the UK after a two year absence, the sky was no limit for Everton at this particular time.

My dad met me at Heathrow on that sunny evening at the dawn of a mid-summer weekend and immediately I felt the pace increase. Not just the driving (my father has always been an impatient person behind the wheel) but in the general hustle and bustle of everyone; taxi drivers, immigration officials, waiters, shop assistants and even the DJ on Radio 1 who seemed to be speaking a different language to the English that I was familiar with. Two years of East African life had evidently dropped me into a permanent state of first gear. For the four weeks back in England in the summer of 1991 I found most people to be in much more of a hurry than I remembered them being when I had left them behind for foreign climes in September 1989. I felt good knowing that my stride was somehow not in line with everyone else, though, and, with my tales of safaris and break-ins and sliding down Mount Kenya on my arse and stormy dhow trips and encounters with hippos by the swimming pool and muggings and, of course, the orange Capri, I suddenly found myself to be a much more interesting person than I ever used to be. I was probably boring the pants off many old friends but they were too gracious to say and I was too full of swagger to notice. Immersing oneself in another culture with the defenestration of all accepted parameters that applied for so many years does give a new dimension to conversation and life in general. As I said, it is called PERSPECTIVE. It also opens up new conversation with other like-minded people who have had their own experience of expatriate life. In a pub in Malvern, I jokingly proffered a 100 Kenyan shilling note to pay for two beers. I was somewhat surprised when the proprietor accepted it and then pinned it on a noticeboard that, up to then I hadn't seen, displaying bank notes from exotic places all over the world. And so an entry into an evening conversation with the owner of the hostelry about various experiences from far flung locations was secured; all for half the price of what the round should have cost!

Even though I may have become a little full of myself as a raconteur, I was sensitive enough to appreciate who my audience was. Thus when I had a reunion with my former teammates of the Sunday League football team that I had played for in Wem in North Shropshire from 1987-89, I steered well clear of African anecdotes and reverted to the more agricultural language and content that the player of Loppington FC were familiar with. I could be quite a chameleon if I wanted to be which allowed me to straddle many social classes. Of course, having the language of football at one's disposal opens up so many more avenues. Vicky came to visit me at my house in Wem, a house that I was now having severe difficulty paying the mortgage on as I had not managed to find a new tenant to occupy it for six months. As you can imagine, the now fabled Braeburn salary was woefully inadequate to cover even as little as £120 per month which is what I was required to cough up on repayments. She had come back to the UK for the summer to attend her sister's wedding which I accompanied her to.

It felt good to be with her in her home town of Watchet meeting her folks. I felt welcome and at ease and, of course, the Kenyan connection, made me feel that little bit closer to my girlfriend, as if we had a secret knowledge to share that no one else could intrude on. She had a wild cousin called Sean who became quite a drinking partner during my weekend in Somerset. He supported Liverpool and took great delight in informing me in the toilets at the wedding reception that Liverpool had managed a jammy 2–1 win over First Division debutants, Oldham Athletic managed by my first ever Everton hero, Joe Royle, while Everton had gone down by the same score at Brian Clough's Nottingham Forest.

So Vicky and I had travelled up to Wem on the Monday after the wedding. The next day we went to Liverpool. Vicky spent a day looking around the Tate Gallery at Albert Dock and other places of interest to an aficionado of art history which she was. Meanwhile I caught up on various friends from my university days and my two years as a trainee accountant in the city. In the evening we went to Goodison Park for the first home game of the season. In a magnificent exhibition of football, Everton put the League champions, Arsenal to bed 3–1. There were several new faces in this new look side and a former Everton trainee called Mark Ward signed from Manchester City particularly impressed. He capped a fine performance with two goals while Tony Cottee scored the other. Vicky tried to analyse the game rationally as we drove back to Shropshire that evening. Her lack of technical knowledge irritated me and her criticism of some aspects of Everton's play positively angered me. We had just played the best team in the country off the park for large sections of the match. Where's your PERSPECTIVE, woman? But that is the problem when someone who is emotionally involved discusses a match with someone who isn't.

That post match dissection disappointed me more than it probably should have. I had had the totally unrealistic expectation that Vicky, by accompanying me to a match, may have gained some understanding of where I was coming from with my pathological fixation with Everton Football Club. Quite where such a thought derived from I have no idea looking back. Did I really believe that the smell of the Bullens Road hotdog stand or the twinkling of the Goodison floodlights in the late summer Merseyside dusk was going to turn her head? That the exotic cocktail of swearing, sweat and uncomfortable plastic seats would transform her into a fanatic over the course of an evening; that she would lose all her sense of reasonableness and, dare I say, PERSPECTIVE at the stroke of Cottee's right boot striking the ball to make the net ripple in front of an adoring Gwladys Street. I really had some growing up to do. But I had to accept that, the fact that there had been no meeting of minds at the end of that match along with the fact that I was beginning to feel extremely comfortable again with all my former friends and colleagues from the Shrewsbury region, meant that the appeal of East Africa began to dim quite quickly. I began to have serious second thoughts on the wisdom of having extended my contract by a further 12 months.

By the time I boarded the plane back to Kenya on 3 September I really did not want to return to Braeburn. People I knew in Nairobi suddenly seemed strange and incompatible again just as they had all seemed when I had first arrived. In contrast my former associates from Shrewsbury Sixth Form College and Loppington Football Club seemed more substantial and dependable. The fact that a long term relationship with Vicky no longer looked on the cards; not just because she hadn't embraced my other love in the way that I had hoped but also because a month spent back in the UK had proved to me that I still loved being single, also made a return to Kenya seem quite unappetising. There was one period during my stay in England when I slept on 19 different floors and beds in the space of 19 days. As I drove around the country in my mum's Mini catching up with friends, relatives and acquaintances from past and present, the car radio was blanketed with news of the disintegration of the Soviet Union and Mikhail Gorbacev: Would he stay or would he go? The question could have also applied to me as August drew to a close. My mind was in turmoil. I needed PERSPECTIVE.

The reason I stayed in the UK until September was that I had been asked to be best man at a friend's wedding in Birmingham on 31 August. It was my debut as a best man and, stealing a few gags used by the best man at the wedding of Vicky's sister a fortnight earlier, I delivered a speech that seemed to be well received by everyone present. Again a new found relaxed confidence took over me as I rose to speak. A self-assuredness that came from the feeling that, after the experiences I had had in the previous 24 months, trying to be mildly amusing in front of a packed room of mainly strangers was not going to faze me. Seeing a good friend from childhood fight considerable local prejudice to tie the knot with a West Indian woman also made me think of many things as I sat observing the wedding reception disco later that evening, occasionally accepting an offer to join in with some inane party dance floor filler or romantic smoocher.

I interrogated myself: was I ready to marry Vicky? No. Was I ready to marry anyone? No. Did I like the idea of marrying someone from a different culture? Possibly. Did I fancy black women? Definitely! Could Everton win the League? The way we played against Arsenal, why not?

At around 10 o'clock I slipped out to catch sight of the evening news on a television in the hotel lobby and, more especially, the football results of the day. My duties had been such that I had not wanted to distract myself by knowing the Everton result. It was an Anfield 'Derby' and I couldn't run the risk of being knocked sideways emotionally by a bad result when I had so many key duties to perform.

And there it was: Liverpool 3, Everton 1. Beardsley with a late consolation. Could Everton win the League? For Chrissake, Cliffy, get some PERSPECTIVE!

My final year back in Kenya on that extended Braeburn contract, season 1991–92, if you like, was an anti-climax for me and for Everton. I fulfilled my main targets for the year of successfully reaching the highest point of Kilimanjaro at Christmas, completing the Mombasa marathon in June and helping Peter Anderson to his A grade in A level Accounting. There were other adventures and stories but the wide eyed newness of it all had waned a little from that sensational first two years of living in Africa. Likewise Everton's first full season back under the guidance of Howard Kendall was a massive disappointment. As I returned to the UK on 21 July, I and my football team were both striving for the adrenalin rush of past glories and excitement. It seems we were both suffering serious financial difficulties, as well. On 9 October 1992, it appeared that all my problems had been solved in one fell swoop. In *The Times Educational Supplement* I spotted a job that was made for me. The Berkeley Institute in Hamilton in Bermuda required a teacher of Mathematics and Accounts with recent experience of working overseas. And they were willing to pay a tax free, telephone number salary for me to take up the challenge. I passed the interview in November and on 2 January 1993, I boarded a British Airways flight destined for the tiny holiday paradise in the Atlantic.

PART 2:
A Clearer Picture

Chapter 11
I can hear clearly now

20 February 1993: Aston Villa 2 Everton 1

I arrived in Bermuda's tiny airport in late evening on 2 January 1993. I was met by the Principal of The Berkeley Institute, Mrs Michelle Gabisi, a warm natured black Bermudian lady with a sonorous voice that was punctuated with the hint of a lisp. She had just been appointed as the new leader of the state secondary school that had enjoyed a proud reputation as the most academically successful black school on the island producing high achievers in all fields of life; something akin to Bermuda's black grammar school. Mrs Gabisi herself, was a member of its esteemed alumni. However, she was being brought in, not to maintain the enviable standards and traditional values of the school, but to try to restore them. Having progressed her career in various teaching assignments around the world, she had now returned to her homeland with fresh ideas and an outlook untainted by the suffocating politics that develop in an institution that is choked by its own history and the insularity of a nation that looks only inwards.

You may have noted the term 'black school' in the earlier description. Yes, I was also surprised by this. The holiday brochures boast of Bermuda as being some sort of last bastion of multi-cultural bliss where the 60 per cent black population mix effortlessly with the 40 per cent white with no prejudice or friction. I also believed this hype. Well, how can I put it politely? It's bollocks! The schools on the island are a microcosm of the whole society. The state schools are predominantly black and are run down, gloomy places. In some cases they are quite violent. There were several incidents of stabbings in the schools during my time living there, thankfully none of them at The Berkeley other than a second year child trying to spear another with a set of compasses in one of my maths lessons. Meanwhile a majority of the white children attended the handful of private schools, where the exorbitant fees provided for immaculate buildings and state of the art facilities. In principle I was glad that I was not employed at one of these elitist establishments and, from my three years in Kenya, it appealed to me that I was in a school of around 550 students where 549 of them were black. Yes, there was just Peter Medeiros as the only white child in the entire school and he happened to be in my third year form class. However, it wasn't long before I began to prefer the idea of ditching my ideals and taking up a contract in one of the privately funded schools.

The Berkeley Institute had not just lost its estimable record of academic excellence for some time now, but it had also lost the plot in terms of providing basic discipline, a positive ethos and decent values. Sadly, with regard to trying to reverse this downward spiral, many of the staff were ex-Berkeleyites and had taught at the school almost since the day they finished being on the other side of the classroom desk so to speak. They could not or would not see out of their blinkers and, while whimsically lamenting the declining standards in their beloved school on occasions, seemed incapable of taking an objective standpoint from where they could do something about it or, more likely, hadn't the will to do something about it. There was a sort of narrow-minded possessiveness that allowed them to be mildly self-critical of their hallowed academy but, God forbid anyone else daring to say a word against the place that educated them.

Having travelled, Michelle Gabisi was viewed with great suspicion by the 'old guard' especially the acting Principal who was now being relegated back to one of the positions of Vice-Principal having failed to show the governors that she had enough original thought outside the Berkeley dogma, to turn the place around. Michelle Gabisi was starting her new job at The Berkeley Institute at exactly the same time as I was. Perhaps she had come to the airport to meet the only other new member of staff on that Saturday evening because she felt that she might need every ally she could possibly muster. She had some far-sightedness that I, in my wide-eyed anticipation was naively lacking. I was soon to receive a rude awakening.

I think it was in my third week in my new post when I walked into my form classroom first thing in the morning to be greeted with the words 'WE HATE WHITE MEN, MR GREEN, GO HOME' written across my blackboard. What dear souls 3E were. The Head of Third Year was a lady called Rhonda Woods and her position dictated that she was my line manager and the one to run to when in difficulties. A hardworking, dynamic woman (not at all Bermudian in many ways), probably a few years older than me, who seemed to have a mesmerising control over the children. The fact that she was black and was an ex-Berkeleyite gave her two distinct advantages over me, but she sure had some talent for communicating with children which I could only admire. Obviously I didn't want to seek her help too often as it would undermine my position, but there were many times over the next 18 months when she came to my rescue either of her own volition or from an SOS signalled from me. *Help me Rhonda*, that iconic '60s Beach Boys song became a popular refrain in my head as I made my way to work each day during my time in a place that I was soon to regard as a zoo masquerading as a school. This hurtful blackboard graffiti, evidently endorsed by all 32 students in the class, was the first time that I officially reported to Rhonda and it appeared to be the point when I accepted that I had 'lost the dressing room' to use a well-known football cliché. That was just three weeks into my tenure… and I never got it back.

Apart from the fact that my take home pay had increased approximately sixfold from my pay packet at Braeburn, all comparisons with my two overseas posts on different sides of the world favoured Kenya over Bermuda by some significant distance. The remuneration was a considerable sweetener, though, given the parlous state of my personal finances as I entered the New Year of 1993. It was the consoling thought that kept my head above water for the next year or so.

If life outside of The Berkeley had been more agreeable, I might have survived more easily but, the raw, wild, alcohol drenched times of Kenya proved a hard *social* act to follow as well. I made some good friends during my time in Bermuda but the nature of the country somewhat dictated the sort of characters who made a success of being an expatriate in this tiny nation. The adventurous, single, young people that had populated the staffroom of Braeburn High School were largely replaced in Bermuda by more staid, family people of an older age bracket. They had reached a different stage in life and were driven by a different motivation. Words such as security, future and nest-eggs filled conversations more than local gossip about who's shagging who amongst the new teachers. The soap opera of Braeburn had been replaced with a documentary on how to put up with the daily crap brought on by the ultimate example of 'an island mentality'. At 31½, with a youngish disposition, I wasn't yet ready for life's documentaries.

I tried to get into football. Amazingly I impressed so much at my first training session with BAA (Bermuda Athletics Association, founded in 1904), a second division side, that I found myself on the bench for a League game against Vasco on the following Sunday. I had not done any serious physical exercise since leaving Kenya half a year earlier and, in an attempt to link up with as many different social circles as I could in order to fend off the threat of loneliness, I had been out drinking vast quantities of beer on the three nights leading up to the big match. And it *was* a big match. In fact, it was probably the highest level of football I have ever participated in in my life. Bermuda may only have a population of around 65,000 people but I was playing for the team ranked at approximately 15th in the whole country. It was also an extremely hot and humid afternoon on Sunday 17 January 1993. All this is a build up to an admission of the inevitable. My half an hour appearance in the second half was an absolute embarrassment. The standard may have been quite high but I never got close to it. I can't even remember the score; I tried so hard to put the whole sorry affair out of my mind although I'm sure we lost as I remember the violent scenes of abusive language and cups and bottles being thrown about the dressing room in the post-match analysis afterwards. I just sat there, head buried in my hands hoping that the abuse and missiles didn't start heading my way. Mercifully they didn't. My performance had evidently been so innocuous that my presence on the pitch hadn't even been noticed by most of my teammates. I never played again for BAA; not so much dropped out of contention as dropped out of the scene completely. A self-imposed exile borne out of utter shame.

So my job was pretty shitty, my social life was pretty unfulfilling and my football career had hit the buffers. I didn't even like the ground floor apartment that I had been allocated by the school on the edge of the capital, Hamilton, with the noisy Canadians partying at all hours above me, but I was tied there for three months so I couldn't move until Easter. Life in Bermuda was not turning out quite as I had hoped. Even the good news in my life at that time came by way of consolation from an incident that I would rather forget.

Because the island is so small (just 21 miles long and an average of one mile wide) the roads are sized accordingly; the place is like one big pastel coated village with windy single lanes. Therefore, most people use motorcycles rather than cars to get around. Within a couple of weeks I had bought myself a little red moped. I had not ridden a motorcycle since I was 16 and on that occasion, it was one ill-fated attempt on a friend's driveway that ended up with me being extricated from under a parked lorry because nobody had told me how to brake! To be allowed to drive on the roads of Bermuda I had to take a short road theory test on a computer. It was a multiple choice exam. The first question was 'In Bermuda we drive on: A. The left, B the right or C It doesn't matter which side of the road.' Needless to say I passed with flying colours.

All this was not ideal preparation for going on the roads on a machine that I was not entirely au fait with. Sure enough, on about my fourth journey I mixed up the throttle with the brake as I tried to park it near a lamp-post. I slipped off the back as it reared up in front of me. I managed to hang on to the handlebars as the front wheel climbed the side of the lamp-post and then bounced down onto the bonnet of a parked car. All the time I was desperately hanging onto the handlebars until I recalled how to bring the wild jumping machine to a standstill. In the end the only serious damage inflicted was to my pride as I sheepishly looked around at the sniggering onlookers in Hamilton town centre. What was the good news out of this? Well, the damage to my bike was minimal and a friend gave me a replacement back light free of charge and, amazingly my insurance company paid to remove the dents and scratches from the car that my moped had crashed down on with absolutely no questions asked. After the corruption and bureaucracy of East Africa this was a serious breath of fresh air; one benefit of living in one of the wealthiest countries in the world compared to living in one of the poorest, I suppose.

The first pay packet arrived at the end of January and, seeing that first huge deposit in my account could not have been more timely. A 1–0 defeat at home to League leaders, Norwich had put Everton back on the fringes of relegation and, just as alarmingly, in front of a mere 20,000 people at Goodison. Things were looking grim for me both sides of the Atlantic and the first thoughts of jacking in this Bermudian adventure and condemning it to the dustbin of experience had begun to surface. Seeing a sum of money arrive in my bank account that would have taken six months to accumulate in Kenya, just about convinced me to stick at it. Recalling my shaky start to life in Kenya gave me a reference point to fall back on, although I didn't have Everton to prop me up emotionally with some encouragement on the field as I had when I first arrived in East Africa. Expatriate life can be unforgiving and lonely especially in the early days of a new assignment and sometimes a crutch is needed. Everton being top of the League did it for me in Kenya and now a $4,000 monthly injection into my personal finances was doing it for me in Bermuda. A Bermudian dollar was pinned to the US dollar and this was at a time when the exchange rate hovered around $1.30 to the pound.

There was one other significant advantage of living in Bermuda compared with Kenya; there was an FM station that broadcast the BBC World Service. Occasionally it was interrupted by a live debate from the Bermudian Parliament, but most of the time it could be relied upon to provide the BBC output. I had my radio dial tuned to it permanently. The voices of the broadcasters, clear and obliging became a source of great comfort after a stressful day of child crowd control. I began to know the programme schedules by heart and used certain programmes as incentives to get through the day. 'Don't worry, this interminable staff meeting will be over soon and you can race home for *The Vintage Chart Show* with Paul Burnett,' I used to console myself at around five o'clock on a Monday afternoon. *Just a minute* with Nicholas Parsons would put a smile on my face before bed on a Thursday evening. And so it went on, a backdrop to my life that brought some soothing perspective to counter-balance the mayhem that I encountered every day at work. I even wrote two long letters to the listener feedback programme, *Write on*, both of which were read out; the one about the distorted amount of news coverage dedicated to the Los Angeles earthquake of 1994 took up approximately one third of the 10 minute programme. The BBC had almost become my best friend in these lonely times, at least from Monday to Friday when I rarely ventured from my apartment. Friendly, interesting people talking to me every morning and every evening. I would turn on the radio in a room before I turned on a light. *Lillibulero* became my theme tune and my lullaby, a regular punctuation mark on each day.

And, of course, it meant that listening to *Sportsworld* on a Saturday was now a pleasurable experience requiring no delicate finger exercise. Because of the time difference the show straddled lunchtime which was disorientating for a while and made for an anti-climactic afternoon as the action was all over by two o'clock. At least I could listen in the peaceful knowledge that I wouldn't need to constantly hover over the fine tuner ready to fight off the peripheral stations as they infiltrated the voice of Paddy

Feeny or to retune completely when a Swahili programme crashed in on the second half commentary without warning.

So, as things settled down, a ritual developed in my life on late Saturday mornings when I would lie on my bed and just listen contentedly and undisturbed to all the sports events taking place around the world with the main focus on the matches taking place in the inaugural Premier League season as they unfolded. At around 1.15pm World Service would switch to the Radio 2 broadcast of the second half commentary. It was on 20 February when I heard the first crystal clear live commentary of an Everton match from Bermuda. Aston Villa were the League leaders and so I had an inkling that their game at home to Everton would be the featured match and I had been looking forward to this moment for much of the week, with a mixture of anticipation at this 30 minutes or so of pure indulgence awaiting me on my radio at the weekend and trepidation at the likely outcome on the pitch. The trepidation proved well-founded. Everton were appalling.

I find that listening to a radio football commentary can be a more rewarding experience than watching the match on television. It requires some element of imagination and effort on the part of the listener. And the commentators are, by necessity, more expressive and informative and often entertaining. When listening to your own team play, though, it can be a tormenting exercise especially when your team is being annihilated by the opposition as was the case here. From the sound of the broadcast it seemed like Everton did not venture out of their own half; it sounded as we had about three players on the pitch and their names were never mentioned in sequence as they never managed to pass to each other. The sound of the Villa Park crowd oohing and ahhing made it sound as if Neville Southall's goal was under permanent siege. By the end of the 35 minutes or so of constant barrage, I was relieved that the punishment was over and we had escaped at just 2–1 (Peter Beardsley made it much closer than it should have been with a penalty). So even the one oasis of joy that I had to immerse myself in in this fast developing Bermudian nightmare had turned into a traumatic half an hour or so of willing Villa not to score. I could certainly hear the BBC much more clearly now, and on 20 February 1993 I could hear clearly that Everton, like me, were heading into a very uncertain future. Something had to change for both of us, quickly.

Chapter 12
Base camp Goodison

18 September 1993: Everton 2 Liverpool 0

Somehow I survived that first six months in Bermuda which covered my first two terms at The Berkeley Institute. And Everton survived as well even finishing with a flourish with a 5–2 win at Manchester City on the last day of the season, a day that was filled with emotion as Nottingham Forest were relegated in Brian Clough's final game in charge. If I were to compare my own personal performance with that of my football team, I would say that Everton found safety with a little more to spare than I did; four points and seven places for the Blues compared with personal feelings of acute loneliness and frustration that often engulfed me and were driving me to think of all sorts of lifestyle alternatives to the one I currently endured. When a Canadian pastor, Reverend Purdey came to speak at a school assembly in March about missionary work in war torn Somalia, I firstly mobilised the whole school into a one day sponsored fast to raise money for the starving refugees and then applied to join the voluntary organisation that sent people onto the front line to give some direct TLC to the people in need. I figured that a quick death doing something useful in Africa was preferable to the slow death from child abuse (inflicted on me *by* the children of Berkeley) that I was currently suffering.

It was a combination of hope and expectation that allowed me to claw my way to the end of the academic year which concluded in late June. Hope came from the miniscule signs at school that Michelle Gabisi might actually be starting to make a slight difference; the general classroom danger level had dropped from about 9.8 to 9.1 on a scale of 1 to 10 since my baptism of fire in January, and the timetable for the next academic year was much more balanced and well thought out than the horrendous combination of lessons and classes that I walked into when I first arrived. The expectation came from the rekindling of my relationship with Vicky. She had started an art teaching job in Costa Rica at around the same time that I went to Bermuda. At least we were in the same vicinity as each other in a global sense and the idea of meeting each other in our new homes had become more and more exciting as each letter arrived from Central America full of warm, comforting thoughts to anaesthetise me from the horrors of a day at The Berkeley.

The holiday was long and I spent a month of it in Costa Rica mainly exploring the west coast of the country with Vicky. When I returned to Bermuda, I was full of doubts again about the future mainly because I didn't know what it held for me. I had two whole years left on my Bermudian contract but it seemed unlikely that I would see it out. Vicky and I had had a great time in each others' company but all the other doubts that were currently haunting me meant that I couldn't think about a long-term commitment. It seemed that Vicky could and did though, and a week after returning to my new apartment in Southampton in the central part of the island, I received a letter from her that amounted to something close to an ultimatum. Seeing the stark choice presented to me in writing of being with or without Vicky, I panicked and immediately booked myself on another flight back to San Jose. So we had another fantastic week together exploring the Caribbean coast this time. Again I returned to Bermuda not sure about anything.

As I stayed in a hotel in Miami for my connection back 'home' my mind was tortured with questions about what to do next. Should I seek a job in Vicky's school? I had had a productive chat with the headmaster who was willing to take me on if a suitable vacancy arose. Should I go to Uganda where a former Braeburn colleague of mine, Jim Park was planning to set up his own school? Should I go to Somalia and do something truly altruistic before I died which would probably happen pretty well simultaneously? I hadn't heard from the Swedish Aid organisation that was responsible for sending people to the frontline. Or should I follow the well trodden path of adhering to the adage 'when in doubt do nought' which has the distinct advantage of being the easiest and laziest option? While all this muddle was clogging my head, scenes of devastation were being shown on the television in my hotel room in Miami as Hurricane Emily was battering the American east coast not far from where I was now staying. The ferocious storm was now heading out to sea. I looked hard at the maps that were being shown on the TV screen. Was it heading for Bermuda? Some projections suggested that my country of residence was about to take a direct hit. That would at least reduce my choices to three and eliminate the easy, lazy option. Alas, by the time I awoke next morning to head for the airport for my 9.15am flight, Emily had started to take a completely different course and would barely tickle Bermuda. Once again all four options were in the frame and I was no nearer knowing where I would be living in 12 months' time, or even at Christmas.

And how to get to Christmas? That was a more immediate and measurable target to aim for. It required positive thinking and a psychological approach that converted the daunting prospect ahead of 15½ weeks teaching in a school that I had come to hate, into something more manageable. It was a formidable mountain ahead and I needed to take it in stages. The first significant target to aim for was just 2½ weeks into term. The 'derby' at Goodison was on 18 September. It was probably going to be live on television. That would be a good resting place, call it base camp if you will.

I then set about developing a positive attitude and a strategy to see me through the term. The first part of this strategy was to be completely ensconced in out of work activities. Soon after realising that I was in no condition to play in the Bermudian second division, I had linked up with a social expatriate football team called The Inlet which played on a Sunday morning. It was definitely more to my standard and I enjoyed the drinks afterwards which would usually enable me to sleep off much of Sunday afternoon before preparing for the battle that lay ahead for the next five days in work. I had become a central figure of the team, not just because I tended to stay longest at the post-match drinking session, but because I had introduced a club fanzine. It was titled *Outlet, the voice of the fan.* The content was supplied by me even though I requested other contributions. Footballers generally do not make good writers. At the start of the new academic year 1993–94 I threw myself into producing a third edition of this light-hearted rag. After struggling with the Apple computers and the staffroom photocopier at The Berkeley, I had about 15 copies of the flimsy publication ready for distribution to the lads. It featured a 'page three' photo of me skinny-dipping at a deserted beach in Santa Rosa on the north west coast of Costa

Rica...a rear view, of course! The second strand of my survival strategy was to do something positive in school; to ride roughshod over the crap taking place around me every day and connect with these kids in another way. I had already started running the girls' football team and had organised the sponsored fast that had accumulated over $4,000 towards the plight of the refugees in Somalia, but perhaps I could raise my game a bit further and do something spectacular to make my mark. The Somalia Appeal was the obvious area to exploit. In those early days of September 1993, the germ of a fund-raising idea began to formulate in my head, a germ that grew throughout the term and gave me solace and purpose whenever things began to fall apart.

The final strand of my strategy to see me safely through to Christmas was to 'go in hard' right from the start. My life is filled with football analogies but this one was very appropriate. Just as a craggy centre-half lets the opposition centre-forward know he's in for a rough afternoon by kicking him in the air in the opening minutes of the match; or at least that was the tactics of the '70s hard men before referees and strikers became over-sensitive to such methods, I was going to stride into The Berkeley Institute and from the opening day of the new school year I would show a new uncompromising approach. I felt that there were two factors on my side that could make this strategy work. Firstly, arriving mid-year as I had done because my predecessor had escaped back to England at short notice, it was always going to be difficult to pick up the pieces. The students of Berkeley were obviously fully aware of how they had chased the previous accounts teacher back onto his British Airways flight and had already smelt my blood long before I had walked through the door of the form room of 3E. If ever there was an image of a sacrificial lamb, it was me on that first morning in January at The Berkeley. Any teacher will also tell you that setting the ground rules at the start of teaching a new class is the key to maintaining discipline in the classroom thereafter. You can go from hard to soft but not vice versa. If the ground rules were not there when I arrived, then it was going to be hard to establish them halfway through the school year. The fact also has to be conceded that I underestimated the challenge and aggressiveness of these young Bermudians and had not been fearsome enough from the outset. This was a new year and a new form class, the slate was wiped clean and I could show them who was boss. Secondly, I felt a confidence in the new Principal. She had struggled to overcome the resistance of her lieutenants, but seemed to have now largely won them over. She was on the whole hated by the kids which showed that she was ruining their party, although there is a balance to be struck between fear and respect and I don't believe that she had gained either from a majority of the pupil population at that stage. There was still some way to go, but Michelle Gabisi had made a promising start and I felt sure that I could rely on her when push came to shove. And, of course, I still had the faithful distress call of 'Help me Rhonda' to deploy which had probably kept me from complete emotional meltdown on a number of occasions already.

So there I was tootling towards The Berkeley Institute before 8am on Wednesday 8 September 1993 with a nauseous mix of dread and fear coursing through my veins. 15½ weeks seemed a hell of a long time, stretching ahead like a prison sentence; my mental survival kit and internalised pep-talks were not holding up too well in the battle with abject pessimism that was determined to grip me. I parked the moped and headed for the staffroom. The greeting I received from the collection of expats did little to raise morale. They were more gloomy than I was about the prospects for the term. The Bermudian teachers tended to bypass the staffroom or arrive later or not at all. There were eight expatriate teachers working in The Berkeley Institute at that time as I recall and we used to meet for our coffee to try to fortify ourselves against the impending doom of another seven hours of verbal abuse that lay ahead. We gained some macabre consolation from each others' tales of woe from the previous day, although the flip side of that for me was that I would feel pangs of debilitating inadequacy if one of my fellow white teachers had had a rare success in the classroom. One guy, Dai Thomas, a Liverpool fan had been teaching science at The Berkeley for 12 years. As the money piled up in his offshore accounts, his face had screwed up to a permanent expression of unrelenting miserableness. He looked significantly older than his 42 years. Our verbal exchanges became a ritual every morning and a signature of my short time spent on the island. 'Good morning, Dai', I would say with as much joie de vivre as I could muster. 'Well, you're half right; it *is* morning', came the deadpan response. Then he might find some cynical observation to draw pleasure from; usually Everton's weekend result, although his team weren't exactly setting the world alight under Graeme Souness at that time.

And so the scene was set for the day, framed in an icy cold negativity. This was a new term and a new year, though, and I was determined to attack it with a bit of vim no matter how short-lived this enthusiasm might be. A new expat had joined the staff and was about to experience his first day in The Berkeley. His name was Vincent Fergusson, a stocky Barbadian technical drawing teacher with a gentle demeanour and deep voice. He had already started to show some doubts about his new place of employment based on the few days of staff inset he had endured but, at least, he hadn't yet been completely ground down. I latched on to him eagerly. Feeling like an 'old hand' can give you a sense of a knowing self-assuredness no matter how unfounded such feelings might be. So I made Vince a coffee and chatted with him until the 8.30 bell reverberated like a particularly unwelcome alarm clock and we headed into combat.

I laid down the law with my form class and then I did the same with the fourth year accounts class and then again with the fifth years and so it went on through the day. I emerged at 3.30pm unscathed and virtually untouched by any unpleasantness; those little bastards had hardly laid a finger on me all day. The tactic was working but it had been exhausting and there were still approximately 75 working days to go before the term ended. Meanwhile Vince was in a state of shock at what had hit him and I went round to his place for a few drinks to resurrect his confidence or help him forget about his day whichever he required. And so my new bludgeoning, take no prisoners approach to education continued; I thickened my skin and loosened my tongue and several felt a lashing. Some ended up in tears, others just open-mouthed but, at least, I wasn't feeling the pain any more. No more Mr Nice Guy from Mr Green.

The battering ram had a bit of a mishap on the third Friday of term. There had been some slight signs that I was losing my iron grip on my form class, so I decided to keep them in for an extra half an hour at the end of the day to give them a lecture on their responsibilities and the consequences if they didn't meet them. By 3.35 they had all come in to the form class, bedraggled and resentful. There had been noises of dissent and the odd swear word aimed at me as they entered but I stood stony-faced, completely impervious and they soon received my unrepentant message. My lecture began. There was a snigger from Peter Medeiros. He was the only child still in my form class from the previous year. There was a policy at the school that progression to the next academic year was conditional on satisfactory grades in the internal end-of-year exams. Peter had not achieved the required standard. As his silly little laugh disturbed my sense of authority, I walked up to him in a rage and bellowed into his face: 'Some people in this form are still learning what is required of a form 3 student but some have no excuse. Peter, the expectations for you are higher than anyone else. You cannot afford to mess up again. You need to be whiter than white'. Remember, this was the only white child in the entire school of around 550. What an unfortunate phrase I had managed to dig up in my fit of incandescence. There was the odd gasp and the hint of a laugh from some corners of the classroom. Obviously I realised immediately my gargantuan faux pas and was wrong-footed or, perhaps mouth-footed for the next few seconds as I tried to extricate the aforementioned foot from my mouth. I don't quite know how I saw out the remainder of that punishment period and I went home mortified with embarrassment. At least there was a weekend in which I could recover, although I spent some time fearing repercussions. Thank God it was 'derby' weekend to take my mind off this terrible moment in my life.

I rode into town to the Robin Hood pub for around 11 o'clock the next morning. It was an extremely superficial and 'white' drinking place but it showed the live transmission of football on a big screen every Saturday. Even though the Mersey rivals were both having an unconvincing start to the season, this was the chosen match for the live broadcast. The place was packed with about 15 Liverpool fans and precisely two Evertonians as well as many neutrals; a fair representation of the country's football allegiances and, as I liked to muse, it was a pretty good reflection on why I never really warmed to the place. Anyway, that's by the by; the most important thing is that Everton played Liverpool off the green grass of Goodison Park and won convincingly with goals from Mark Ward and Tony Cottee. I think I'm right in saying that it was the first time we had won by more than a single goal at home to Liverpool in the 23 years that I had supported them. And Bruce Grobbelaar and Steve McManaman started fighting each other on the pitch. Beautiful! I rode the five miles or so back to Southampton so proudly that afternoon with my Everton scarf flapping from under my helmet. I spent the rest of the weekend relaxing and enjoying the afterglow of a 'derby' success completely rejuvenated for the next week at work. The mind-numbingly stupid moment from Friday was put behind me completely once the summoning to the Principal's office did not happen on the Monday morning; a possibility that had festered in the back of mind like a rotting vegetable all weekend. Yes, apart from that almighty stumble, I had made it to base camp with something to spare. Just 13 more weeks to go.

Chapter 13
The final straw

4 December 1993: Everton 1 Southampton 0

So there I was fumbling around the hospital cash machine at around midnight trying to work out where my ATM card had gone. A woman politely came up behind me and explained that I had put it in my wallet no more than 10 seconds earlier. I sheepishly thanked her before shuffling away through a door towards the maternity ward. I quickly realised that this was another wrong move and wandered around for a few more minutes until I located the exit of A&E. As I walked out into the warm air of a Bermudian October night, I was greeted by two police officers. Panic shot through me like a lightning bolt as I was offered a seat in the back of their car. Apart from being picked up for walking on the M6 when I was hitch-hiking to the 1984 Cup Final from Liverpool, I had never had a ride with the 'busies' before. That little flirtation with the men in blue ended with a slap on the wrist and a helpful lift two more junctions towards my desired destination. Nine years later this brush with authority surely wouldn't have such a benign ending. The tone of the two Bermudian policemen was soothing and cordial, though and I was overflowing with gratitude as they dropped me next to my bike still parked at the scene of my accident. They wished me a safe journey home. It was indeed safe. Riding at 10mph on deserted roads with my concentration levels turned up to maximum is not likely to cause further bodily damage even if that body is still full of alcohol, concussion and shock. The helpfulness and nonchalance of the Bermudian constabulary had given me an almost 'African' moment. In fact, even better than an African moment as it hadn't concluded with a bribe to salve my conscience and secure my release. I laughed to myself as I gingerly entered my apartment at 2.30am. Well, as much of a giggle as the pain of major road rash on my right arm and four stitches in my chin would allow.

Exactly how the accident had occurred was not entirely clear. I was riding home along Harbour Road after my regular Thursday four-a-side football session with a group of expats followed by four pints of Fosters in Flanagans when I seemed to pass out. I vaguely remember some gravel and other road debris scraping against my right arm as I slid on my side. I then remember someone telling me to lie still and not move my head and then I remember the inside of an ambulance. Finally I remember a surgeon inserting stitches into my chin. Obviously fatigue and lager had a role to play in this affair but there must have been an element of stress as well. Despite my best efforts at the start of the term of trying to engineer a mindset of positive thinking and a sense of purpose, six weeks into this marathon half of a term I had 'Let the bastards grind me down' as Ronnie Barker used to so famously quote in the iconic '70s sitcom *Porridge*. He, of course, was referring to the institution of prison. Well the institution of The Berkeley was starting to seem like a prison to me. At least this close encounter with the tarmac of Harbour Road had given me an excuse to have three days off. Obviously I hammed it up and I didn't mention the role that alcohol could possibly have played in the mishap and I received nothing but sympathy and concern from Michelle Gabisi and the rest of the school's hierarchy. I felt relieved at having some respite from work but also guilty at the fact that this was essentially a self-inflicted incident that was causing my absence.

On the day after the accident Vince visited me after work to see how I was. When he related the story of The Berkeley Founders' Day that he had just experienced, I felt very grateful that I had missed it. It was supposed to be a celebratory day to recognise the school's proud history. Sure enough there was plenty of tub-thumping in honour of 'our wonderful school' but there were also fights and scuffles in the assembly and Stanton Summersall being taken away in an ambulance after being hit over the head with a metal bar by a classmate called Akoni Cupidore. The students all had such theatrical names and, it appeared, a penchant for drama. I was so relieved that I hadn't witnessed the whole self-indulgent, depressing spectacle. Perhaps someone was smiling on me when they caused me to black-out the night before, thus sparing me of the nightmare of The Berkeley's Founders' Day.

By the time I returned to school the following Wednesday, I was sporting a beard for the first time in my life. It raised many comments including some nasty ones from the kids but that was to be expected. I couldn't shave for a week after the stitches were removed because of the scar.

The half term holiday arrived after 8½ agonising weeks. There had been one day off at the beginning of October for the Bermudian General Election and I had added my own three days off for post motorbike crash disorder. There had still been 39 working days to endure. The students of The Berkeley evidently found it as tiring as the staff, going by the way their behaviour degenerated. It was a mighty relief to all of us when we reached 3.30 on the afternoon of Friday 5 November with the prospect of nine days of recuperation ahead of us. There were two days of inset at various locations around the island to attend on Monday and Tuesday but, as long as there were no Berkeley pupils present, I could suffer some staff training without rancour. Having managed to make it to 3.30 on that final afternoon, my rush to the Hamilton bars was delayed by Michelle Gabisi calling me into her office to inform me of a complaint from a parent concerning an incident when I had called my form class 'animals'. I responded 'guilty as charged' and then said that I couldn't promise that it would not happen again. I really had had enough. I drank just that little bit harder and faster that evening mainly with Vince. The sense that I was not receiving the full unconditional support of the Principal in a matter of child discipline for the first time was a distressing sign which seemed to register more sharply as the night progressed and the alcohol weaved its melancholy way into my head. Calling children 'animals' is hardly a method of discipline that would be found in any tome on child psychology, but at this point all I wanted from my boss was an arm round the shoulder and some words of encouragement. Vince, coming from a country of a more, let's say, 'old fashioned' approach to juvenile behavioural management, agreed with every sentiment I uttered as we wended our way through the bars of Court Street that night. I needed a mate like this right now and several times I must have told him just that as I became more tired and emotional.

The next days were filled with much self-examination. I had survived the two months of teaching at The Berkeley but only just. The 'derby' win had lifted me, as had the visit of Vicky for my birthday in the final week of September. Once those fillips had passed though, I seemed incapable of pulling myself through. The motorcycle accident had been timely but still I had reached the end of the half term with nerves frayed and a dismissive attitude towards my responsibilities. Outside of school I was enjoying the Sunday morning exercise with Inlet Football Club and the Thursday night four-a-side sessions in the gym of Saltus Grammar School but, otherwise, I embarked on the activity of drinking myself into oblivion every Friday night with increasing devotion. The Saturday morning ritual of crawling to the bathroom for the aspirins and the toilet to discharge at either end the poison from the night before had become repetitive and futile. I was in a serious rut. Something had to change. During that half term week I met a six foot Canadian nurse in a bar. I went out for two dates with her. The second one ended with her coming back to my place for a meal. At about 10 o'clock I drove her home on the back of my bike. It had been a good evening but somehow, both of us knew we didn't want to take it any further. As I rode back, a motorbike came round the corner in the opposite direction on Harbour Road almost at the very point where X marks the spot of my infamous derailment. The bike was doing about 50mph on my side of the road. I swerved out of the way and almost had a head on collision with a pursuing car doing equal speed. It was the closest I had ever come to death. It was fortunate that I was sober on this occasion. I stopped by the side of the road and waited until the shaking had gone out of my body which took at least 10 minutes. This scrape with death had happened at almost exactly the same place and almost exactly one month on from the previous incident. The whole eeriness as well as the scariness of the moment stunned me. If Vicky had a guardian angel, he must have got the wrong end of the stick with me and the Canadian nurse. If I had had any thoughts of seeing her again (which I didn't), I probably would have reconsidered after that. I may have wanted to end my time in Bermuda but I hadn't yet reached the stage of wanting to end my life completely. Not until I'd done something really worthwhile on this planet, at least.

Somalia was out of the question by now as I had received a letter saying that my services were not required by the organisation that Reverend Purdey was associated with. Possibilities in Uganda, on the other hand, were starting to take shape. Jim Park's letters telling me about the ground work taking place and the proposed opening of Hillside High School on 2 February 1994, filled me with excitement and I started to send money to buy shares in the project. A lack of capital seemed to be a problem for the fledgling business and I started asking other benevolent types whether they might be interested in investing in a school on the edge of Kampala. This included my parents.

I didn't realise what consternation this had caused back home but an epic letter from my sister soon put me in the picture. Apart from saying how unfair I had been to even ask our mum and dad to be involved financially in what she clearly considered a hare-brained adventure so soon after they had bailed me out with my mortgage while in Kenya (although I had now paid them back completely), she took it as an opportunity to tell me how to run my life and how not to be so selfish. To be honest, it seemed that she was questioning the point of my whole existence. In hindsight it seems that she had an uncanny sixth sense of what was happening to her brother 3,500 miles away as I had been asking myself the same question. Her sledgehammer approach of telling me to 'pull myself together' was not appreciated at the time, though. The letter arrived two days after the nearly fatal moment on Harbour Road; the second one, that is, and about two hours after I had verbally handed in my notice to Michelle Gabisi. My memory of the way this momentous event happened is not clear. I cannot be sure that my intention as I rode into Hamilton on that Monday morning was to resign but I know, following the heart-stopping incident on Harbour Road two days earlier, that I had spent the whole of the Sunday seriously thinking about leaving the island forever. As I walked into the reception of The Berkeley Institute, Michelle noted my melancholy mood. Normally I raised a cheery 'Good morning' if I saw her as I signed in, usually as one of the first to arrive at around 8 o'clock. On that day my greeting was more of a morbid Dai Thomas type of effort. It alarmed Michelle who immediately called me into her office. I left 15 minutes later having explained why I wanted to leave and that I would work to the end of the academic year to give her time to find a replacement. This was also for selfish reasons as I knew that Hillside High School would not be in a position to accommodate me until at least next July going by the slow progress currently being made according to Jim's letters. By now my sights were very much set on returning to East Africa. The idea of helping to set up a school in Uganda was possibly that philanthropic act that I was looking for to fulfil me. Financially it may have been risky but it didn't have the life threatening element of entering a Somali war zone.

This turned out to be the resigning season. The day after Michelle received my news, The English FA received the same announcement from Graham Taylor as the

England manager. Unlike me he was likely to be pushed, anyway. I assume that I was not going to be asked to leave The Berkeley, although maybe if I had tried to see out my contract, it was inevitable that I would have done something to have persuaded the authorities that it was in everyone's interest for The Berkeley Institute and Cliff Green to part company. Some moment when my resistance was cracked by a nasty confrontation with a Berkeley child who pushed their luck too far and I lashed out physically or verbally to an extent that made my position untenable.

Such an incident almost occurred on the Friday before the resignation and had probably been the catalyst for that Monday morning denouement with the Principal. It had happened on the last lesson in the morning when I presented the fourth years with a mathematics test. In schools that I had attended so far in my life as teacher and student, a class test was a time when the teacher could relax a little. Bermuda was different. The concept of not communicating to each other in the classroom seemed alien to these kids even during a test. I tried to impose rules more familiar to me and insisted on silence throughout. I had just about achieved this. However, when students reached the end of the test they felt that this gave them carte blanche to chat to each other, even to chat to those that had not completed the test. I disagreed with this idea and insisted on silence until the bell for the end of the lesson was sounded. Anyone found talking during the one hour lesson would have their test treated as null and void and receive a zero mark as far as I was concerned. I announced this rule to the class as the first student told me that he had finished. As I completed this announcement, Harry Hunt immediately spoke to the boy next to him. I went over and whipped Harry's script from his desk and triumphantly ripped it up in front of him and threw it in the bin. Harry Hunt stood up and shouted something along the lines of 'You can't do that' to which I replied something to the effect of 'I just have'. His next lines I can quote verbatim. 'OK, white boy, you just watch this.' He then strode out of the class and slammed the door behind him. He returned soon afterwards with Michelle Gabisi. The lesson was concluded without further incident but lunchtime was taken up with a long conference with Michelle, Harry Hunt and me. I just about had the backing of the Principal but it was a split decision.

Looking back on it, I can see that my method had been somewhat confrontational and gave little scope for a way out from either side. At the time, though, I simply wanted support from The Principal. The support came but it was unconvincing. By the end of that evening a little rhyme had formulated in my head, it was four words long, started with the words Harry Hunt and the second line rhymed with the first. I was taking this all so personally. So the showdown with Harry Hunt proved to be the final straw for me. For Graham Taylor it was Luxembourg scoring in the first minute against England in a World Cup qualifier. England went on to win 7–1 but the fact that England went a goal behind against the international minnows was a defining moment in what had become a disastrous reign for the affable Mr Taylor. The fact that England hadn't qualified for the 1994 Finals in the USA obviously meant that he had nowhere to go but out of the door of Lancaster Gate never to return.

Howard Kendall was the third to fall on his sword. He hung on for a few days longer, but for him the final straw was something to do with wanting to sign the Manchester United reserve striker, Dion Dublin but being told that the club couldn't afford the £1.5 million fee. I had just ridden back to my apartment having watched a sensational top of the table clash at The Robin Hood that ended Manchester United 2 Norwich City 2. As *Sports Report* concluded the results they broke in for a newsflash. It was shock news to me and to the BBC as I recall as they said that they were hearing from Goodison that Howard Kendall had resigned immediately after Everton's 1–0 win at home to Southampton. The day had started so brightly as well with Tony Cottee scoring in the first few minutes of the match; it was 11 hours of football and the next calendar year before we scored again.

That resignation of Howard Kendall after a completely unfulfilling second spell as manager at the club was a turning point for me. It was as if things couldn't sink any lower. Vicky arrived in Bermuda three days later and stayed for nearly four weeks making it a memorable Christmas for me. I worked hard on my big sponsored event. The first fund-raiser had been a one day fast to give the over-indulged Bermudian children some idea of what it is like to go hungry. For the second event I felt it apt for them to experience some idea of what it is like to walk a long way as many of the Somali refugees had to. Geographically Bermuda is limited in providing opportunities for long walks but, at least The Berkeley Institute was quite central being on the edge of the capital, Hamilton. With meticulous planning and enormous energy I managed to get the entire school to walk seven miles to school on the final morning of the term. On Friday 17 December 1993 around 300 pupils and teachers walked from a point on the west of the island, and around 300 pupils and teachers walked from a starting point seven miles east of Hamilton. I had presented an assembly to explain the logistics to the entire school, I had designed and printed the sponsor forms, I had mobilised the media and given interviews on television and radio and, in the end, I had motivated the students and staff of The Berkeley to raise over £6,000 for the starving, desperate people of Somalia. I had finally found light at the end of the tunnel and the prospects for 1994 looked a whole lot brighter. Meanwhile Everton, rudderless and mediocre began to nosedive down the League losing four games in a row over Christmas. After a period when the mood of my club mirrored my own, our paths were once again diverging.

Chapter 14
The Great Escape: Part 1

7 May 1994: Everton 3 Wimbledon 2

It's a sad indictment on the fortunes of my beloved football club since the heady days of the mid-1980s that one of the best-selling videos/DVDs in the club shop features our two great escapes in 1994 and 1998 when, on the very last day of the season, we avoided leaving·the top flight of English football for the first time since promotion from the second division in 1954. While Manchester United and Arsenal could make a whole catalogue of home viewing full of great goals and trophies over the last 20 years, since the technology and marketing nous of the top clubs allowed for such compilations to be made and sold, Evertonians are limited to little more than video biographies of the iconic (but regretfully largely unsuccessful) Duncan Ferguson, our solitary piece of silverware from the win against Manchester United in the 1995 FA Cup Final and those two last day redemptions.

I had engineered my own personal great escape some considerable time before Everton performed their 11th hour extrication from the Premier League's trapdoor. It meant my last six months at The Berkeley Institute were much more bearable than the first year had been. Turning a blind eye and a deaf ear to some of the nonsense going on in and around my classroom proved somewhat easier when I had the knowledge that I had a point on the calendar to aim for when my exit from the island was assured. I can't say that, in any way, I began to warm to the pupils in my charge but, perhaps with a new detached nonchalance, I could at least be more philosophical as to why we just had not 'got on'. Parents' evenings gave me an insight. At Shrewsbury Sixth Form College and Braeburn High School these occasions had been, on the whole, an opportunity for constructive dialogue between teacher and carer. The motivation for parental interest may have been different but it was equally powerful in both cases; at Shrewsbury the families were generally middle class with high aspirations for their child's success; in Kenya the pupils I taught were, in the main, offspring of high flying parents who expected their children to meet the same standards that they themselves had achieved, especially given the considerable amounts of money being invested in their education.

At the very first parents' consultations that I attended at The Berkeley Institute I detected a completely different attitude. Education was free. It was also seemingly dispensable in the eyes of many parents that attended. The island boasted of 100 per cent employment so there was no fear of going without a job. When even a road sweeper could earn $30,000 per annum tax-free, what was there to strive for? Quite often the child would be accompanied at the consultation evening by just a single mother. Not only would this woman be quite ignorant of her child's needs or abilities, she would be grossly overweight. Obesity was a massive issue in Bermuda; a symptom of decadent over-indulgence. There was usually evidence of matriarchal discipline and domination as the child would usually look quite cowed in the presence of their overbearing mother but there was also often the appearance of an emotional disconnection. The mother often had little interest in the content of her child's mathematics book or anything else of educational nature but would prefer to use her allotted 10 minutes with the teacher bemoaning the absence of a feckless 'wacky backy' snorting father.

It is impossible to give a snapshot of a nations' society in one paragraph and I could be accused of stereotyping here, but, in my opinion, there were certainly a lot of pubescent youths in Bermuda who had quite hollow existences with little or no contact with a male role model and a disenfranchisement from their only family female role model. With a little black American angst thrown in to the mix, often manifesting itself into an anti-white victim mentality, it was clear why I and all the other white male teachers in The Berkeley experienced a perpetual undercurrent of non-compliance in our classrooms. In summary we were on a hiding to nothing because we were male, white and saw a purpose in education. In the heat of battle, though, when a 15-year-old angry young man is telling you to 'fuck off' it is not easy to instantly consider the empty, possibly violent home life of this wild adolescent confronting you and allow sympathy to intervene.

From the moment Vicky and I had parted at Bermuda's airport for her return to Costa Rica on 5 January 1994, I had faced life in Bermuda with a new resolve. I started a routine of running from the south coast to the north coast every morning before breakfast. This might sound impressive but it actually amounted to about 1½ miles as I lived on just about the narrowest part of the island. I developed a strict discipline of work from Sunday to Wednesday, let myself go a little on Thursday with the four-a-side football workout at Saltus and then got completely 'off my face' so to speak every Friday evening. Saturday was recuperation time with the now regular live Premier League match at The Robin Hood as the main entertainment. Sunday morning consisted of a 90 minute game for Inlet, a quick drink and then back into the routine for a new week ahead.

Vince introduced me to the bars of Court Street every Friday. The expats that I had first met up with in Bermuda had told me it was a 'no-go' area for whites which had instantly made me determined to go there. My association with Vincent gave me my passport to enter that part of Hamilton and, although I was refused service in some of the bars and looked at threateningly by many, I liked the fact that I had broken the taboo as one of the only white faces in the district. I also liked the company of Vince and the Barbadian friends that he introduced me to. Vince was a much harder and heavier drinker than me but, apart from giving me the opportunity to experience the edgy thrill of a night on Court Street, he also introduced me to the concept of abstaining from alcohol for the duration of Lent; a ritual that I have continued to observe ever since as an annual act of self-discipline and internal body cleansing.

All in all 1994 was looking like a much better prospect than the previous year and I started to prepare for the second half of it with relish. I managed to acquire donations of old text books from several schools on the island to send to Hillside High School and enrolled several friends and relatives on a scholarship scheme whereby needy children local to our new school on the south west tip of Kampala had their fees paid for by overseas sponsors. Obviously it was a way of boosting the finances of the school while giving people the opportunity to salve their consciences by serving a worthwhile cause. For all my criticism of the nation and its people, I have to say that Bermudians were extremely generous in this respect. To me there seemed to be a certain equitable symmetry in one of the richest nations in the world redistributing wealth to one of the poorest. I had to be careful not to mix up the selfish profit motive of Hillside High School which ultimately had to be the objective if it were to sustain me, with its philanthropic element. Sometimes the line became dangerously blurred, I fear.

So, there was my escape plan signed and sealed. What about Everton's? It became obvious by Easter time that an escape would be necessary. As I fell off the wagon, Everton had come completely off the rails. Mike Walker was in charge. The white haired, rather dour character who had magicked Norwich City to a European success against Bayern Munich and to the top four of the Premier League had taken the step *up* to manage Everton who were sinking fast towards relegation. Apart from a 6–2 thrashing of the 'out-of-their depth' Swindon Town (yes, Swindon Town v Wimbledon was a Premier League fixture 17 years ago!), there had been few signs of a revival. A derby defeat at Anfield on 13 March signalled the start of a calamitous decline.

After participating in a pop quiz at The Robin Hood when I realised how my photographic memory for pop trivia had faded badly during my five years abroad, I got into a deep and gloomy conversation with an Evertonian called Wayne. It is a strange fact but a fact all the same, that when I meet an Evertonian expat, the unifying attraction of sharing the same 'religion' overrides everything else. I don't bother to find out about their job, their history, their life; they could be an escaped rapist avoiding extradition for all I know (although I would like to deceive myself that such lowlife do not follow Everton). All I need is their name so that our conversation about our football team can progress with a modicum of chumminess. And our football team can provide enough material to fill many hours of conversation. And so it was with Wayne. To this day, I have no idea how he occupied his days in Bermuda and I have no idea where he is now. I can barely remember what he looked like. None of that matters. Our common detailed knowledge and passion for Everton was the glue that bound us for the few months that we were acquainted with each other. On this, our first meeting at that Robin Hood quiz night, we lamented the state of our club and what had gone so spectacularly wrong in the past seven years. We both concluded the evening exceedingly inebriated and with the absolute conviction that Everton would be relegated. At this stage there were just five games to go and we had just lost 5–1 to Sheffield Wednesday and 3–0 to Blackburn and were a point off the bottom three.

The following Saturday Tony Cottee scored against his beloved West Ham to give Everton three priceless points. He did the same at QPR the following week to put us 1–0 up but we capitulated to a 2–1 defeat. A dismal 0–0 draw at home to Coventry City was followed by a 3–0 'massacre' at Leeds United when we were 'lucky to get nil' as they say. This Elland Road mauling put us into the bottom three for the first time all season and there was one match left: home to Wimbledon on 7 May 1994.

All week I had been anticipating this match. Once it had been confirmed as being the live televised match, I looked forward so much to my visit to The Robin Hood that Saturday morning. Somehow I felt that, by watching it, I could influence the outcome in our favour. Insanely I had organised some private mathematics tuition on that Saturday morning. It was with a girl called Odia. Pronounced as it is spelt. A very apt name in the context of this day. I mean, what was I thinking of, having another engagement on the morning of the most significant day in Everton's history in my lifetime? Indeed, as I raced that morning as fast as it is possible for a two stroke engine to race from Odia's house to The Robin Hood with my faithful Everton scarf flapping in my slipstream, the enormity of the occasion was starting to get to me. I was becoming extremely nervous. I remember seeing people playing golf as I headed into Hamilton and thinking 'How can they be smiling and pre-occupied with something like a game of golf when Everton's very existence in the Premier League was about to be decided?'

After the roller coaster five years I had had when my commitment to Everton had been tested to the limit by the fuzziness of the World Service and the intensity of my worldly experiences, suddenly all those deep feelings for my beloved Blues had returned at this hour of need. I hadn't slept well all week; I just couldn't bring myself to contemplate us playing in a lower division. Here I was, on the brink of trying to make a difference to the world by building a school in sub-Saharan Africa and yet suddenly I was consumed with fear and worry over the plight of Everton Football Club. Where was the perspective there? What a mixed up contradiction my life was.

I hurriedly parked my bike and rushed up the steps to the entrance of The Robin Hood. It was already 11.10am and Wayne's ashen face said it all. We were 1–0 down after 10 minutes thanks to a ludicrous penalty given away by Gary Ablett. At the very least, I thought we could keep it tight for the first half an hour. Soon it was 2–0. This time a comical own-goal. Everton's nerves were shot worse than mine; the players looked devoid of confidence, incapable of playing a single pass. I am sure at that point I gave up. The

Bermudians watching had some strange fascination in the game. They had probably heard of Everton as a quite famous football club and, seeing the look of abject despair on the faces of Wayne and me, they took pity. There was not a large gathering in The Robin Hood that morning but those present started to root for Everton. Just before half time the referee gifted us a lifeline when Anders Limpar took an outrageous dive in the penalty area and he presented us with a spot-kick. Graeme Stuart converted. The cameras missed Barry Horne's sensational equaliser from 25 yards midway through the second half, it was so out of context with the rest of the match. With nine minutes left, Everton were still going to be relegated if they didn't find a winner and then Graeme Stuart shot, Hans Segers went down in instalments in the Wimbledon goal and Everton's Houdini act was complete.

At that point Ipswich were to be relegated but then in the very last minute at Stamford Bridge Chelsea scored a winning goal against Sheffield United to send them down instead. A truly sensational 10 minutes. It was now lunchtime but I had no interest in food. I drank solidly for six hours until I ran out of stamina and money. Somehow I rode the five miles back home and cried real tears of joy when I staggered across the threshold of my apartment. I was so happy and so relieved all at once. It was a truly memorable day in my personal Everton history. Perhaps the best ever, even better than the trophies of the mid-80s. Those were filled with joy, but somehow when joy is mixed with relief it makes for a more potent combination and the fact that I experienced this with just one other fellow-Evertonian made it feel better than when I shared the successes of 1984 to 1987 in Liverpool with thousands of others blessed with the same blue blood.

In that glitzy pub in the centre of Hamilton, I had become the focus of attention. My anguish and then ecstasy witnessed by so many who were then keen to ask what all the fuss was about when the game was over. Complete strangers buying me drinks and then I reciprocating just to have the chance to tell them what being an Evertonian was all about. As with the askari at the bar in Nairobi who I drank with all night after the 1–0 Cup win against Liverpool, I also had some naïve belief that I might just convert a native to the wonderful world of Evertonianism, and once again, no doubt, I failed. Being an ardent football fan abroad can have moments like this that cannot be equalled back home. A bit like comparing missionary work in the colonies to preaching in a church in British suburbia. Perhaps that's why I still had the wanderlust; With Everton now safe for another season it was all systems set for Uganda.

Chapter 15
Slam Dunc

---

21 November 1994: Everton 2 Liverpool 0

Many a time had I chewed the fat with Braeburn colleagues over a vat of Tuskers at The Castle Inn doing simple calculations on how the owners of the school who employed us were so amazingly rich. For some the conversation would become embittered with questions as to why the salaries we were paid were so paltry. For others like me, it opened up possibilities and ideas of how to follow the example of the Braeburn shareholders except do it better. For me, better meant doing it with a more philanthropic bent; paying the workers a wage that allowed them to support their families properly, lowering fees to a level that permitted more of the local community to make use of the international standard facilities and education on offer and investing in the local teachers so that ultimately the indigenous population could run the school for themselves.

Well, that was my vision at least. Problem was, I had never actually discussed whether this was the vision of those that I had now gone into business with to build Hillside High School in Bunamwaya, a small trading centre about six miles south-west of the centre of Kampala. In my haste to leave behind the nightmare of Bermuda, I had sent my money to Uganda with little thought as to what was happening to it when it was received at the other end. My trust had been placed in Jim Park, a former colleague of mine at Braeburn who had lived in East Africa for well over two decades. He had first worked in a school in Kigezi in the south of Uganda in the early '70s but had been forced to leave when Idi Amin's brutal reign took hold. He then moved across to Kenya. He was 15 years my senior but still had the enthusiasm for life of someone half his age. He took an active part in sport mainly rugby and had an acute appreciation of the benefits of a hedonistic existence that can be enjoyed by an expat living in East Africa. From his earlier connections in Uganda, Jim had linked up with a Ugandan businessman called Wilbrodiz Rugogamu; Brodiz (pronounced Brods) for short. Brodiz was to be the financial powerhouse behind the project using money from his lift installation business called MEMS to fund the building of the school. He had brought on board an Indian business partner called Naran Shankla and Jim had persuaded an elderly English architect by the name of Doug Parry to purchase some shares, move across from Nairobi to Kampala, and design the school. This was the theory that had been contained in the copious letters posted to me in Bermuda by Jim over the previous 12 months ever since I had expressed an interest in becoming the fifth shareholder. The reality on the ground was rather different. I discovered this as soon as I arrived in Uganda at 8 o'clock in the morning on 10 September 1994. Brodiz, Jim and Doug met me and, as I sat in the back of the Hillside minibus explaining effusively what I had been doing in my short stay in the UK in terms of drumming up interest in the scholarship scheme and even putting an advert in *The Times Educational Supplement* inviting investors to put their money into a the Hillside project, Brodiz and Jim were probably trying to warn me that things were not going too well; and I probably wasn't really listening. To be fair, Jim's letters had indicated something of a financial struggle taking place but, such was my blind determination to be involved in the romantic notion of 'Starting up a school in Africa' that I had been very selective in how I received the content of Jim's missives. The fact that I had been so active in seeking more sponsors, investors and donations shows that I was partly aware of the difficulties I was about to encounter.

The school didn't actually exist. Lessons took place in a house rented from Brodiz's brother on land adjacent to the nine acres of land allocated to build the school. The rented house had crumbling concrete floors and walls and no glass in the windows. Jim described it as a cave. He was being generous. So, where had all the money gone? Foundations, lots and lots of foundations laid out like some lost Roman village uncovered by an archaeologist's trowel. There were foundations protruding no more than a few inches above the ground like a three dimensional map of Doug's beautiful master plan covering vast areas of our site but only one finished building; a small toilet block. The nearest to a completed classroom was a wooden structure that looked too small to be a classroom anyway. The location of our field full of foundations was beautiful, looking into the Mayanja Valley but I couldn't help feeling that it would have been nice if at least some of this spectacular vista could have been obliterated by the skyline of the roofs of classrooms. Clearly my arrival had brought a fillip to everyone, though. Perhaps they thought my pockets would be full but I had actually arrived with virtually nothing as I had already sent the contents of my bank accounts to the Hillside High School account in advance of my arrival. The acuteness of the situation became very clear to me over the next few days as the four main directors (including me) of this non-existent school would require credit at the local bars just to see out the evening in a sufficiently anaesthetised state. Brodiz asked me on our very first evening out: 'So, Cliff, what made you get involved in this wild goose chase?' Reassuring or what.

I met the fifth director, Naran, on my second day in Kampala. A charming man who was pleased to meet me, as if he felt I would bring some sense to the madness of what had gone on so far regarding the formation of Hillside High School. It was clear that there were already major tensions between him and the other shareholders and he had now diverted his attention elsewhere. He was well educated in the field of project management and another company that he owned had just been involved in building another school in the city, Rainbow International School; a school that I was to become very familiar with. He was a major shareholder in Hillside but was no longer prepared to devote any energy or further money to it. He clearly saw me as the best chance of safeguarding his investment. Indeed I had been brought on to the board of Hillside for my financial expertise as well as my finance. I might have failed in the profession of accountancy but I had been teaching the subject for the past four years and, at least I knew my way around a balance sheet and a profit and loss account. I was soon installed as the company's financial controller. It seemed in the early days this involved little more than settling various bills accumulated by my fellow directors in the local drinking holes.

More seriously my role through the day involved sorting out the mess of figures that was supposed to represent the accounting records of the business and install a proper accounting system; all manual, of course as there was not a hint of technology to be seen anywhere in Hillside. We shared an office in The Diamond Trust building with Brodiz's other business but it didn't even have a phone. That semblance of modernity had been cut off and there was no money to reconnect it. As for the school tucked out on the slopes of Bunamwaya, electricity had not even reached such a remote place. Sometimes lessons had to be suspended if a storm cloud loomed overhead rendering the interior of the classrooms too dark to continue. If the rain followed, then the furniture would have to be rearranged to avoid the torrent of water that would be swept in by the tropical winds through the glassless windows.

I also spent many hours in those early days in Kampala, traipsing round various offices trying to collect monies owed to Brodiz's other business for lift installations already completed. Although, it may appear that the whole Hillside project was being run by a bunch of nincompoops, there was actually some logic behind the financial planning. On paper Brodiz was a very wealthy man. Sadly the predominant asset of MEMS came under the heading of 'debtors'. As several of these debtors were either the Ugandan government or businesses depending on payments from the government, it meant that much of the money owed to MEMS would probably never be realised. Through dogged defiance and many hours sat glaring in the receptions of offices around the city, I did manage to extricate a few million Ugandan shillings from some of MEMS's clients. Usually there was some kick-back necessary to secure the release of funds and, such was the direness of the Hillside situation, whenever money was collected it was instantly swallowed up by our own creditors. MEMS's debtors paying off Hillside's creditors and neither business benefiting much in between.

You may be wondering about where the primary source of money for a private school was going at this stage. Where were all the school fees as we entered our third term in existence? Well, here the picture was also somewhat more cloudy than I had anticipated. We had just three fee paying students at this time. Apart from other students paid for by the overseas benefactors that I had persuaded to get involved, the rest of the pupil population of our little school were free scholarships given to 10 children from the local village; a gesture to generate good PR with the surrounding community. It was also a gesture to make the official opening of the school in February not a completely futile exercise as there were no other children apart from these 10 'charity cases' to be educated at Hillside when the doors were initially opened. Financially I am not sure how we survived the remainder of the year up to Christmas.

Every now and then Brodiz would produce some money from somewhere. We didn't ask too many questions but simply accepted gratefully. Jim managed to acquire some consultancy work for another school setting up in Kenya and he also received a few meagre royalties for the English language text books that he had had published in the region over the years. I also received a payment from Bermuda for some exam marking that I had done before I left and, of course, occasionally another payment would come in from one of our overseas sponsors. Whenever money did arrive it would be put straight to paying overdue debts and wages. The remainder was shared among the four resident directors for a night of Bell beers and fried chicken or pork in one of the parade of tiny bars of Nakulabye or Kabalagala.

We were defining the term, 'hand to mouth existence' and, for me, I could also add the term a 'riches to rags tale'. Just a few months earlier I had been living on a king's ransom in the idyllic surroundings of Bermuda. Occasionally I reflected on this very point but the classrooms of The Berkeley Institute always conjured up pictures of a jungle. A hostile, aggressive, even scary jungle, and I could reassure myself that I had made the correct choice. I also reflected on my lost love. Vicky had given up waiting for me and had found another boyfriend in Costa Rica. She informed me as soon as I arrived in San Jose in July for what I had imagined was going to be a romantic three weeks' holiday together before I headed for East Africa. I still accompanied her on an expedition to Ecuador but, as you can imagine, it was a difficult situation. I tried to forgive her for choosing such a cruel way to terminate our three and a half year relationship, albeit often quite a tenuous one. Eventually I succeeded. I also internalised life's lesson that 'a woman's needs are manyfold' and eventually she will lose patience with a man's indecision. 'Faint heart never won fair maid' as they say.

Of course, my relationship with Everton could not be ended, even if I wanted it to. We all have our cross to bear and, no matter how outlandish my existence may have been at that time and how disconnected with the UK it was, I still needed the drug of knowing how Everton were doing. I had managed to catch three matches during my three weeks in England in between Bermuda and Uganda, including seeing new signing, Nigerian World Cup star, Daniel Amokachi being paraded in front of the Goodison crowd before the game against Nottingham Forest. This was a seminal moment for the club as it dispelled some of our unfortunate racist undertones that had arisen from the behaviour of a mindless minority of our fans and the fact that we were the only Premier League side not to have a black player in its squad. With virtually no disposable income and electricity being a rationed commodity in the village where I shared a house with Jim, access to Everton via a television set was completely out of the question. At that time satellite stations had not been set up to transmit Premier League football anyway. There was an FM radio station broadcasting selected extracts of World Service but they were not always the extracts I required. Jim and I would often sit on our living room verandah overlooking the tranquil valley, hearing the chirping of cicadas, occasional croaking of frogs and the brush of a warm breeze as we would mull over the events of the day, the prospects for the future and our stories from the past. Occasionally Jim would bring out his unwieldy shortwave radio and we would listen to the BBC news or a favourite programme such as *Letter from America* which would provoke some further discussion on a topic raised by the inimitable considered discourse of Alistair Cooke.

On 1 November we heard through the crackle and pop of a sports bulletin that Everton had finally won their first match of the season, 1–0 at home to West Ham. Yes, the *first* of November and our *first* win. It was the 12th game and fourth month of the season. I had already accepted that there was no way for Everton to escape relegation this time and, despite this welcome three points (which doubled our tally for the season), I spent several hours of that evening explaining to Jim what it all meant for the team with the greatest history of any when it comes to longevity in the top flight of English football. Jim is an avid reader and a student of everything. He absorbed the information I gave him and became very interested in the affairs of Everton Football Club from that time on including news of Mike Walker's sacking just a week later.

It was just three weeks later that Everton's second win of the season arrived. We were reaching the end of term and absolutely scraping the barrel in terms of finance and energy. It was a Monday in the second half of November and our budget determined that it would be a subdued evening. It had already been a notable day in that I had received a letter from Vicky informing me about her new life with Sam and I had also booked my ticket back to the UK for Christmas. I had to leave the country after 9 December as I did not have a work permit and would have become an illegal immigrant after three months in the country.

I went to bed with mixed emotions knowing that there was a sports bulletin at around 1am when I would hear the result of the 'derby'. Because of all these other things going on in my head such as the prospect of abject poverty and the finality of my recent big romance, I couldn't sleep anyway. When I caught the result through the ether of BBC's long waves that Paul Rideout and Duncan Ferguson had battered Liverpool into submission and a 2–0 defeat at Goodison, my cause of insomnia switched from stress and worry to delirious joy. Suddenly my head was full of pictures of the flashing cameras under the Goodison floodlights as big Dunc netted with a towering header. I had obviously not seen the goal and up to that point had never even seen Duncan Ferguson. This was his first goal for the Blues since his £4 million transfer from Rangers but I already had the feeling that he was going to be an Everton hero. Anyone who saves their first Everton goal for a 'derby' has to be destined for legendary status in the eyes of Evertonians. The fact that it was also the first game with my first and, perhaps greatest hero, Joe Royle as manager added to the feelgood factor. Any hope of sleep was destroyed by optimistic thoughts of the future of Everton rather than the pessimistic thoughts of where to find a new love life…or my next meal. Faithful old Everton had once again salvaged my sagging morale in the nick of time.

Chapter 16
Welcome to the club, Freddie

9 April 1995: Everton 4 Tottenham Hotspur 1

Supporting a football club doesn't make sense in many cases, including mine. Non-believers will often rationalise the whole irrational process with a statement such as: 'It's just 22 men kicking a ball around a field.' It is not easy to argue with such a description or defend why this apparently pointless exercise can cause such extreme feelings in those that are emotionally attached from the sidelines. The aggression and anger brought out in those that *participate* can be explained by the basic competitive element in every human being, a survival instinct that makes even the most mild-mannered person want to do better than a colleague or adversary. In other words, the essence of sport and why it exists. When the little grey haired lady gives high fives to her grandson after fluking a hole in one on the local putting green, it may be just fun but there is a tiny morsel of genuine joy at having achieved something that no one else has in that particular contest. Supporters of the grannie may share her joy but only because they are, no doubt, friends and relatives of the old woman. Extending this idea further, it is understandable when parents become fervent supporters of a football team because their son or daughter plays in it. Although their main focus is on the performance of their offspring, they develop an allegiance to the whole team because the team's success is a vicarious measure of their child's success even if their child is not one of the star players and indeed may contribute very little to the team's success.

Now expand this discussion to try to explain the support of a professional football team. Firstly there is the clear cut case of 'supporting your local team'. Thus people living in small provincial towns can easily support their home town team as it represents an integral part of their identity. Even people with no particular interest in football will accept a little of the reflected glow brought about when the team with the name of the town where they live disposes of a famous Premier League side in the FA Cup. Some miserable buggers may prefer to moan about the inconvenience of extra policing and early closing of businesses in their high street in preparation for the invasion of thousands of marauding louts affiliated to a large visiting club, but most will welcome the spotlight cast on their previously unheard of corner of Britain. I'm sure some old codgers in Hereford who have more concern for farming than football and have probably never visited Edgar Street, will still reminisce over a pint of bitter, the day that Ronnie Radford scored that last minute goal which led to the overthrow of the mighty Malcolm McDonald and his Newcastle United team in 1971.

So, we've explained the logic of supporting a football team that has some intrinsic connection with the supporter either through blood or birth. Local association could also explain where the support of many large teams comes from; thus 'one club cities' such as Newcastle and Sunderland are easy to explain. There won't be too many people born and raised in Newcastle-upon-Tyne who do not support the club of Jackie Milburn and Alan Shearer, even *after* that Hereford humiliation. The same can be said of many London clubs where clubs located in certain areas will generally attract supporters from their own catchment area. But, what about clubs that are literally on each others' doorsteps? Fulham and Chelsea, Chelsea and QPR for example. And then we move to other cities. How do Mancunians decide whether to support City or United or Birmingham residents make a choice between Villa or The Blues? And what about Everton and Liverpool?

Much literature has been published on this very topic. This book is not designed to investigate these cases in depth. In many instances there are family reasons. For some families in Liverpool the origins of their support of Everton go back to the Catholic roots of the club, although in 130 years of history the religious connection has probably faded. Families of Evertonians will be inclined to bring up their children to support their team although there are many examples of 'mixed' families in Liverpool. There could be some geographical element to the decision. Certainly someone brought up in a two-bedroomed terraced house on Gwladys Street would probably choose to support the team that plays in the stadium that overshadowed their living room throughout their childhood, I would imagine. The potent whiff of success draws many people to support a club. That is why, in so many of the aforementioned provincial outposts, there will be a plethora of Manchester United supporters. The local team is merely their 'second team'. A team to connect with especially when there's the potential of a Cup giant-killing in the air. The team whose result you always look out for. When I lived near Shrewsbury for two years and worked in the town, Shrewsbury Town became my 'second team'. During the 1987–88 and 1988–89 seasons I would go to the quaintly named Gay Meadow to watch a Second Division match if Everton were not at home or playing in the vicinity of the West Midlands or maybe Manchester. Throughout my travels around the world I have always listened to the World Service football results at least long enough to find out the Shrewsbury Town score and I will always take a cursory glance at their position in the League table whenever I have managed to come across an English newspaper. Don't get me wrong, there has never been the stomach churning nervousness that builds up just before I am about to learn how Everton have fared, but there is a curious anticipation nonetheless.

The question is, why is Shrewsbury Town my *second* club? Why isn't it my *first* club? Why is Everton my first club and why is it so much my first club that it tortures me and delights me and gives me a way of getting through some weeks but also makes Mondays at work not worth living on occasions? How did I saddle myself with this yoke? Why did I inflict myself with this torment, this perpetual source of crushing disappointment and embarrassment, interspersed with the occasional crumb of pleasure? Even the successes, few and far between as has been the case for Everton in the past two decades, cannot surely counter-balance the long periods of frustration and anguish. The mystery of this is, I do not fall fully into any of the above categories. I am not Evertonian by blood. My father has only a passing interest in football and that is with Millwall, which some would say is two ways of saying the same thing. It is not a birthright. I was born and brought up in Andover, Hampshire for God's sake.

At the very beginning there was an element, though, of being attracted to success. I started to support Everton towards the end of the 1969–70 season as Harry Catterick's wonderful team was about to win the League title by the length of the Mersey. However, that success soon turned into 14 years of famine, a trophy desert that I could have avoided. I was only eight when I fell in love with Joe Royle in his gold shirt in the *Soccer Stars* album that I so meticulously completed that year; surely I had every right to change my allegiance when the promise of that great team was broken so spectacularly the following year when we finished 14th. Surely a child of my tender years would be forgiven for trading their affections; we are all entitled to make a mistake in life. No one else in Andover had taken the bait that Ball, Kendall and Harvey had so tantalisingly placed before them; they all supported teams by blood or birth, such as Arsenal, Chelsea and Southampton. Those that followed success were maybe a little more circumspect than me and assessed the football landscape more carefully before taking the plunge. As a consequence, they took their football identity from Leeds United and Liverpool and had a decade of success to look forward to. For me, though, it was Everton. Perhaps some congenital desire to support the underdog and to fight lost causes gave me a perverse joy in standing up for Everton throughout my schooldays; a lone figure, mild-mannered until someone had the temerity to insult his beloved Blues. Mild-mannered until he got into a major fight with Nigel Burke for pushing his unflattering comments about Bob Latchford just a little too far after we had lost the League Cup Final in a second replay in 1977. So, Bob Latchford was barrel-like but he was never *fat*. More significantly he was my hero and, ipso facto, beyond criticism.

So you see, I and people like me give an arsenal of ammunition to the argument that supporting a football team is a futile and illogical pastime. Enjoy the spectacle of the game but don't get emotionally involved. You have no sensible reason to. It's entertainment, not submission of the soul. My mother said it to me endlessly during my teenage years especially when I went into a state of morbid non-communication after Everton lost the FA Cup semi-final replay to West Ham in 1980. She was dumbstruck and quite disgusted when I announced that I was going to go to Liverpool University to study mathematics. And to study Everton Football Club from closer quarters, she concluded…and she was right.

So, because of this apparently arbitrary decision that I made when I was in the first year of junior school, a decision made after being allowed to stay up and watch *Match of the Day* for the first time ever and seeing Everton win 1–0 at Wolves with Joe Royle scoring, I have had my whole life shaped by the goings on at Goodison Park. I have never met any of the players and have no other cogent reason to support Everton. I am proud of the club's history but I didn't know that when I joined the club, so to speak, in 1970. I like the club's style and philosophy although, sometimes when the likes of Gordon Lee and, dare I say it, Joe Royle were in charge, could we really describe ourselves as The School of Science? Sometimes I have found myself hanging onto the old clichés about Everton wanting to play football 'the right way' when, deep inside, I know that we are no different to any other club especially when gaining the three points is all that counts; further evidence that there is no logic, no reason, in all this. So what do I conclude. I'm a mad man? Brain-damaged, demented, delusional? Well, I've managed to hold down serious jobs and have meaningful relationships with people in my life. Most people who meet me might think I'm a little eccentric or odd, but not a raving lunatic. I have given up trying to explain it. All I know is that this unremitting attraction towards Everton Football Club is not manufactured or contrived or temporary. It is innate and genuine and probably permanent.

It is the reason that when I went to The Bamboo Village, a bar, restaurant and sports club in Kampala, on Sunday 9 April 1995 I jumped around and shouted at the top of my voice as first Matt Jackson and then Graeme Stuart and then Daniel Amokachi and then Daniel Amokachi again scored against Spurs in the FA Cup semi-final at Elland Road. It is no doubt the reason why an impressionable young Ugandan A level student by the name of Freddie Bukenya who accompanied Jim and myself to watch the game on a big screen became an Evertonian that day. Was it the smell of success or the fact that an African icon had scored two of the goals or was it seeing the effect that these men in blue shirts were having on a seemingly well-balanced and respected adult in a bar 4,000 miles away from where they were playing football? I don't know. I do know that it had nothing to do with blood or birth and I do know that Freddie has become an obsessively devoted supporter of Everton ever since. Amidst the wash of trophy hunting Manchester United, Chelsea and Arsenal fans that clog up the streets of Uganda, Freddie is a lone voice for the team that has a more impressive history than any of these teams. There I go again; contentious arguments to prop up my beliefs. What is the definition of 'history'? Who cares. I believe, and so does Freddie, and that is all that matters. Welcome to the club, Freddie. Sorry for the agony you have had to go through but I hope one day you will realise your dream of visiting Goodison Park.

Chapter 17
How I came to hate United

3 February 1996: Wimbledon 2 Manchester United 4

I suppose all of us have some anger within. Most people manage to find a safe conduit for their aggressive urges in the form of adrenalin inducing pastimes, the occasional surreptitious kick at an inanimate object or family pet or maybe, more subtly, by diffusing their pent up ire in the words of poetry or other creative activity. By doing so they channel their negative demons in a safe and environmentally friendly manner (although the family pooch with a mouth full of leather might disagree) and are able to function in society without too much difficulty. Then there is Wayne Rooney. It's appropriate that I should mention his name at the beginning of this chapter as he is an example of someone who brings out the worst sort of anger in me. I am generally a gentle, human loving individual. My only real anger from the age of eight was all directed at Liverpool Football Club. It is a phenomenon that I have never been able to explain but, even though I lived over 200 miles from Liverpool and had no prior knowledge of the geography and history of the two clubs on Merseyside (indeed it was about two months *after* I had decided that Everton was 'my team' that I found out that the club actually heralded from Liverpool), I instinctively knew that to support Everton meant that I should have an execration towards Liverpool. I think the catalyst was provided by the 1971 FA Cup semi-final when Everton, down to approximately nine men through injuries (remember only one substitute was permitted in those days) lost 2–1 to Liverpool at Old Trafford. It all seemed so unjust and the seeds of abhorrence of Liverpool were sown for evermore. How I supported Arsenal in that Cup Final. How I enjoyed Charlie George's spectacular goal complete with celebration, ahead of its time in theatricality.

Is it age that has made me more irascible, more curmudgeonly? The abrasions of worldly experiences wearing away the optimism of life and appreciation of its beauty. Because over the last 15 years or so I have found so many more things and people to get worked up into a negative froth about. Strangely, though, they are virtually all related to football. Perhaps it is not so strange after all that an aspect of life that has dominated me so completely, provides the fulcrum on which all my strongest emotions, including the negative ones, turn. The insidious intrusion of obscene wealth into the game has upset many 'true fans' and there will be more on that topic later in this book, but well before that, I found that my hatred of Liverpool was being supplemented by a new strain of vitriolic fever passing through my veins. And I believe that I can pinpoint the moment when the sickness was officially diagnosed; the tipping point, when feelings of dislike towards Manchester United Football Club, brewing beneath the surface for a while suddenly exploded into an ugly metamorphosis that altered my character for ever.

The day was Saturday 3 February 1996, the place was The Shires, a small hotel perched high up on the side of Muyenga Hill in Kampala where live Premier League football was shown on a small television situated above the entrance to the main eating area. It had become a regular place for me to retreat to on a Saturday afternoon and evening, and even other nights of the week; a sanctuary in which I could unwind from the constant strain of trying to keep Hillside High School afloat. I had become such a regular that, when I walked in, I would be handed the remote control to select my television channel as I desired. I became a familiar figure with the staff there. Once, when watching a rerun of *Four Weddings and a Funeral* on the movie channel one night, I made the observation that the character played by Hugh Grant was me. I was, of course, speaking metaphorically; my life was pretty aimless, single and yet to find true love at that point. Ugandans are not generally good at picking up tone or implied meaning, tending to take the spoken word literally and the barman became quite agitated asking me about other films that I had made! This little story also goes to show that *muzungus* all look the same to many Ugandans. I actually have not even a passing resemblance to Hugh Grant.

So what happened on the first weekend of February in 1996 to crystallise my antipathy towards Manchester United so irreversibly? It was a fairly innocuous day. I had been working in the office in town as usual during the morning. It was a particularly frustrating accountancy task that I had been absorbed in and, as I left the Diamond Trust Building into the warm dusty air of Kampala Road, I had not completed it, which meant I went into the remainder of the weekend with a nagging feeling of being unfulfilled. In fact, so much so that I would return to my spartan city office again the following day for six hours to solve the puzzle and balance the trial balance. I headed straight out to The Shires in the battered Hillside Toyota pick-up, walked into the deserted restaurant area and settled myself into a bar stool with a cold bottle of Club lager. I ordered a snack and then turned my attention to the television. I flicked to Supersport 3.

The build-up to the Final of the African Cup of Nations was on. The room began to fill up as there was obviously much local interest in this match. Not as much as there would have been if a sub-Saharan nation had been represented. In fact most of the Ugandans that day watched as neutrals as South Africa, still tainted by apartheid in the eyes of most black Africans and the predominantly Arab nation of Tunisia took to the field of the FNB Stadium in Johannesburg. Two late goals from Mark Williams brought some life to a turgid Final and decided the destination of the trophy in favour of the 'Rainbow Nation'. The fact that South Africa had been a last minute substitute for Kenya as hosts had not helped raise their popularity in the area. Although Kenya voluntarily withdrew for financial reasons, the suspicious mind of many black Africans soiled by years of corrupt oppression from their rulers came to a different conclusion. The theory that this was just a white conspiracy to put South Africa in the shop window and demonstrate their capacity to host a World Cup was quite prevalent. Maybe the awarding in 2004 of the biggest football show on earth to the most 'un-African' African nation gives some legs to this theory. By 2010 the whole continent rejoiced and celebrated at a World Cup being played on their soil but, back then, the support for *Bafana Bafana* in Uganda was lukewarm at best.

Two Shrewsbury gap-year students, Lea and Robert who I had persuaded to come to Uganda in January to teach at Hillside for a term, met me at The Shires having been dropped there by a teacher from Rainbow International School whom they had linked up with. Lea was a keen Liverpool fan while Robert was a mildly interested observer of football with no particular allegiance to any team. Educated at Shrewsbury School, Robert was refined and well-spoken and I remember feeling a tinge of shame as I drove the three of us away from The Shires that evening in a storm; not an actual climatic storm outside the vehicle but a storm within the pick-up cabin generated by my anger and expletives. It came about when the post-match analysis of the African Cup of Nations was over and the presenter, former Manchester United goalkeeper, Gary Bailey, announced that the live Premier League game now to be broadcast was Wimbledon against Manchester United. The emergence of satellite TV on the continent beamed across the whole of Africa from Randburg in Johannesburg meant that a single English Premier League match was broadcast live each Saturday plus the live Sky game from Monday evening if there was one. The timing of the launch of DSTV, one suspects, was deliberately intended to coincide with South Africa's hosting of the rugby World Cup in 1995 and the Africa Cup of Nations in 1996. I do not believe that DSTV was responsible for the selection of matches that it broadcast but, nonetheless, it came across as a form of football indoctrination to some of the more sensitive followers of the game like me. Having had 10 of their previous 11 matches broadcast live, I was beginning to get sick of the sight of Manchester United. They weren't even leading the League but were actually some distance behind Newcastle United at the time. But, while Newcastle enjoyed intermittent coverage, the United from Manchester were privileged to a blanket exposure that, to me, was completely disproportionate.

There was no particular reason why the 12th match in this sequence should be the one that pushed me over the edge. There are snapshots in my head of key moments in my life when a sea change occurs to my view of the world. I just remember that instance when I made my dramatic, childish exit from The Shires with a bewildered couple of student teachers in tow, as the one when I knew I would hate Manchester United for the rest of my life. I had no sensible reason to have believed that Southampton v Everton would be the favoured match for the television schedulers that weekend or, indeed Newcastle at home to Sheffield Wednesday. I didn't share Lea's appetite for Liverpool v Spurs, although there was a strong argument that that should have been the chosen match on merits of international interest. This argument isn't meant to disrespect Wimbledon. If Manchester United had not been shown for a couple of weeks, I would have had no quibble with this match being on television. It's the fact that it was becoming clear that the only two opportunities for the likes of Wimbledon to have their moment in the spotlight during a season, would be their two fixtures against Manchester United. Some of us with a taste for the less well marketed and less successful brand of football club were being overrun by this Manchester United media juggernaut.

And so a germ that had festered for a while in my sub-conscious exploded in an outburst of unpleasantness not very becoming of someone of my supposed intelligence especially in the presence of one as balanced and civilised as Robert Taylor. There is no cure for this anti-Manchester United sickness. Indeed with every new piece of silverware accumulated at Old Trafford and every million more pounds they generate from their ubiquitous merchandise (I even saw a wallet in a craft shop in Mombasa embossed with the Manchester United crest for pity's sake), the bitterness becomes ever more caustic, ever more incurable. My dislike of Manchester United now exceeds my loathing of Liverpool.

Once again I'm left to analyse the possible causes of such ridiculous feelings of irrational hatred in a supposedly well-rounded adult. Firstly I should say that a scientific reasoning will only go a limited distance in explaining away this behavioural abnormality. I believe that there is still an element of raw emotion in everyone that is so innate to be beyond rationalisation. I have never been one to follow the crowd; my life has been quite a lone furrow in many respects. When I feel that I am being herded into a zone that represents the norm, the accepted masses, I develop an instinctive need to pull out. I am attracted to those who sing their own song and respond to a different drum. I am naturally irritated by those that follow the accepted dogma blindly but equally by those that try to persuade them to follow. This inescapable aspect to my psyche coupled with my expatriate existence has combined to make me detest Manchester United and everything to do with the club. The streets of Nairobi and Kampala are packed with supporters of Manchester United and it has become so much more distinct since the emergence of satellite television across the continent. DSTV has become a kind of technological missionary, spreading the word to the masses. By choosing the programmes and the content, the South African television station has unfettered access to the minds of millions; an absolute power to educate, indoctrinate and manipulate. In the arena of football, this has meant compelling huge swathes of the continent to support Manchester United Football Club.

It's easy to take on a victim mentality when supporting Everton, but the argument that we have been unbelievably unlucky in our timing, historically holds some water. Two world wars and thus the suspension of competitive football commenced directly after we had lifted the League title meaning we had no opportunity to defend it. Everton have actually been in possession of the League title for longer than any other club if the 11 blank years when no football was played due to world conflict are taken into account. When at our peak and widely accepted as the best club in Europe, Heysel happened and we were banned from testing ourselves against the top clubs on the continent. By the time the ban was lifted, the football landscape had changed and Everton were down among the also-rans just as the big money started to flood in from television and European competition. And so I lament what might have been had satellite television mobilised its global tentacles a decade previously. Would a generation of Evertonians have been spawned worldwide from watching the likes of Graeme Sharp, Kevin Sheedy and Peter Reid in the bars and restaurants from Kampala to Kuala Lumpur? And where would Manchester United be now? This question will never be answered and we have to live with the reality. The reality is that many, many people have taken on an obedient faithfulness towards Manchester United in all kinds of far-flung places due to the bombardment of the brand, the wall to wall transmission of every little detail of the club.

In places where people are starving, the hardship of everyday living can be put on hold for just a few hours on a Saturday afternoon for a cold beer and a view of the Red Devils in action. What a massive distortion of priorities, a complete contortion of perspective. I'm a fine one to talk, though, aren't I? I've hardly shown myself to be a model of measured mind. If the worldwide microscope had been focussed on Everton instead of United, I would have no rancour. In the end, perhaps it comes down to one simple word that I've been trying to avoid; jealousy. If those wretched television satellites had beamed in pictures from Goodison every week instead of Old Trafford would I even be having this discussion? Would those 'sheep' that follow Manchester United be spared the ovine analogy if they had been brain-washed into supporting Everton instead?

We are where we are though, and the fact is, from the moment Gary Bailey announced that the satellites were aimed at Selhurst Park on that Saturday afternoon in February 1996, Manchester United were going to leave a nasty taste in my mouth for the rest of my life. The new corrosion that beset me from that day onwards was intensified for the remainder of the season when Manchester United overhauled the huge advantage of Newcastle and won the title provoking the unforgettable rant from Kevin Keegan on the way. My feelings were set in stone in the opening game of the following season. Everton, who had finished sixth were at home to Newcastle with transfer record-breaking signing, Alan Shearer making his debut for the visitors but, as it happened being eclipsed by Gary Speed who scored on his Everton debut that day. Surely a match that pitted sixth at home to second from the previous season was certain to be the chosen televised match. You must be joking; the Manchester United obsessed TV programmers chose instead their darlings in a match away to, yes, you've guessed it, Wimbledon. The fall guys again. The rest, including Beckham's famous lob (which, to this day, I have never seen), is history, as they say.

Chapter 18
Baby on a Barclaycard

22 March 1997: Everton 0 Manchester United 2

So how did I get into this mess? How did Everton get into this mess? The short answers are Hillside High School and Andrei Kanchelskis respectively, but let me elaborate.

Firstly, to which mess do I refer in March 1997? Personally it refers to occupying a bedsit in Leeds with new wife and new baby son with accumulated credit bank balances to my name of approximately £300 and a credit card bill just about to cross that level in the opposite direction and no prospects of a dependable income to rely on in the foreseeable future. For Everton it was eight points out of 36 since reaching sixth place in the League on my wedding day on 21 December and elimination from the FA Cup at home to struggling Championship side, Bradford City and no prospects of a dependable three points to rely on in the foreseeable future.

Hillside had been a roller coaster adventure with a number of interesting sideshows attached. Friction between the five main directors brought on almost exclusively by the lack of money available to fulfil our vision, had caused more heat than light and the ugly confrontations had started to tear the whole project apart. The fact that the school never achieved a student roll greater than 150 during my 2½ years of struggle with the business, meant that we were always chasing our tail financially. Every shilling that came in to the coffers instantly exited, earmarked well in advance for repayment to a creditor at the front of an ever-extending queue. The opportunity to build and plan was thwarted at every turn by the need to fire fight.

The school wasn't so much under-capitalised as non-capitalised. The initial money put up had been buried into the ground in layers and layers of foundations on the optimistic hope that further money would materialise to actually build some walls and roofs. In the meantime Brodiz's brother was swallowing up the equivalent of about £300 per month in rent collected for the use of his 'grotto' as a school. A building with potholed floors, no interior doors, no electricity and no glass in the windows. Some of these issues were addressed during our tenure but the fact is we had been operating a school from little more than a concrete shack. Naran Shankla, determined to maintain dignity and his smart suits, kept well out of the mire. He would just attend board meetings and rile everyone, especially me, when he would ask accusingly where all the money had gone. Brodiz, genial and charming throughout would grapple with trying to keep the team together and put in any money he could muster from his other business. We managed to put up a few basic structures from such injections. Doug would whine about the ugliness and question the structural soundness of these monstrosities as he saw his beautiful master plan being systematically dismantled. The rest of us would mutter something along the lines of 'needs must' and thank Brodiz profusely for his commitment to the cause as we moved on. Doug would then hit back with spiteful comments aimed at Jim over the lack of discipline in the school and how inadequate he was as a headmaster. I was also having my doubts as to Jim's management methods but tried to keep my criticism on a professional and less personal level. Jim, himself was uneasy with Doug's homosexuality especially in the context of him being a part owner of a school in a country where homosexuality is outlawed.

I managed to bring in another shareholder by the name of Paul Mugambwa. He had made his fortune in coffee and was looking for a social project in which to invest some of his wealth. The day I persuaded him to part with 50 million Ugandan shillings in exchange for shares in Hillside High School was one of great celebration. At that time, such a sum was worth around £30,000 which could have built at least two basic classrooms. Almost from the moment he made this decision, though, Paul seemed to develop cold feet. It took the whole of my time with the project for this ebullient Ugandan businessman to pay the amount he had promised which meant each sum that he deposited was eaten up by creditors rather than put into bricks and mortar which is what was really required. I spent many hours of time and inches of leather traipsing around banks and other possible financiers with my business plans and cashflow statements in hand, but every time I drew a blank.

The closest we came to finding someone to help fund our project was when the European Development Fund said they would provide $20,000 for classroom construction. We had wanted at least one nought on the end of that, but beggars can't be choosers, and I pursued this scrap of hope for all I was worth. Brodiz and I ended up having a meeting in a house with some guy called Tados who was representing Mr Kayemba, the gentleman at the EDF who had shown an interest. Nothing came of the meeting and Brodiz, who was obviously seeing this meeting at a completely different level to me, explained that Kayemba would most definitely have run away when Tados reported back to him how naïve and honest the *muzungu* had been. In other words, Kayemba couldn't see how he was going to make his 10 per cent out of it. About a year later I was asked to assist in an investigation that resulted in Kayemba being sacked from the EDF for massive corruption!

So my endless trips to the bank had brought nothing but dust coated shoes, tired legs and ever increasing cynicism. I would go to the British High Commission's 'happy hour' every Friday evening to try to network with possible funders and investors. By the time Brodiz, Jim and Doug collected me I had a pile of business cards, the prospects of a hangover and not a sniff of anyone remotely interested in being involved in Hillside High School. I wrote to people back home to see if they were interested in assisting in our upstanding venture. Vicky's mother lent us £5,000 and sponsored the previously referred to Freddie Bukenya. A former colleague of mine at Shrewsbury Sixth Form College bought 10 shares. All of this helped us fight some day to day cashflow battles but we could never win the war that required major capital funding.

In conclusion, my main achievement as financial controller during my time in post was to retrieve the situation I inherited of salary arrears and have everyone paid on time every month during my time in charge which, in Uganda, is by no means the norm. And I suppose you could say that I succeeded in keeping our creditors sufficiently at bay to ensure that, by March 1997 the school was still in operation (and still is to this day).

The situation became a whole lot more difficult after 31 March 1996. That is the day that Brodiz passed away. Just four weeks earlier I had been in a roadside bar in

Nakulabye, a suburb of Kampala. I was with Brodiz and a good friend of his called Patrick; a very personable man in his mid-30s who worked for the Uganda Revenue Authority and had a passion for football. He had taken me to a couple of Ugandan Superleague games, one of which became very exciting when the police started firing live rounds to prevent some potential crowd trouble at the interestingly named Wankulukuku Stadium. This Saturday evening out with Brodiz and Patrick occurred in the middle of Lent so I was stone cold sober and became a spectator of the oral exchanges taking place around me. It is fascinating to observe the incremental deterioration of people's articulacy as the accumulation of alcohol takes its toll. So as this increasingly bizarre conversation flowed around me, I was doing mental calculations in my head of what Everton's 2–0 win at Middlesbrough had meant; three defeats in 18 matches and fifth place in the League according to me. The verbal interaction between Brodiz and Patrick came to mean much more to me less than a month later. There had been much discussion about death. It hadn't been of a morbid tone but rather about finding positive ways to rationalise it and to face it. Exactly what Brodiz might have been told that day or just before by his doctor I don't know, but three Saturdays later he mysteriously failed to attend the Hillside Soccer World Cup that I had organised and when I went to visit him with Jim the next day at his home, he was barely conscious. A week later he was dead. At the wake I spoke to Patrick. He looked more upset than most. He looked almost frightened. About three months later I learnt that Patrick had also passed away. AIDS kills people in many different ways. For some it is a slow, agonising demise, for others, with the aid of antiretroviral drugs it can be managed almost right up to the point of death. Jim and I (and probably Doug) hadn't realised it, but Brodiz had been spending huge amounts of money every week to keep himself alive. I had no idea that he was even HIV positive. He had succeeded in maintaining this brave façade almost right up to the time he succumbed. Less than two weeks before he died, he enjoyed a night out with my parents who visited Uganda at that time and me, laughing about the tales of Hillside and eulogising my great input. My mum and dad could not believe it when I called them a few days after their return to the UK to tell them that Brodiz had died of AIDS.

The last few days when Brodiz was shifted from one hospital to another to find a final resting place were simply awful. As the antiretrivirals gave up working, the hospitals refused to offer painkillers as they were not sure who would foot the bill.

Indeed the change in hospitals was for the same mercenary reasons. He was relocated from a private to a public hospital but even those run by the state have to be paid for out of the private pocket. The tossing and turning in excruciating pain that I witnessed as I visited Brodiz virtually every night of the last week of his life, finally came to an end early on a Sunday afternoon. I had gone to visit him and found an empty bed. I went to the morgue and found him lying there exactly as he was in life, with his wide round face and the hint of a cheeky smile etched into his features. I wanted to cry but I had to organise the coffin, clear the hospital bills and sort out other formalities. There were crowds of family around but few were capable of thinking coherently. He was a big character in every sense and clearly a massive loss to his family and community. For me it was the first time I had experienced death at such close quarters and the first time I had seen a dead body. The fact that it was of someone who had become a great friend and who had provided me with the opening for one of the most amazing episodes of my life, made it a time of extreme emotional turmoil. I had much to learn from Brodiz; his charisma, optimism, humour and sheer love of life even when he had secretly lived with this death sentence for so long. He had fought for the freedom of his country from the tyranny of Amin and Obote and had earned millions from a successful business but lost so much of it in his desperate attempt to leave his estimable legacy before the fast approaching sands of time could bury him. He had barely turned 40 when he made his final journey to heaven.

From the depths of despair, Jim and I fought to keep Hillside going. I was appointed the managing director of Educational Services Ltd, the company formed to run Hillside High School and we soldiered on. Soon after Brodiz's death, I experienced emotions from the other end of the human spectrum; I fell in love, deeply and totally. Her name was Violet and she was a beautiful 23-year-old from Mbale in the east of Uganda. She had recently graduated from Makerere University. She arrived on the doorstep of Hillside High School at the behest of Brodiz's former girlfriend, Marilyn who had been a roommate of Violet's and had found out that the school was desperately seeking a geography teacher following the spectacular departure of the previous one who Jim had had to frogmarch off the school premises after he had tried to incite a riot among the sixth formers in support of a personal grievance he had with Hillside.

Violet turned up offering her services for nothing as she wanted to gain experience in her chosen profession. Jim took her on immediately. On 6 May 1996 I set eyes on her for the first time in the crumbling staffroom of Hillside High School and that was that. The term 'whirlwind romance' was coined for what happened next. If nothing else, I am good at learning from my past. After the faltering three years of my relationship with Vicky, the one word that had been discarded from my romantic dictionary, was prevarication. No more indecision, no more hesitation when it came to affairs of the heart. I had reached a different stage in my life, of course. My existence in Kenya had been made up of a series of anecdotal dots. Since then these dots had continued to punctuate my life but had increasingly been joined together by an underlying thread that was working its way towards being some meaningful life plan. The exact path I was following still wasn't entirely clear, but having a wife and children certainly came into it. There is also the carnal aspect to this scenario that didn't apply to my relationship with Vicky. Basically I couldn't keep my eyes or hands off of Violet. Within two months of our first meeting we had set our wedding day and were expecting our first child. The order in which those two things occurred I cannot remember now and is irrelevant.

With love in my water, my appetite for the Hillside battle diminished. I could no longer devote such long, often fruitless hours trying to make a silk purse from a sow's ear. The writing was on the wall long before Violet and I blew our last £1,000 on our wedding and a honeymoon which included six friends from England travelling around Uganda with us in the Hillside school bus over Christmas and New Year. When I flew back to England on 9 March after a difficult discussion with Jim when I expressed my steadfast opinion that Hillside had no future and that he was not of headmaster material, I had not *officially* given up on the wild goose chase as Brodiz had so succinctly described the Hillside escapade. However, when I arrived at Dave Anderson's house in Leeds where he had converted a Victorian tenement into student flats, I had *mentally* just about given up the ghost. Violet had already been living in one of the flats for over a month in preparation for the birth of Christopher who duly arrived early on Thursday 13 March. I witnessed the birth and then went back to the one roomed apartment in Dave's house and lay there staring at the ceiling rigid with fear. I had no money, no job and no idea what to do next. Fortunately Oxford University Press followed up on their request for me to write a mathematics text book for the Ugandan O level syllabus and, when Christopher was just two days old, I had a visit from a representative of the publishers during which he agreed to give me a

£500 advance to start work on the manuscript. And so that is what I filled my days with endlessly as Violet and Christopher and I managed in our one-bedroomed flat in Leeds. And that £500 plus my Barclaycard is how we survived the first few months of Chris's time on this earth. In terms of narrow squeaks, this was a hair's width.

Meanwhile, not a million miles away, Everton had been freefalling down the Premiership table. Such was the tumult in my personal affairs, I had taken no more than a passing note of what was happening at my esteemed football club. I had not even realised that Andrei Kanchelskis had ended his 18-month flirtation with us. Apparently a gargantuan error from the Ukrainian that had assisted Bradford City to end our interest in the FA Cup had been the final straw in an increasingly fraught relationship that he was enduring with Joe Royle and the club as a whole. He departed soon afterwards for £8 million to Fiorentina. It seemed that this was symptomatic of a deeper malaise at the club and suddenly, from a position of seeming upward momentum the wheels came off. I had been aware of the trail of destruction from the series of results I had seen in various newspapers but I had no idea what was actually going on on the pitch. I had been shocked and mystified by the rapid descent. As we faced Manchester United at home on Christopher's second Saturday outside the womb, things had become very grim indeed. Violet and I listened to the commentary on Radio 2 in our bedsit as Chris slept. Two howlers from goalkeeper Paul Gerrard gave the League leaders a comfortable win. Joe Royle resigned six days later. From hero to zero so quickly; not so dissimilar to me. What a ferment I and Everton had lived through in the past couple of years, and neither of us were out of the woods yet.

Chapter 19
The Great Escape: Part 2

10 May 1998: Everton 1 Coventry City 1

1,462 days on from the previous last day drama, 40,109 people filed into Goodison Park wondering if they would be solemnly observing the sleeping giant finally going to its resting place in the Championship after more than 40 years of dining with the elite of English football at the top table. A stumbling institution enfeebled by a chairman without his heart in the club and some poor choice of managers. Howard Kendall had left the club in mid-table in December 1993. By the time Mike Walker took over about five weeks later, we were on the brink of relegation. The silver haired Walker seemed to have little talent for motivation and contrived a somewhat fortuitous last day reprieve. When Mr Walker relieved all of us of his duties in November 1994, Everton were on Premier League's death row. If you were to combine the second half of that season with the first half of the 1996–97 season, Joe Royle's Everton lost just eight games and won an FA Cup. The season in between was possibly better. What went wrong from my wedding day onwards on 21 December 1996, I am not certain but I do know that we only just limped over the line at the end of that season under the guardianship of caretaker manager, Dave Watson. There then followed the longest, most excruciating management appointment in the history of football.

I was back in the UK with wife and baby during that close season when virtually anyone who had 'manager of a professional football club' written somewhere on their

CV was linked with the Everton vacancy. Unsurprisingly, most of them were not in the slightest bit interested and only a candidate with no management experience at all apparently came close to taking up the challenge…but then Andy Gray decided that the repose of the Sky studio was a more comfortable option than the Goodison dugout. Having searched everywhere for someone to take on the unenviable task of trying to revive our great football team, Peter Johnson, our Liverpool supporting chairman found Howard Kendall at a loose end and drinking in the last chance saloon. It appeared to be the last chance for both Howard and Everton and we fell into each others' arms. The season that followed was an unmitigated disaster. From the moment we lost our opening game at home to newly promoted Crystal Palace, we rarely raised our heads above the relegation parapet. As we entered May our destination was out of our hands. A 4–0 capitulation at Highbury the week before had cemented that position. Was Howard Kendall to suffer the same ignominy as Brian Clough, when he concluded his glorious association with Nottingham Forest with an alcohol blurred relegation season? It was widely accepted that Everton's final match of the season at home to Coventry would be the last one ever under the charge of its most successful manager in its history.

The build up to this most crucial game was not auspicious for the Green family. I fell under the spell of a mysterious virus and our son, Christopher who was barely a year old, smashed his head on the side of the bath and required three stitches above his right eye. The omens were not promising. We were now living in the girls' boarding house at Braeburn High School. Let me quickly explain. When the chips were down at Hillside High School, our host in Leeds, former headmaster of Braeburn and very good friend, Dave Anderson, put the feelers out to former colleagues at Braeburn. It didn't look hopeful until a late resignation from the Braeburn Head of Accounts opened up an unexpected avenue back to the school where I had enjoyed such a memorable baptism to my life as an expatriate. My reputation was good among the decision makers at Braeburn who were largely the same people that I left behind there in 1992. A contract was in the post instantly, no questions asked and I even accumulated two additional responsibilities of boarding house assistant and clubs coordinator to add to my portfolio and, more importantly, my salary. I had approached this new opportunity at Braeburn as a married man with ambition as opposed to an unattached dosser, my status when I first applied to Braeburn in 1989.

I suddenly discovered what immense potential I had if I put my mind to it and acted just a little more like a grown up. Meanwhile the driving force behind this newly discovered dynamic approach to life, my wife, Violet, secured the post of Head of Girls' Boarding by the end of our first term at the school. Suddenly we had gone from paupers to earning a reasonable income. I owned my first ever television before Christmas 1997 at the grand age of 36. Obviously Violet's post meant that we lived in the family house allocated to the head of girls' boarding which was embedded in the girls' accommodation block.

I am not sure if DSTV provided an inferior service to subscribers in Kenya to that offered to their Ugandan counterparts, but I was to wake up to a terrible shock on the Sunday morning of the last day of the 1997–98 season. Because Arsenal had already won the League on the previous weekend when Everton were offered a side tent at Highbury as the hosts performed in the marquee seemingly unaware that their visitors from Merseyside were even part of the carnival, the South African satellite television providers deemed it unnecessary to show any live Premier League football on the final Sunday. Who won the League was all that concerned them; they had little interest in who fell out of it. I was dismayed and angry in equally large measure and frantically thought of ways to solve this problem. Internet was still in its infancy and I had no access to it. Mobile phones were pretty immobile and unwieldy and didn't always have the capacity to reach the UK from East Africa. More significantly, we didn't possess one. Anyway, catching the result at the end of the match was not what I wanted.

I couldn't see how I could possibly cope with the tension of waiting for the voice at the other end of the phone in England delivering the outcome like a judge delivering his final verdict. 'You have been sentenced to a minimum of 12 months in the Championship for your part in supporting this team that was obviously going to disappoint and frustrate you. Yours is a foolish act which you appear to have been unwilling or unable to control. This should be a lesson to all of those who continue to indulge in the futile and self-destructive pastime of supporting a football club.' I couldn't allow any friend to hear my weeping on the other end of the line should the news be negative. And the fact was, there was a major possibility that this would not go Everton's way. Basically Everton had to better the result of Bolton Wanderers. Bolton were away to Chelsea so that half of the equation seemed quite simple but

Everton were at home to Coventry City. All week I had analysed the psychology of the teams involved in these two crucial fixtures. Coventry were mid-table; surely they would be 'on the beach' mentally speaking? Then again they would be relaxed and carefree and anyone playing with a smidgeon of confidence could blow away Everton who seemed to be devoid of the stuff. Chelsea also had nothing to play for. They were in fourth place though and surely much too powerful for Bolton. I could comfort myself that Bolton were almost certain to lose, but I could not come to any kind of reassurance in my head that we could achieve even a draw at home to Coventry City. We had only won two home games since January and lost more than we had won during that time. We had not won anywhere for a month. Our self-esteem, team pattern, self-belief were all shot. And now I was faced with the prospect of not being with those players in their hour of need. Even when over 4,000 miles away, I always feel that I have some sort of influence on the game and my players when I can see them on the screen live. Everton would probably have been relegated in 1994 if I hadn't been there with them in The Robin Hood Bar in Hamilton. I have commented in a previous chapter of how I enjoy listening to a radio commentary, how it exercises the mental muscles to conjure up pictures of what is being described through the airways. It requires an element of exertion from the audience that television pictures do not demand. A viewer can have a television on and see the pictures but not really watch and still gain some recall of the images. If you hear a radio but do not listen, you gain nothing from the experience. All this may be true, but when the situation is as stark and critical as the possible relegation of Everton Football Club after more than four decades of top flight football, the immediacy of the information becomes paramount. With the radio the information comes through an intermediary. Not only does this cause an agonising delay but it means that the information is also open to interpretation. Thus the commentator can say 'goal' and then correct himself when he realises that it is not, in fact a goal due to an outrageous save by the goalkeeper or the intervention of a linesman's flag. That moment of misinformation can cause untold agony to the listener with an emotional investment in the outcome. When the match is on the television, the information is transmitted to the brain by its own trusted messengers, the eyes. Any deception is self-inflicted; the great save can be seen without needing to use an auxiliary communicator who might initially get the information wrong albeit for a fraction of a second.

You might think this is splitting hairs and dealing in triviality but, when your football team's future is at stake, every microsecond counts. To add to my horror, it wasn't entirely clear whether World Service was even going to broadcast coverage of these end of season matches. It had been a relatively new innovation to move all the final matches to a 4 o'clock kick-off on the Sunday of the last weekend of the season. Indeed, Everton's first great escape in 1994 was the final time that such last day theatre was to be played out on a Saturday. It was not easy to access BBC World Service programme schedules especially in the days before the world wide web. Saturday *Sportsworld* was a three hour fixture in the weekly timetable, the timing of which was engraved in my brain. A Sunday equivalent didn't generally exist unless there was a major sporting event taking place on the Sunday such as the Open or the men's final at Wimbledon or the British Grand Prix. If the BBC attached the same level of importance to the final day relegation drama that DSTV evidently did, then I wouldn't even have radio access to this destiny defining moment.

What to do? My agony at having Everton's future in the balance now compounded by the fact that I had no idea how I could find out what was going on at Goodison that afternoon. I did some marking of exercise books, I took Chris for a walk around the school grounds but I could not train my mind on anything other than what was to happen in the two critical football matches taking place at opposite ends of England at 6pm East African time. I could not even take advantage of the huge Sunday lunch on offer at the boarding house canteen which was one of the perks of Violet's position. I could not eat, I could not settle. So much for my new found maturity and purpose in life. My whole life was suddenly at the mercy of the outcome of these two key football matches and I was reduced to this pathetic imitation of a normal human being with no substance or perspective.

Kick-off time arrived. Just as I had feared, World Service was on its regular Sunday programming; news or religious affairs or something. All I know is, it *wasn't* football. I went up to the staff clubhouse where the television was connected to DSTV. I was acting on a last forlorn hope that maybe there had been a change of heart from the powers that be in Johannesburg. But it was golf being shown. Fucking South African Masters or something! I don't know, but it was not the events taking place at Goodison Park, that was for sure. As I walked back across the field to the girls' boarding house, I reflected on the fact that the game was now 10 minutes old and anything could have happened. We could be 4–0 up and almost safe or 4–0 down and virtually relegated. Neither scenario was likely but that's what happens when your imagination is left unharnessed in a situation of stressful ignorance.

On terrestrial television there was a station that broadcast Sky News. I switched it on in our living room at quarter past six knowing that there was a sports bulletin imminent. After the adverts, there was a summary of headlines. Unbelievable; a snippet of Goodison Park and someone in a blue shirt curling a ball into the top corner. Who the hell was that? 'Possible lifeline for Everton' came the newsreader's voice. The flesh was soon put on the bones. Gareth Farrelly, a Kendall signing symptomatic of that era in our history, no pace, no skill, a model of mediocrity, had chosen his greatest moment in an Everton shirt to coincide with one of our most crucial matches just as Barry Horne had done four years earlier. Chelsea v Bolton was still goalless. It reached half time like that. With 45 minutes of the season left we had been saved, surely. BBC World Service then obliged with a special *Sportsworld* after the five o'clock news. Unlike Uganda, Kenya still had no FM transmission of the BBC. This was to be a throwback to my early days in Braeburn. I carefully tuned my shortwave radio and, through the aural squiggles and doodling, I could just about hear what was transpiring at Goodison Park and Stamford Bridge.

The commentary kept switching from one venue to the other. The first goal of the second half went to Chelsea. We now had a three point swing on Bolton. In the dying minutes Everton were awarded a penalty. This would surely seal it. Nick Barmby missed it. He was soon to sign for Liverpool. A fifth columnist surely? Chelsea then doubled their lead. It was still all over despite the efforts of that little scumbag, Barmby. But hang on a minute. Dion Dublin scored with a brilliant header. The silky Coventry striker who had inadvertently caused the end of Kendall ll, was now playing a role in the final throes of Kendall lll. Injury time was three hours or something. When the whistle finally ended the torture, I ran around the house punching the air with joy. I grabbed Christopher and went back up to the staff clubhouse to celebrate with friends. A recording of Chelsea v Bolton was already showing on the TV there. A group of teachers were watching it as if live. I ruined it for them by giving the game away. 'Bye bye Bolton' I exclaimed and then redeemed myself by buying drinks for everyone.

Violet joined in the fun that evening. She had shown an interest in supporting Everton from the moment we started dating. If it was a form of entrapment it worked, but I like to believe there is more to it than that. Violet is a competitive person and needed a team to get behind. The idea of supporting a minority club in the face of the hordes of Manchester United, Liverpool and Arsenal fans appealed to her sense of 'taking on the world'. Like me, Violet is not one to follow the crowd. She had shown great dedication, sensitivity and commitment to the Everton cause during our two years together but I think that even she was surprised by the powerful effect that this gut wrenching day had had on her husband. If she feared that she had bitten off more than she could chew, married some brain-damaged maniac, she didn't let on.

As the family wound its weary way back across the field that evening, our fellow staff members said goodbye and well done on our survival. Christopher, with bandaged head, waved back murmuring 'Bye Bye Bolton'. A new Evertonian had been born on the day the club nearly died.

Chapter 20
Suffering in silence

7 March 1999: Newcastle United 4 Everton 1

I have a confession to make. I stood on the Kop at Anfield. In fact I did it several times. When I arrived at the University of Liverpool in October 1980 to begin my degree in Mathematical Statistics, it was the first time I had lived outside of Andover in Hampshire. For 18 years I had lived in a small market town. I had occupied a three bedroomed semi on a housing estate where most people within 20 houses in either direction were well known to our family and we were well known to them. Many of them had children who I regularly played with. It was a friendly, secure and quite insular environment. I only ventured out of this cosseted world in my head with visions inspired by the three carefully regulated terrestrial channels broadcast on our black and white television set until 1974 when we finally splashed out on a colour one in time for the World Cup hosted by West Germany.

Perhaps it was a break for freedom at the age of eight that led me to take that outrageous decision to idolise Joe Royle and follow Everton Football Club, a quest for an identity that would make me stand out in a place as benign as Andover. The fact that my parents were not locals but had migrated from London just before my birth probably added to my desire to be regarded as something of an outsider.

So, back to the point of the first line of this chapter. When I arrived in Liverpool, I was more wide-eyed and wet behind the ears than most. I'd only travelled this far north three times before in my entire life; once to Blackpool and twice to the Lake

District, each time for a holiday. Even though I had innately acquired a loathing for Liverpool Football Club, I couldn't help but be intrigued by Anfield. My curiosity was of the nature of a Japanese tourist rather than as a football fan. And describing it this way, my conscience allowed me to consider a visit. In fact, I went to Liverpool's first home League fixture after my arrival on Merseyside. Bobby Robson's League leaders, Ipswich, were the visitors so I figured it was a game worth compromising my morals for. I stood on the Kop and managed to suppress my joy when Ipswich scored and didn't allow my glumness to be too evident when the home side found the net in a 1–1 draw. I recall the exhilaration of being part of a fluid mass of stumbling people tumbling down 10 or so steps in response to a near miss or great save. Much as I despised the team, I had to admit it had been an experience worth paying £1.50 for. The Gwladys Street, having a smaller capacity didn't quite generate the same atmosphere. Obviously in view of Hillsborough, 1989 it would be insensitive to advocate for the reinstatement of terracing at football grounds. What I can say though, is that I am glad that I had an opportunity during the peak of my football watching days, to observe matches all over the country as part of this molten mass of people usually situated behind a goal. It gave a sense of belonging and unity that seating never can; being one molecule in a whole liquid of people sharing one passion and one desire was as much a reason to spend so much of my student grant on following Everton as watching the actual fare being served up on the field of play which, let's be honest, wasn't too entertaining for an Evertonian in the early 80s. Even though the colour was wrong, I had to privately admit that the Kop was something special when it came to the physical experience of watching a match live.

Later in the term I went with a bunch of mates to witness a European night when Liverpool swept away Alex Ferguson's Aberdeen in the European Cup. I hated the fact that I had been among Liverpool fans as they celebrated and vowed never to stand on the Kop again. I broke that vow during my second term at University when I learnt that, in order to have a chance of acquiring a ticket for the Anfield 'derby', I would have to accumulate some priority vouchers by attending home games leading up to the Everton game. I watched a 2–2 draw at home to Birmingham and also saw one of the biggest shocks ever witnessed at Anfield. Bottom club Leicester City came and conquered. 2–1 was the score at the home of the club that had won the League for the previous three seasons and had not lost at home for three years. I still recall 30 years on, the unadulterated agony of wanting so much to express my spiteful joy as the winning goal hit the net in the second half under the Kop but being virtually sat on by my two friends who could see the exultation spreading through my veins as a guy called Jim Melrose netted the winner. The Kop had turned into a library at that point and any expression of joy would surely have been handled with more than just a disdainful tut. Like a cartoon character who, for some obvious reason, has to contain an extreme feeling of pain or joy until a later time, I was almost exploding as I came out of Anfield at the end of that match.

And so we fast forward to the last year of the century and there I was in the Braeburn boarding house on the evening of Sunday 7 March. All the FA Cup quarter-finals were shown live on DSTV that weekend. They had saved Newcastle v Everton to last. Well in advance I had realised that this meant very bad timing for me as the game was not only in the middle of the boarders' prep time but in the middle of a prep time that I was scheduled to supervise. For some reason I didn't manage to swap my duty with anyone else and so I was faced with this exasperating scenario of having to ensure 120 boys were studying in silence while Everton were involved in a match that represented the closest we had been to success for four years. Once again Everton were in relegation trouble in Walter Smith's dire first season in charge and any sniff of success in a Cup competition had to be inhaled long and hard to eke out whatever pleasure it may bring. With an Alan Shearer inspired Newcastle who were fairly formidable at home, that pleasure was very likely to be curtailed on this Sunday. And now there was every chance that I would not be able to witness the last rites of yet another premature end to an Everton season. I was determined, though. I had a plan that may have compromised my professionalism and my right to pick up my entire pay packet for that month but an Evertonian has to do what an Evertonian has to do in these circumstances.

I turned up for duty on time as normal for that Sunday evening. I then turned on the television in the boarding house television lounge, tuned to Supersport 3, turned the volume to zero. I then cajoled the younger boys into their study area which adjoined the TV lounge and made sure that they were all seated in silence with books ready for the two hour session of study ahead. I then did a quick skirt of the senior boys' rooms to make sure that they had all settled down to work as well. I then also settled down; in one of the comfortable lounge seats in the boys' TV room to watch the game from St James's Park. Every now and then I would do a quick circuit of the corridors and study area to ensure no indiscipline was afoot, but I never took more than a two minute chunk out of the match. An injury or some other stoppage in the game was the signal for me to do one of my lightning checks. I didn't miss any of the goals. Everton actually played very well and, when David Unsworth equalised with about 20 minutes to go, that old 'Anfield feeling' was revived. I moved around the TV lounge clenching my fist and then I kissed the television screen several times. I so wanted to share this happiness but had to keep it within and there was not a sound that emerged from my throat. It was all followed pretty quickly by a mime of despair as Newcastle smashed in three at the other end to make it a rather flattering 4–1 scoreline for the home team. Another season over, another massive heartache to contend with. And I had to deal with the immediate aftermath of yet another mortifying blow inflicted on me by my football team by completing my boarding house supervision duty as if nothing else had been occurring for the previous two hours or so. Once again I had been occupying a parallel universe while most of those around me were oblivious to the emotional turmoil sloshing around inside me.

Everton had played well, though and the encouraging signs were illuminated further with the arrival of Kevin Campbell on loan from Trabzonspor soon afterwards. Up until that 'silent night' in the FA Cup, Everton had score 20 goals in 28 League matches in season 1998–99. That defeat at Newcastle was the springboard for Everton to score 22 times in the final 10 matches with Campbell scoring nine of them. We avoided relegation by some distance and there was optimism for the future. Another false dawn? Probably. Whatever it was to be, Violet, Christopher and I, plus our recent addition to the family, Vincent, were going to witness it in a different job in a different country.

Things changed dramatically at Braeburn during the remainder of that academic year. It seemed that El Nino that brought flooding throughout East Africa for much of our first year at Braeburn brought significant winds of change within the school itself during our second. In a restructuring exercise that no one had seen coming, Violet was to have her job description radically altered and her pay packet slashed. I had been trained for the post of Director of Studies which I was to take up in September but the additional money that that post attracted did not compensate the loss of pay and benefits caused by Violet's new arrangement. Then Uganda came calling and, once again, a providential door of opportunity was opened for the Green family. On 1 August 1999 I became the Headmaster of Rainbow International School in Kampala, Uganda. Violet became the Head of Boarding at the same school. I was excited at the prospect of running my own school. Violet was excited at the prospect of returning home. Christopher and Vincent were excited by everything!

PART 3:
Perfect Vision

Chapter 21

Welcome the ugly world of grown ups

16 April 2001: Everton 2 Liverpool 3

'So, have you found a buyer for the school, yet?' asked Mr Patel, a rather fearsome looking Indian gentleman with some unfathomable job title that I deduced could be paraphrased as 'IFC boss for East Africa'. IFC stands for International Finance Corporation and is a branch of the World Bank dedicated to handling what it regards as small projects. In 1994, IFC had lent $800,000 to Mrs Alemayehu to set up Rainbow International School. She had been operating a small primary school from a rented house on the edge of the Ugandan capital, Kampala since 1991. A country that was dragging itself off the floor after many blood soaked, brutal years of chaotic tyranny suffered under Amin and Obote, was seen as a land of opportunity by many and, in the early nineties, Uganda was swelling with the influx of expatriates. Some with genuinely altruistic motives but most with the scent of money in their nostrils. When a country is on its knees, it needs entrepreneurs to help it to its feet. Mrs Alemayehu was offering a bit of altruism and opportunism. The starting of a school has to have an element of social conscience attached but the idea that there is money to be made from a private school would not have escaped her. I know exactly her thought processes; they had all applied to me when deciding to become involved in Hillside

High School. So her little school soon mushroomed into something very large that only serious financial backing could support. The World Bank, conscious of its obligation to demonstrate a caring, compassionate side particularly in the developing world, had been willing to provide that backing. It seems that they had agreed the deal with Mrs Alemayehu just a few months before I turned up with my cash projections asking for something similar for Hillside High School. The response I received at the time was that they had just lent a considerable sum of money to an international school in Kampala and were not prepared to lend to another one until they could assess the success or otherwise of their venture with Rainbow International School. How ironic that just a few years on, I was leading this school, a potential rival to my own. Perhaps Mrs Alemayehu had been just an opportunist or simply a poor financial manager, but the fact was, not a single shilling had been repaid on that loan when I arrived to begin my three year contract as the school's new headmaster on 1 August 1999. The bombshell delivered in the first line of this chapter by the humourless Mr Patel and his entourage of smart suited bankers, arrived just 27 days into my tenure. It was delivered to the ashen faced Mrs Alemayehu who owned the school and who had just hired me as the person charged with steering her flagging project away from the choppy waters that it had entered. I was appointed primarily to handle the educational welfare of the school but, no doubt, this middle aged, slightly neurotic German woman with an Ethiopian husband, had half an eye on my background in accountancy when she chose me as her third head teacher. I looked at her in this meeting feeling a mixture of pity and an acute need for self-preservation. Mrs Alemayehu looked as if she was at the mercy of some sharp dressed mafia presenting an ultimatum in the cloaked threats of people who always get their way. As for me, I was wondering if my ambition to head an international school was about to be aborted after less than a month.

As she stumbled around looking for an answer to this question posed by Mr Patel and fumbled around for a much needed nicotine boost, I, who had remained acquiescent in the meeting up to that point, interjected; very clumsily, on reflection.

'I know that Mrs Alemayehu has not managed this project very well but, with over 300 children on roll, I do not see why we cannot turn it around and start to repay the loan.' It was quite courageous, perhaps foolhardy, to be undermining my employer in front of such exulted company when my feet were barely under the table, but the brazen approach worked. The IFC bankers seemed sufficiently reassured and a stay of execution was bought. In the end, their social remit meant that closing down a school was not something they would relish. So, as a result of my bold claim that I could ensure that the school would repay $100,000 in the next year, Mrs Alemayehu still had a school to own and I still had a school to run. However, when one of her particularly unpleasant creditors took the law into his own hands and sent the boys round to the school nine months later to try to extract computers and other assets from the premises in lieu of a debt, I could no longer save her. IFC's patience ran dry and they decided to exercise their legal rights as preferential creditors and put the school into receivership. It was probably the gunfire around the school reception as the security guards tried to fend off the attack by the bailiffs while classes were in session that finally swayed it. It was more than just IFC's *money* in danger now. So, Mrs Alemayehu was ousted and I found myself running Rainbow International School on behalf of the World Bank. How the tables had turned and what a difficult situation I found myself in.

I really grew up quickly in that first year at Rainbow International School. At the age of 38½ I had finally entered the world of adulthood; a world where people are not truthful or honest or kind to each other; where people scheme and plot and smile at you while planning to do you serious damage. I had been cocooned from this before. Although I had had interactions with fellow adults for many years by now, they had not involved weighty issues such as the management of millions of dollars, seriously big business decisions and bankruptcy. And they had never before involved being in the same room as representatives of the World Bank demonstrating my knowledge of cash flow forecasts, budgets and profit and loss accounts. For nearly twenty years I had been studying and then teaching these subjects but now I was using them in the real world in real situations. OK, so I had practised accountancy in Liverpool all those years earlier, but preparing a set of final accounts for a small photographic studio in Southport was a far cry from discussing financial projections of an international school in sub-Saharan Africa with members of the biggest bank in the world. Hillside High School had just been playing at 'the real world'. It was an exciting adventure that became rather scary and frenetic as my personal responsibilities expanded but, still it was essentially a project set up and run with friends. In fact, the mood swing of those involved in Hillside seemed to take a fatal plunge from exhilaration to exasperation at exactly the time that Brodiz passed away in 1996. And here was another salient point that was not applicable to Rainbow. Brodiz was fundamentally a 'good guy' and all the people I had worked for or with up to this point in my life had been essentially straightforward, trustworthy people. At Rainbow, partly due to the ridiculous set of circumstances I found myself embroiled in, I was starting to touch a new world inhabited by some of the human race's lower life.

The fault lines caused by the ruptures of the tectonic changes at Rainbow during my first year in charge, were sometimes very difficult to handle. I had not been used to nastiness and unpleasantness in my life apart from that offered to me by the kids in Bermuda; but, at the end of the day, they were just kids and could be excused and rationalised. I had become demoralised by loneliness and a lack of personal direction on occasions but that pain comes from within, it is not inflicted by others. Suddenly here at Rainbow I was contending with a whole mass of Alemayehu loyalists telling me what a bastard I was to have ousted their friend from her own beautiful school, destroying her vision and her ambition in the process. Looking back, though, there is nothing I would have changed about how I responded to that bizarre situation that I faced. I needed a job and I had for some time harboured the ambition of running my own school. With its precarious financial situation, most people would have viewed Rainbow as a place to be avoided in 1999 rather than an opportunity to resurrect a mismanaged institution. But I was prepared to sign Mrs Alemayehu's contract of employment and, for that act of bravery or idiocy, I could convince myself that my carefree attitude to risk had been rewarded on this occasion. At Hillside High School such a cavalier approach to life had led to failure and the loss of a relative fortune; you win some and lose some. Moreover, if I hadn't taken up the gauntlet thrown down by IFC to try to save the school from financial ruin, Kampala would probably have been minus one international school and plus a lot of unemployed people and disappointed children and parents.

Mrs Alemayehu's flippant attitude towards her own debts also ameliorated my guilty feelings to an extent. 'It's IFC's fault. Why did they lend me the money in the first place? They should have checked whether I could manage a project like this before they gave me all that money', was her rather warped defence proffered when I put forward strategies that might have allowed for a repayment on the loan to have been made. As the belligerent creditor who attacked her school had once said to me: 'The problem in Uganda is, you lend people money and they regard it as profit'. He had a point. And he had his own inimitable and heavy handed way of dealing with it. He didn't retrieve his money but he did cause the demise of Mrs Alemayehu as the captain of her ship called Rainbow International School. And he did indirectly instate me at the helm as the receiver manager of the entire school. I was suddenly thrust into the role of trying to rescue Rainbow International School on behalf of IFC.

During academic year 2000 to 2001, I had to contend with an emotional battering. The saving grace was that, in general I had a majority of the parents and students on my side as well as the entire staff; or at least I thought I had the full support of the staff. Having a fair and transparent salary structure embedded into a performance management system had been new developments that I had introduced. Suddenly employees felt valued and connected to the project they were part of. Rainbow International School found some forward momentum. The idea of teamwork had been invented. There are always some that 'don't get it', though. Several anonymous letters arrived either giving various weird inside gossip as to what was going on under my nose in the classrooms or the staff room or simple, outrageous threats and accusations against me personally. Among all this collateral generated, no doubt, by Alemayehu supporters, I had to try to make the school more financially robust. This could only be achieved by encouraging many more students through our doors; a daunting task in the wake of the negative publicity the school had received during the receivership process. I mean, how do you recover from a front page headline in the biggest selling newspaper in the country of: 'GUN SHOTS AT RAINBOW INTERNATIONAL SCHOOL'?

One way is to try to prove to the world that the school is still flourishing and doing well and that the change in regime is for the benefit of all. Fulfilling some of the long standing promises that Mrs Alemayehu had held as a carrot to disillusioned parents when they threatened to withdraw their children from the school, was one way of doing that. Thus, within three months of being installed as the receiver manager of the school, I had manoeuvred sufficient funds to build a swimming pool and jiggled the timetable to allow for the introduction of A levels. The funding of the swimming pool had involved some personal sacrifice in the form of a short term loan. I was also the only person on the entire payroll of Rainbow International School to suffer a pay freeze in my three years in charge; a freeze on what was a fairly meagre income in the first place for someone in my lofty position. I had been promised receivership fees from IFC but I never claimed them as they would have had to be paid from the Rainbow coffers. The positive vibes that I was trying to generate to the Kampala public provoked a reaction and the student roll began to rise.

Some hard-faced business had to take place as well, particularly in the area of the collection of school fees. I had already encountered this most difficult of quandaries at Hillside. The puzzle goes something like this: A private school needs the fees to run the school and to educate the children. If the fees are delayed or not paid these services are compromised, but they are not compromised only for the people who have not paid but also for all the people who have dutifully paid their fees in full and on time. When a school is walking a financial tightrope as Rainbow was at this time, these compromises are very real. A marginal reduction in income can mean a marginal decrease in provisions so, for example, text books are shared, science experiments are carried out in larger groups, even furniture can become a problem. If the people who are late paying, have their children removed from the school, then those that have paid will have a full, uncompromised service. So, where's the puzzle? The provision of education is essentially a social undertaking; how do you tell a parent who has paid school fees for their daughter faithfully and punctually for six years but has now lost their job and so has asked for a temporary period of grace, that their daughter can no longer come to school? Apart from the psychological and educational damage inflicted on the child, what about the potential harm that that parent could do to the reputation of the school when he tells his story of how his child was kicked out of Rainbow because of an unfortunate but temporary financial crisis that he had encountered. Many parents, of course, play on that sympathy card but many are genuine cases. The hardest part of the problem, is deciding which is which. And, having decided that a case is genuine, how long can you allow the debt to build up before it is unmanageable on both sides. Once you do finally decide to pull the plug, you can be sure that that debt will not be recovered, unless you are prepared to try to recover it through the courts; an unpalatable business for a school to dirty itself with.

I inherited from Mrs Alemayehu a debtors' ledger laden with such difficult cases. One was from a compatriot of hers called Mr Muller. He had had his oldest child in the school from its inception in September 1991 and now had three children attending Rainbow. He was more than a term behind with the school fees which amounted to quite a considerable sum of money. Mr Muller was unemployed but owned some property in the Ugandan capital. Keen to avoid confrontation with a former friend of Mrs Alemayehu and looking for a creative solution to recouping our money, I arranged to rent two of Mr Muller's houses for the purposes of our expatriate staff. The rent would be offset against his school fees debt. However, the agreed rental still fell well short of the school fees due on his three children and, without topping it up with a further $250 per month cash, his debt would spiral out of control. He agreed to this arrangement convincing me that he had other investments which would allow him to make this monthly top-up. We reached Christmas and he had not made a single repayment. After many warnings, I terminated the agreement. The Rainbow tenants were rehoused elsewhere and Mr Muller's children were removed from the school. Early in the new year of 2001, we received news that Mr Muller had hanged himself in the garage of one of the vacant houses. His youngest son had been the one to find him dangling there when he got up that morning. A traumatic sight for a five-year-old to witness and a terrible situation for the school to handle. The extended family arrived on the scene (Mr Muller's wife was Ugandan), the children were reinstated into the school and the old debt was written off. Within a term the relatives had reneged on their instalment plan of school fees that I had agreed with them and the debt began to sky rocket again. Don't let anyone tell you that fee collection at a private school is a straightforward, black and white affair.

Soon after the suicide of Muller, I received my first death threat. It was written in rather obscure language but the meaning was clear: keep stealing the money while you can because you will be dead soon. I had managed to deflect much of the debris hurled at me during the previous six months helped by the strength of Violet and the joy that our two little sons brought me, but this was entering a new dimension. My personal existence on this planet was now in question. I set about with vigour trying to find the culprit. I think I succeeded although, to this day, there is a nagging doubt that I didn't. My investigation was so forceful and persistent and my manner so possessed with determination, that a lot of the poison festering in the woodwork of Rainbow was squeezed out. The pinning of the case and subsequent sacking of the receptionist eliminated any doubt that I meant business and that I was staying at Rainbow for the long haul. Mrs Sewali may have been the sacrificial lamb in this but, what I found out about her during my blitz of interviews and inquiries, convinced me that it was worth lancing that particular boil in order to stop others popping up at untimely moments. The tactic worked as the letters and nastiness abated. All except one letter, that is; a letter from Mrs Sewali's lawyers saying that I would be dragged to the High Court of Kampala at my own expense and embarrassment for the persecution of their client.

Compared to the drama of my personal life, Everton were experiencing a life of unrelenting boredom under Walter Smith. As the modest income of Violet and me had increased slightly on the sum that we had earned at Braeburn, we invested in the unspectacular luxury of satellite television. The particular package we could afford only offered three channels, fortunately one of them was Supersport 3. I now had three or four live Premiership matches to enjoy every weekend. Very often this proved the salvation of me. One o'clock on a Saturday lunchtime was when I finally put the affairs of Rainbow to bed for a day and a half (although Violet still ran the boarding house so there was sometimes business to attend to there). Until my return to office on Monday morning my hours were filled with family time and a succession of live football matches on television. Everton were rarely featured having disappeared into the whirlpool of mid-table obscurity. The 'derby', of course, had to feature, though. Earlier in the season we had been whipped at Anfield with Barmby scoring one of the goals for the Reds. Some serious revenge was in order as we approached the Goodison return on 16 April. It was a Monday night game which meant, with the two hour time difference, it was due to kick off at 10pm Ugandan time. Everton played well, big Dunc roughed them up all night and, as we entered injury time, it was 2–2. Then Liverpool were awarded a free-kick 30 yards from the Everton goal, fairly central. Gary McAllister took it. A sense of inevitability struck me as McAllister's boot struck the ball. Sure enough, the ball seemed to take an age to reach the goal but still fast enough to beat the despairing dive of Paul Gerrard.

I had to go into school the next day to lead three hours of staff training before the commencement of the new term. Muller, Sewali and now McAllister had knocked the stuffing out of me. I felt like curling up and going back to bed when I awoke from a fitful sleep barely six hours after the Goodison 'derby' had concluded. But I didn't curl up and I didn't pretend that all life's problems could be kept at bay by the width of a duvet cover. You see, now I was made of stronger stuff, now I had joined the tough, uncompromising world of the grown-ups. Even a maddening 'derby' defeat could not floor me; not quite.

Chapter 22
Lost weekend

10 March 2002: Middlesbrough 3 Everton 0

Steve Simonsen, Alessandro Pistone, David Unsworth, Alan Stubbs, David Weir, Peter Clarke, Tobias Linderoth, Paul Gascoigne, Joe-Max Moore, Tomas Radzinski, Scot Gemmill. That was the Everton line-up at The Riverside on the second Sunday afternoon of March 2002. It was an FA Cup quarter-final and we were 3–0 down and dead and buried by half-time. And looking at the team sheet it is hardly a surprise. We had a few key injuries to the likes of Duncan Ferguson, Thomas Gravesen and Kevin Campbell but, even so, the team that took to the field merely emphasised that we had a squad depth the width of a razor blade. Most people without a keen interest in Everton would probably have never heard of Peter Clarke or Tobias Linderoth. Joe-Max Moore sounds more like a circus owner than a footballer but sadly the American's performances were never so colourful. The defence would be familiar to non-Evertonians as being granite like and uncompromising and most will be able to drag the names of Radzinski and Gemmill from the depths of their memory but then wouldn't remember why they had been able to recall them. And then, of course, stuck in the middle of this mishmash of mediocrity is the shining jewel; someone even your old grannie with not the smallest grain of football knowledge or interest would have heard of. Alas poor old Gazza was in the dying stages of a swansong and could add little light to the dullness that surrounded him. I remember thinking as I sat there in my living room watching the horror show unfold on our little television in the shabby lounge of the living quarters of the Rainbow boarding house: how did we get to this state? Was this the sum total of three and a half years of sweat from that dour, craggy manager, Walter Smith? Injuries or no injuries, this was a sad indictment of his toil. He had inherited a squad that had avoided relegation by a whisker on the final day of the season, but this feeble surrender at the Riverside gave me the impression that we had barely moved forward since that great escape. He may have won enough pots to fill a hotel kitchen in Scotland but south of the border, where there are more than two candidates for the League title, he just didn't cut it. A pleasant, honest, impenetrable guy, but not one of Everton's greatest managers.

And this poor imitation of football from my beloved Blues came in the midst of a dire weekend. I had spent much of Saturday suffering from malaria. In July 1999, after 10 years on the African continent, I had finally contracted my first dose of malaria when holidaying in Mombasa just before we moved across to Kampala to start work at Rainbow. It was a severe attack during which I couldn't eat for a week and was even throwing up water. From that time on, the parasite was in my blood and the illness would recur every three months or so. A bout of this debilitating disease struck me on this particular weekend rendering me bed-ridden for the first half of it. I could generally recognise the symptoms well in advance and medication would limit the worst effects to less than a day. So, by Sunday, I was in the recuperation stage. I needed a big result at Middlesbrough to complete my recovery.

The day had begun on a promising note as I gave Violet two dresses as presents from Christopher and Vincent for Mothers' Day. However, I had already detected another malady infiltrating my body at this point. It was in the region of my mouth and was the initial stages of toothache. Wishful thinking soon succumbed to the jolting realisation that this affliction was only going to get worse as the day progressed. By the time Everton had finished drowning at the Riverside, I was feeling pangs of excruciating pain and began to chew on a handkerchief for respite. Violet phoned around for a dentist but none were available on a Sunday. She secured an appointment with Dr Aliker for eight o'clock the next morning. There was a massive amount of torture that lay ahead of me before my meeting with the dentist. I spent much of the night striding around, groaning as I gnawed on that hanky. Reruns of the four FA Cup quarter-finals were shown on Supersport 3 throughout the night. I half watched them as they gave me a countdown to the moment when the agony would be over, 90 minute steps on the road towards oral redemption. The rerun of the Everton game seemed to take twice as long as the others; it was almost more painful than the toothache. Violet came out of the bedroom at one point around midnight to see how her husband was faring. She was soon distracted by some noises from downstairs where the boy boarders slept. She went down to investigate. She came back after some time looking quite disturbed. I had heard her shouting at someone but had been too indisposed with my rotten molar to find out what the fuss was about. Well, the fuss was actually about the fact that she had found one of the senior boys, Anthony, lying virtually unconscious in his own vomit stinking of Waragi. He had evidently sneaked a small bottle or two of the lethal banana gin back with him after visiting home for the weekend. Two friends in the same dorm had also sampled some of the alcohol but had only reached the silly giggling stage. Violet soon removed the giggles and soon brought Anthony round to his senses. It wasn't his first offence. Indeed, he had, for some time, seemed determined to push the boundaries of the school rules to a limit where his position as a pupil of Rainbow was rendered untenable; he was not a scholar and had a pretty messed up home life; he was very keen to remove himself from the chains of academia and his own home as soon as he could so that he could go and make his own way in the world. Well, he had achieved his goal that night. So I had an expulsion (or permanent exclusion to use modern educational parlance) and two suspensions on my plate as well as a visit to the dentist to contemplate. In the condition I was in, I had to make the visit to the dentist a priority and so I requested that Violet put a report in writing of what she had just witnessed in the boys' dormitory ready for me to deal with whenever I came round from the anaesthetic.

It was around 11 o'clock the next morning when I was finally released from the leather upholstery of Dr Aliker's operating room. As with all dentists, the large, jovial man who was the father of two children attending Rainbow, was much too cheerful and insistent on conversation for my liking. I was glad when he got down to the real business thus making it impossible for me to respond to his idle chatter without cracking further teeth on a mirror or other metallic object thrust into my mouth. Again, as with all dentists, it didn't seem to prevent him from carrying on with a one directional conversation making the client feel somehow discourteous or inadequate in not participating. He elicited the occasional groan of physical pain as he extracted the offending tooth and dug around in a root canal. He elicited groans of mental anguish when he joyfully heralded the progress of Arsenal in the FA Cup and mocked Everton's demise. The anaesthetic was only a local one and I was permitted to return to my car immediately after his excavation work had been completed, ready to be driven home by Violet. She collected the antibiotics and painkillers from a pharmacy and we arrived home with my mouth feeling as if it was the size of a football and my pockets feeling extremely light. I wrote the letter of expulsion for Anthony and gave it to Violet who went with it and the miscreant to his father's house for both to be deposited. The other two boys sat in the school reception all day as I decided that I would deal with them the next day. I spent the rest of the day in bed making up for the lost night of sleep. The next day I learnt that Walter Smith had been sacked. It's a strange quirk of history and the way my memory interlinks events concerning my personal affairs and those of Everton Football Club but I will forever associate Walter Smith's reign at Goodison Park with toothache. Not a bad analogy.

So that uninspiring team sheet that opened this chapter was the very last to be penned by Mr Smith's own hand. He probably conjured it up in his head as I was wrestling with the fever of malaria. Bill Kenwright was penning Mr Smith's termination letter when I was horizontal again, this time struggling with the numbing pain of an anaesthetic and then the throbbing ache brought about by root canal treatment and an extraction. It is surely the most brutal and decisive act that the avuncular Mr Kenwright has ever taken in his life. So, in the weekend when Walter lost his job and, to be honest, the plot, I lost a tooth and a night of sleep, Violet lost her temper with three errant students, one of whom lost his place in Rainbow and Everton lost an FA Cup quarter-final and so lost interest in the rest of the season. Once again a premature end to proceedings on the field for another season but at least, after this lost weekend, I and all Evertonians had the appointment of a new manager to look forward to; a new man to steer us through to the end of the season. But who would it be?

Chapter 23
A brave new world

23 March 2002: Derby County 3 Everton 4

It was, of course, David Moyes. He was proudly unveiled by the Everton chairman, Bill Kenwright on 14 March, one day after Christopher's fifth birthday. It was something of a present for our son, as he had just started to demonstrate an affinity with his father's football club. Perhaps a responsible, compassionate father would have directed their son away from a life of potential torment and disappointment at that point but I was neither responsible nor compassionate when it came to football. Chris would 'enjoy' the suffering for a lifetime just like his dad. Father and son chats over a pint in a pub outside Goodison before and after yet another 90 minutes of anguish in the approximate year of 2017 were already formulating in my head. Talk about 'Making plans for Nigel'; talk about child cruelty.

At this stage Chris could not engage in any deep conversation on the merits or otherwise of our newly appointed manager from Preston North End. I discussed the topic with some enthusiasm with members of the Rainbow staff and with Violet who was now a devoted and knowledgeable Evertonian. The parallels with the Howard Kendall appointment when he first arrived as Everton's manager from Second Division Blackburn Rovers 21 years earlier drew great comfort. A young, enthusiastic manager who had transformed a struggling Lancashire club on limited resources to reach the cusp of the promised land of top flight football. He had not had the same success as a player that Kendall had enjoyed but, interestingly he had played for

Shrewsbury Town in the Second Division in a period coinciding almost exactly with my time in Shropshire. As I was stacking up my appearances at Shrewsbury Sixth Form College from 1987 to 1989, Moyes was accumulating 96 appearances for the Shrews, although he stayed an extra year to achieve them. I vaguely remember a lean, flame-haired centre-back playing for the home side when I visited Gay Meadow on the handful of occasions that I went to watch 'my second team' when Everton were playing too far away. Little did I know that I was watching someone who was to become one of the greatest Evertonians of our time. As most will recall, on being named manager of Everton, David Moyes immediately showed his political as well as his managerial nous when he dubbed Everton 'The People's Club of Liverpool; the club that the people on the streets of Liverpool support'. In one platitude he had alienated the Reds, embraced the Blues and given Everton a moniker that has stuck ever since.

He also brought a refreshing approach to the way Everton played football. After the soporific fare provided by his predecessor, anything remotely positive on the pitch was going to appear entertaining, but this really was a contrast; from funereal to fun at the wave of Kenwright's magic wand. David Unsworth scored in under 30 seconds of Moyes' debut at home to Fulham and the tone was set. We went on to win that game 2–1 and then had to pay a visit to Pride Park the following weekend. Even though Everton were pretty well clear of the relegation mire, an extension of Smith's tenure could have had us in a late scramble for safety again such was the downward momentum. Derby were one of the teams deep in trouble. John Gregory's men would have liked nothing better than to grab the pants of a team like Everton and drag us down into the quicksand with them. In a sense, therefore, this was almost a relegation battle. If we won, we would just about be able to breathe easily for the final seven games; if we lost, we would remain twitchy for at least another week. What would Walter Smith have done in such circumstances? Been so obsessed with the opposition that he would have put in six defenders and hoped for a 0–0. What did David Moyes do? Ignore the opposition and concentrate on what we were going to do. He put out an attacking line-up and outscored the opposition in a seven goal classic. It was so good that I watched it twice!

The state of my health gave great symbolism to the state of my football team over these two weeks. From bed ridden and depressed during the final throes of Walter Smith's leadership to fighting fit and on top of my game as Everton travelled to the East Midlands in the opening chapter of a brand new era.

I had watched the Rainbow senior boys lose 9–0 to Vienna College in the morning. That didn't upset me as much as you might expect. In an attempt to integrate Rainbow International School more with the local community, I had organised a league involving five Ugandan schools as well as Rainbow International School. The international community in Kampala is small and there are effectively only three international schools in the city offering secondary school education. I had found it rather insular to be constantly having fixtures against the same two schools. So, at the start of the academic year, I had circulated information to five of the more well known and respected Ugandan private schools in the area. The League was bedevilled with indiscipline and cheating from the outset. PE is not a recognised school subject in Uganda. It is not even included on the country's national curriculum. Some old colonial ways were adopted and never released even after 40 years of independence. In many ways the society is very staid and traditional, like a throwback to the '50s or even more distant times in the UK. There is nowhere that this is more evident than in the field of education.

The schools very much reflect the attitudes of much of the population in believing in firm, almost sadistic discipline and considering vocational subjects such as music, drama and physical education as irrelevant and unnecessary and not representing 'real' education. The majority of children, of course, love to do exercise and play sport. As a result there is this massive surfeit of energy in Ugandan schools with no obvious release valve. That is why in Ugandan schools when discipline breaks down, it breaks down big time. Knowing that there's not likely to be a fair hearing at the end of their action, students take no prisoners; it is not uncommon for schools to be burnt to the ground as a result of the children's anger and frustration having no place to go. It is something of a microcosm of the entire population of many African nations. If people are suppressed hard and long enough, they will eventually rise up in revolution. With no democratic fora in which to use more civilised methods to demonstrate dissent, the masses will eventually express themselves by physical means. They will mistrust those that oppress them so that even if a democratic process is offered such as an election, the result will not be believed. Hence the frequent perceived need for bullets instead of ballots for the proletariat.

Sorry, I got off on a bit of a diversion there. What has this got to do with Rainbow losing 9–0 at home to Vienna College? Well, in addition to the aggressive angry young

Ugandans that take to the field to represent their schools at sport, they are often led by a pretty frustrated teacher. He will be a teacher of geography or French or some other academic subject because there is no such thing as a PE teacher in Uganda because there is no such subject to teach. He will have an interest in sport in the partisan, 'win at all costs' sense. Having come through the Ugandan educational system, he will not have been imbued with such concepts as teamwork or respect. His rock hard winning mentality will not have been softened by alien ideas like fair play or 'it's the participation that counts'. In other words, Vienna College which was situated in Namugongo to the north-east of Kampala incidentally (it's name comes from the fact that it originated from the brainchild of an Austrian) arrived at Rainbow International School on that Saturday morning in an uncompromising mood. With a team of strapping six foot sixth formers, they were obviously going to flatten our motley crew of year 11s and 12s with physiques ranging from moderately muscular to emaciated. At this stage our entire sixth form consisted of 11 students, six of whom were girls. Their coach smiled politely as he greeted me and then set about demolishing our team. I did not expect him to show any mercy and he did not disappoint in that respect. The away team was supposed to provide a referee so I knew the officiating would also be dubious. I was not disappointed in that respect either.

African society is very much 'dog eat dog'. There is little compassion shown towards the subservient or the opponent. The Rainbow football team could be described as both in this particular contest and they were duly put to the sword by a combination of strength, skill and suspect refereeing. As an observer I was not so aggrieved, though. There was nothing that happened that I couldn't have predicted at 9 o'clock that morning. I had set a target for us to keep the score below double figures which was achieved and I had simply told our boys at the start that all I required was for them to do their best and not to give up. I believe they achieved those modest aims. No doubt the Vienna coach would have found such a team talk wimpy and pointless but then again he wouldn't have entered into a match where such a low level of attainment was anticipated from his team.

Some may question why I had allowed the Rainbow kids to enter a competition which involved a weekly slaughter at the hands of bigger and better players. In hindsight, I might ask the same question but, at least it gave me a measure of our progress. By the time, I left the school in 2011, Rainbow International School had a reputation as one of the strongest footballing schools in Kampala irrespective of the opposition. It also meant that the main objective was achieved of maintaining links with the local community and thus ensuring that Rainbow did not exist in an elitist expatriate bubble that so many international schools tend to do. Sadly Rainbow has gravitated back towards the comfort zone occupied exclusively by the international community over the past year since I left. It is a natural pull and requires strength from the leadership to resist it. I had sensed this change in direction was coming and was outnumbered in my efforts to do anything about it. It was one of the underlying reasons for our family choosing to leave Rainbow when we did; but more about that later.

Alongside the swimming pool that I had had constructed in my first few months as receiver manager of the school, I had also managed to stretch the school finances far enough to build a restaurant. We named it Colours Club. It served two purposes. Firstly, it became the dining room for the primary school and secondly, it provided a place for the Rainbow community to socialise out of school hours. We had furnished it with a pool table and a television offering DSTV. Having been responsible for its construction, I gained special satisfaction in spending time there. On this particular Saturday, Colours Club was to be the venue for the school disco. The disco was to start at around 7pm, I went up to the club at around 5 o'clock, in theory to oversee the preparations for the disco but, in reality, to plonk myself on a bar stool, order myself an ice cold Club lager and watch Derby County v Everton on the television situated high up above the pool table. This wasn't as irresponsible as it may at first sound. There was a School Council that organised the disco and they were supervised by two designated and dedicated teachers. I didn't really have to be there at all but I always liked to have my presence felt at every school function. The match was unbelievable. Everton raced into a 4–1 lead in the second half but, such was our frailty at that time, we still managed to make a game of it. Derby pulled it back to a single goal margin and we were hanging on until the final whistle. At one point when we led 4–1 I remember the head girl, Leila Kassam coming up to me. She was a keen Arsenal fan and had a sharp wit. She asked me some question about the arrangements for the disco. I was so transfixed by the television screen that I distractedly said something like: 'Sorry, Leila, I'll deal with that after the match. I haven't seen Everton play like this…' 'EVER' said Leila, concluding my tailed off sentence with a laugh.

The fact was, I hadn't seen us play like this for probably 15 years. It wasn't so much the performance; we were up against relegation fodder after all, it was just the mindset that we had adopted. To be 4–1 up with 20 minutes of the match remaining and to still be 'going for it'. It reminded me of the cavalier days of Bracewell, Reid, Sheedy, Steven, Heath, Gray and Sharp when we had no fear for the opposition and simply had the confidence and belief that we would score more goals than the other team. There was some rookie Premier League manager naivety at play here, of course. The following week we went to St James' Park with the same approach and got turned over 6–2 but I don't think I've ever been so encouraged by a four goal thumping in my life before or since that match. OK, it proved what was obvious; that the strength of our squad was way below the likes of Newcastle United but I would rather us go down fighting and scoring two goals than cower in the corner and lose 1–0.

At that time DSTV had two of the Saturday 3 o'clock kick-offs showing live simultaneously on two different channels. It would then swap the games and play a rerun of them in full directly afterwards. So I rushed home to watch this action packed 90 minutes all over again on the other channel as the TV at Colours Club had to be switched off for the disco. I went back to school to monitor the dying embers of the disco and make sure everyone left the premises safely. There were no incidents of note and, all in all, it had been a near perfect day in this brave new world.

Chapter 24
Lucky escape

30 August 2004: Manchester United 0 Everton 0

It's regrettable when it happens but thankfully it only occurred once in my 12 years as the leader of Rainbow International School. To what am I referring? Taking a school assembly wearing odd shoes? Having a fees defaulter hang himself soon after his children were excluded from the school because of the outstanding debt? Having the school bankers go bankrupt taking approximately £17,000 of our much needed money down with them just before the monthly salaries were due? Receiving a death threat? Witnessing a gunfight in the school car park? Thanking the student band in front of the whole school for their contribution to a special assembly when they hadn't actually played at all due to lack of time? Telling the country representative of IFC to f*** off when he refused to sanction the construction of new science laboratories? Being summoned to the High Court at my own expense and embarrassment for persecution of a staff member? Having to expel the head girl for fighting and swearing in the midst of the parents at school Sports Day? Although each of this eclectic selection of incidents and accidents did actually occur in the crazy, crazy world of Rainbow International School during my 12 years in charge and, thankfully, they all occurred *once* only, they are not what I had in mind when I posed the question at the beginning of this paragraph. Some of those stories have already been told in this book and others are perhaps for another book. As this book is essentially about supporting Everton FC from overseas, the answer to the question that opens this chapter is related to that topic.

The regrettable occurrence that I had in mind was the time when an Everton match was being broadcast live on DSTV but I was unable to watch it due to work commitments. In Chapter 20, I recalled the time at Braeburn High School when I tried to watch an Everton match and carry out my boarding duties simultaneously. At Rainbow, because I had more control over my own destiny as the person in charge, I always managed to ensure that such a conflict of interests never occurred. The one exception was on the August Bank Holiday of 2004. In Uganda there is no such holiday. There are plenty of other national holidays, 13 in total if the two Muslim festivals of Id are included, but there is no day off on the last Monday of August unless, of course, it happens to be Id al-Fitr. Given the two hour time lag of East Africa compared to the UK during the summer months, this still didn't represent a problem as long as the football match kicked off at three o'clock i.e. five o'clock in Uganda. For some reason which I cannot recall now and possibly didn't even know at the time, Manchester United v Everton was a midday kick-off. It was taking place on the first day of staff training for the commencement of the new school year. I had set the programme in stone on the school calendar months in advance, long before I knew that Everton were going to be playing at two o'clock Ugandan time on the same day. I had spent all morning leading various sessions on staff development and was half thinking about sneaking home to catch the game on DSTV. However, a combination of the queue of prospective parents waiting for me in the school reception and the acute guilt I would have felt having told the teachers that they were expected to remain in school until four o'clock carrying out general preparation for the upcoming academic year, meant that I had to resist the temptation. I have always believed in leading from the front and setting the right example. Bunking off straight after lunch while my staff continued to slave away on their wall displays and attendance registers would not have squared with this philosophy.

With each conversation I had in my office with a prospective student or parent that afternoon, I had half an eye on the clock wondering how many goals down we were. You see, this was a game that we had to lose. Manchester United have gained more Premier League points against Everton than any other club. We are their favourite opposition. Up to that day in 2004 we had drawn one and lost 10 of our away games against Man United since a shock 3–0 win at Old Trafford at the beginning of the inaugural season of the Premier League. For Everton The Theatre of Dreams represented the Stadium of Nightmares, The Arena of Horrors, The Coliseum of Failure; call it what you will, we always got zilch from those visits. It was, therefore, tantamount to receiving news of a victory when I called Christopher in between appointments at around four o'clock to learn that we had drawn 0–0. Firstly I was so proud of my seven-year-old son as he so eloquently furnished me with every match detail after informing me of the score. He was already mature enough, if that is the right word, to understand the significance and magnitude of Everton's achievement and articulate enough to describe every highlight and nuance of the game, like how impressively this new guy, Tim Cahill played in midfield and how big Dunc put himself about and nearly scored an improbable winner.

Even by the standards of previous seasons, this was the greatest home banker ever. Everton had started the season as relegation certainties having finished bottom of all the surviving teams in the Premier League in the previous season. Manchester United were, along with the Arsenal Invincibles, favourites for the League title. Everton had suffered a summer of turmoil with Wayne Rooney determined to leave but not admitting to it until the transfer window was about to close. A bid from Newcastle finally triggered the transfer request that we all knew was coming. By the time this game at Old Trafford was taking place he had probably already joined the home dressing room as Sir Alex had moved in for the kill. With no time to spend any of the transfer proceeds, it looked like this might be the *coup de grace* to slay Everton.

I have fast forwarded two and half years to reach this chapter and it is no coincidence that the time vacuum from Chapter 23 covers almost exactly the period of Wayne Rooney's first-team career at Everton. Let me get one thing straight from the start; Wayne Rooney is a brilliant player, one of the best English talents produced ever and I am proud of the fact that this talent was discovered, developed and nurtured at Everton. Apart from his obvious technical prowess, he has great intelligence on the field belying one who seems so witless of it. The sobriquet of White Pele is an exaggeration and probably embarrasses Wayne himself. For Everton, though, he was a disaster and that is why I am happy to gloss over his 67 appearances, 15 goals, 15 yellow cards and one red card that he accumulated during his time at the club he supported as a boy. Those statistics tell their own story; a goal every four and a half games and the youngest player in Everton's history to be sent off. More cards than goals. Even his record of being the youngest Everton scorer was surpassed by James

Vaughan in 2005. Worse than all of this, though, was the detrimental effect he had on the team as a whole. He was precocious but he was also, it seems, disruptive. The magnitude of Manchester United and the reputation of Alex Ferguson were the only forces that were going to suppress this monster that was developing. In the one full season he played for Everton, we finished fourth from bottom and were dumped out of the FA Cup by Shrewsbury Town of League Two (Fourth Division in old money). He was moody and inconsistent and clearly felt that Everton were not good enough for him. He probably had a point but for simple fans like me it was hard to accept that he wasn't prepared to give at least a little more of himself and more of his time to the cause of the team that he had allegedly idolised as a child. His subsequent tantrums, indiscipline and sulks at Man United show that we had a lucky escape when he finally moved down the M62 on summer transfer deadline day, 2004. Within the almighty crèche of Old Trafford, he has been controlled…just. That is probably because he has been more humbled by the talent around him than he was at Everton. We have heard murmurs from time to time that he is dissatisfied with the quality of players available at United. No doubt he will look for greener pastures again before his career is over.

Ignoring the personal Evertonian aspect to my grievance with Rooney and the fact that he sold his soul to Man United before giving even two years of first team service to the club that had brought him up, I believe that Rooney's actions were symptomatic of a behaviour that developed around the turn of the century that has caused and continues to cause the football industry to self-destruct. At present we are only halfway there; there will be many more Portsmouths and Leeds Uniteds and Southamptons before the damage caused by the money madness of the past decade is finally reined in. While I can be upset with Rooney for his complete absence of loyalty towards Everton, he is just a product of a system where the people in charge had just lost track of financial reality. In which other industry, does a teenager get offered a weekly salary that most of us would take five years to earn? And we same ordinary mortals are expected to pay for that obscene salary with turnstile prices that are rising at a rate that is probably 20 or more times the rate that our pay packet is increasing. In what other industry are the employees of the businesses within it able to make their employers go insolvent at such an alarming rate by their ludicrous wage demands? Banks, maybe? But it was the bosses that generally paid themselves too much not the wages of their underlings that contributed to the banking crisis and, even then, that was only one factor in a complex structural collapse. In top flight professional football the cause of most of the financial ills is much simpler. The players, being manipulated by their agents, simply ask for too much money. What other industry could accommodate businesses paying over 100 per cent of their revenue on staff salaries? Clubs such as Chelsea and Man City have solved the problem by finding owners with very deep pockets who regard their football club as a hobby to be indulged in not an enterprise to be run by the normal rudiments of business. Not every club can find such a benefactor and some have ended up badly burnt trying to keep up with these clubs that play by different rules.

As football club chairmen are coming to their senses and realising that they cannot actually compete with clubs who are effectively being run on donations from their very rich owners, they are accepting that they have to compete on a very unfair playing field. Now that they are awakening from never never land, we are operating in a kind of monetary apartheid where the players such as Rooney, clearly driven by money, will only consider mixing with those clubs that meet their approval in terms of their wealth. To be fair, Manchester United have earned their financial strength through more conventional revenue streams rather than charity from their owners, and, for that reason, are now starting to lag behind Chelsea and Man City in terms of salaries. That's why they will probably lose Rooney who will continue to sell out to the highest bidder until he finds that no one is actually willing to bid for him anymore. When I referred to Rooney as a monster, it was in the metaphorical sense, although it is easy to see where the nickname Shrek arose from; he, like many others before and since in the past decade, is the monster that has threatened to destroy the top end of English football as a meaningful contest. The argument presented by those not alarmed by the increasing divide between football's rich and poor is that, if the likes of Chelsea and Man City didn't pay these ridiculous wages, the top players would ply their trade elsewhere in Europe. That fatuous reasoning has a simple riposte. Good riddance. Let them go to Spain or Italy or Russia. The English Premier League's greatest attraction is its competitiveness; having lived overseas for 20 odd years I know that for a fact. Allowing Abramovich and Sheikh Mansour bin Zayed bin Sultan Al Nahyan to monopolise the transfer market dilutes the competition completely. In the '80s and '90s teams like Norwich, Ipswich and even Watford competed for the top four. Do we really have to accept that those days are gone forever and that the League title will only ever be won by one of maybe four clubs until the end of time? As an Evertonian, I know that we will never compete with the likes of Man City and Chelsea unless we find a sugar daddy or, alternatively, those clubs lose theirs. And, if we were to find some staggeringly rich benefactor, wouldn't any ensuing success feel somehow hollow; gained by illicit means and would the fabric of our proud club be stripped bare forever?

For our Christopher, the Rooney episode had a profound effect on him. We had bought him a Rooney emblazoned Number 18 Everton kit for his sixth birthday. It convinced him once and for all that Everton was his team and Rooney was his hero. That debut goal against Arsenal in November 2002 had set off the chain of events. Unlike his father 30-odd years earlier, though, who had a genuine centre-forward hero to worship in Joe Royle, Chris's chosen idol was to disappoint him so utterly and completely. From the moment Rooney signed for United, Chris stopped wearing the shirt and despised the player. He had been so badly let down. This was absolute betrayal and for what reason? Rooney had worn that tee-shirt with 'Once a Blue always a Blue' splashed across it when he was 16. It didn't make any sense to a seven-year-old that he would now go and play for a different team and, to compound it all, one that wore red. The idea that money could be the underlying factor was an alien concept to one as young as Christopher. I had to hurt my son further by explaining away Rooney's act of treachery as the player simply wanting to play for a better team. It hurt me to say it as much as it hurt Chris to hear it because I knew it was true. What he and I and many distraught Everton fans felt was: why couldn't he have stayed to try to make Everton as good as Man United? That, of course, would have required patience, imagination, determination, vision and, yes, a word that is almost extinct in the modern footballer's vocabulary, loyalty; qualities not readily found in young people of this era, certainly not young talented footballers like Rooney who have a myriad of lucrative opportunities thrust at them as soon as they turn professional. Chris showed that he was made of stronger fibre, though. From the moment that Rooney penned that contract with the Red Devils, he became even more staunchly supportive of Everton. His heroes ever since have been the likes of Tim Cahill, Phil Jagielka and now Jack Rodwell. Players with more modest ability but also a more modest temperament. People who I am happy for him to have as role models. I sometimes reflect on what might have been if Rooney had continued to be Chris's hero. It really was a lucky escape.

That transfer, of course, provided some much needed funds to Everton at the time as the club seemed to be lurching from financial crisis to financial crisis. Probably the transfer fee received was Rooney's greatest contribution to Everton Football Club. Ironically something that he had no control over. Before the transfer readies from flogging off our errant protégé rolled in there were all sorts of horror stories of Everton about to go to the wall. Leeds United were one of the teams to finish below Everton at the end of the previous season. Relegated just two seasons after reaching the Champions League semi-final. Everton had not reached such heights and so could not suffer such a cataclysmic decline, but the signs of a financial meltdown on a scale that Leeds were about to face were apparently there, nonetheless.

During the 'Rooney reign' at Everton, there had been two major events in my life, one personal and one professional. On 5 November 2003 our beautiful daughter, Clair was born. I like to think that she is so special that the UK celebrates her birthday with fireworks every year! Almost exactly six months previous to that, Rainbow International School was sold by IFC to private investors, an Indian company called The Midland Group of Companies. One of the conditions of purchase set by IFC was that the successful bidders would have to keep me on as headmaster for the sake of continuity and stability. During the tendering process, I met many prospective buyers of the school. I furnished them with the financial data and the recent history of the school and had some pretty high level discussions with some high profile business people within East Africa. It was a period when I learnt a great deal about the negotiation techniques and procedures that are necessary in the transfer of a major undertaking like an international school that was now being valued at more than a million dollars. I believe the experience developed me as a person giving me confidence and belief in my own ability to converse convincingly about and explain financial data and to understand and make judgements on what I felt was best for the school. In the end, of course, I did not make the final decision as to which bidder should win the tender. It was IFC's debt and it was their decision as to who was to pay it back in order to secure ownership of the school. Inevitably, despite all IFC's blather about non-financial criteria being considered, the school went to the highest bidder. They are bankers after all. Their social conscience as part of the World Bank wasn't going to get in the way of the bottom line of their Profit and Loss Account. When push comes to shove, their shareholders take priority over the wellbeing of a local community in sub-Saharan Africa. It should be remembered that at the time of the take-over Rainbow had around 300 Ugandan students on roll among a total of 650 and employed more than a hundred Ugandan staff. The vision of the founder of the school and one which I fervently upheld was that Rainbow would always be an integral part of the local community unlike many other international schools. The welfare of many local people was dependent on the school's survival and success. In the end, whether by design or otherwise, IFC did safeguard the future of all these people by selling the school to the Midland Group. The owners of this company quickly learnt that financial rewards would only be gained by showing commitment to the whole Rainbow project as it existed in 2003.

This new world that I entered when negotiating the sale of Rainbow International School on behalf of the World Bank had perhaps given me ideas of self-importance well beyond my station for when, just over a year later, Everton appeared to be needing some financial assistance, I called a Ugandan businessman by the name of Michael Ezra. His name had come to my attention when he made a £60 million offer to buy Leeds United in February 2004. That deal fell through but the Kampala gossip was that this guy was seriously loaded with business interests in venture capitalism and real estate among others. In 2006 he apparently bought a Mont Blanc commemorative wristwatch from an Emirates auction for an eye watering $250,000. His secretary answered my call telling me that Mr Ezra was out of the country and that she would get him to call back when he was back in office. He never did. With Everton's story soon moving on and Rooney's departure loosening the club's financial straitjacket, my fleeting fantasy of sitting in the Goodison Board room brokering a deal with Mr Ezra and Mr Kenwright thankfully also faded. A story in Kenya's *Daily Nation* in 2011 stated that Ezra had been arrested for issuing a bounced cheque and there are other rumours that he is wanted by Interpol in Dubai. Whether these allegations are true I cannot say and, no doubt Mr Ezra would still pass the 'fit and proper person test' for the Premiership ownership rules, given some of the other characters that have been allowed to pass it, but I can't help feeling that for me and my football club, Mr Ezra's failure to return my call was just one more very lucky escape.

Chapter 25
Bitter sweet

11 May 2005: Arsenal 7 Everton 0

2004–05 was the first season that DSTV showed every single Premier League match of the entire season either live or as an uninterrupted delayed broadcast. Each Saturday the lunchtime game and the tea time kick-off would be shown live and, at 3 o'clock UK time, three or even four matches would be shown live on different channels simultaneously. Every Sunday the live games on English television in the UK would be duly transmitted via the South African satellite to be viewed across the dark continent as the action unfolded in England as would a Monday night game if one was scheduled. This meant that on several weekends there would be eight of the 10 Premier League matches available to the DSTV viewers live. The other two fixtures would be shown as a delayed broadcast and all the live matches would also be repeated, sometimes twice, at some time on either Supersport 3 or Supersport 7 between the time that the Saturday afternoon kick-offs ended and the first Sunday match began. Thus those two channels would have a conveyor belt of Premier League matches going on one after the other in two hour slots throughout the night and into Sunday. If Supersport 3 was showing a live match on Saturday tea time, Supersport 7 would be showing a repeat of one of the three o'clock kick-offs at the same time. It sounded like a footballer supporters' Utopia and, in many ways, it was. The only drawback was that it was hard not to allow my entire day and a half break from work at the weekend to consist of wall to wall television football. Sadly I often failed to fight this temptation and from 2.45pm or 3.45pm (depending on whether it was BST or GMT) on a Saturday until eight o'clock or nine o'clock on a Sunday evening I would become a couch potato sitting or lying there in our living room watching this wallpaper of English football on our television screen for hours at a time. Some would say it was a rather sad and futile existence; I often concluded the same; but with the constant bombardment of unforeseen problems hitting me from all directions at Rainbow International School from Monday morning to Saturday lunchtime, wallowing in my life's greatest passion from the comfort of my sofa seemed like ideal therapy and I wasn't going to beat myself up about it.

My whole weekend would revolve around the matches being shown on TV. A shopping trip could be curtailed with a rush back to the house to avoid missing the kick-off of a key game. Attendance at an evening party would be delayed or even cancelled completely because it overlapped with the second half of a match that I particularly wanted to watch. My whole social life was being dictated by the match schedule of the English Premier League. Midweek games would present more of a problem. While two or three games would be broadcast live simultaneously, the delayed matches would go on through the early hours of the morning of what was usually a working day. During the English winter when the clocks reverted to GMT, even the live matches would end at the unsociable hour of one o'clock in the morning. Because Everton were predicted to be a struggling team in this particular season, their matches at the beginning of the campaign were often not selected as one of the live games; there were several times that I set my alarm for some unearthly time in the middle of Saturday night/Sunday morning to get up to watch Everton's 90 minutes of action. If they had been involved in a dull 0–0 draw my resolve would have been stretched and I would have had to ask myself whether there was any point in disorientating my sleep patterns to watch a chanceless game of turgid football.

Fortunately, during the early part of that season the question never arose, as Everton surprised everyone by winning 12 of their first 19 matches and reaching Christmas in third place. And as Everton approached 40 points before the turn of the year, it seems that my team also entered DSTV's radar and were more often than not involved in one of the featured live matches. More accurately we entered the radar of the Premier League who sell the various live packages to satellite television providers around the world such as DSTV. There was just one Everton match in the whole

The eccentric Victor Soskin in between bouts of sea-sickness on the dhow to Zanzibar. Victor's conversation began to torment me as much as the sun and boredom of a 25 hour voyage.

In February 1991 I lost a good friend. The orange Ford Capri after the Danger Brothers took her for a night out!

Christmas 1991 at the peak of Kilimanjaro. I was a somewhat unorthodox mountaineer.

The entire teaching staff of Hillside High School when the doors opened in January 1994. Behind is the 'school' which was an unfinished and unfurnished house rented from Brodiz's brother that Jim called a cave.

The Board of directors of Hillside High School in November 1994. From right to left: Doug Parry (architect), Brodiz Rugogamu (businessman and Chairman of the Board who sadly passed away on 31 March 1996) Jim Park (headmaster who is still running the school to this day) and me (financial controller which in the early days involved little more than just settling various bills accumulated by my fellow directors in the local watering holes).

Freddie Bukenya who is now 36 and a devoted Evertonian. 'Sorry for the agony you have had to go through, Freddie'.

Wedding day, 21 December 1996 with the theme of blue and white. Violet and I defined the term 'whirlwind romance'.

Celebrating my 40th birthday at Colours Club in September 2001 as the storm that had engulfed me at Rainbow was just starting to subside.

Chris on holiday in the Seychelles aged 2. Our 'baby on a Barclaycard'. He was already showing signs of being an Evertonian when he murmured 'bye bye Bolton' after Great Escape 2.

Violet with the boarding house chef, Henry. We tried to recruit new Evertonians by giving them old Everton shirts. In the Walter Smith era there wasn't much to sell. I will always associate his reign at Everton with toothache.

Violet showing off the new tyre cover on our blue Pajero soon after we entered 'a brave new world'.

March 2003. Chris proudly wears his Rooney kit. Like many Evertonians, he was devastated by Rooney's betrayal 18 months later.

The victorious Simba Telecom team after that last minute win in March, 2007. Chris is back row fourth from left and Vince is back row third from right in front of his coach, dad.

Chris, Vince and Clair in Kampala in 2006. Vince showed his mental steel when he defected to Arsenal about one year later.

Chris and Vince in front of Rainbow International School when much younger. The famous motto *Nil Satis Nisi Optimum* is displayed at the front of the main entrance. It will no doubt soon be removed as has been most of my legacy at Rainbow.

Leaving party at Colours Club, 15 February 2011.

Being seen off by an entourage of around 50 Rainbow staff at Entebbe airport on 14 March 2011.

season that I didn't see in its entirety. On 4 January we had a midweek match at home to Portsmouth. Violet and I watched the live match that evening on Supersport 3 which inevitably was Manchester United v Tottenham including that 'goal' by Pedro Mendes that the linesman and referee managed to miss when Roy Carroll clawed the ball back from a yard behind the goal line. From that injury time controversy, the action ended on the referee's whistle and the DSTV programme switched to the Randburg studios where even Gary Bailey had to admit that Tottenham deserved to win the match 1–0. Violet and I had lost interest in that issue, though as we just wanted to know the score from Goodison Park and whether Everton had sneaked back into third place with a win at home to Portsmouth. The latest score we had seen on the ticker tape across the bottom of the screen as we watched the goalless draw from Old Trafford was 1–1. All the games had finished now so we were more or less resigned to the fact that we had dropped two home points and remained fourth behind Man United, Arsenal and Chelsea. At around 12.55am the Premiership results for the evening were shown. As we internalised the information, Violet and I leapt into the air yelling in delight. Everton 2 Portsmouth 1 was the score. It is amazing how the combination of 17 letters and two numbers arranged in a particular order on a television screen can relieve so much tension and bring so much joy all in one explosive second.

DSTV were not always very good at informing its viewers of which matches were to be televised and we stayed up until 1.30am when the first repeated matches began but Everton's match was not one of them. Therefore, we deduced it would be shown at 3.30am at the very earliest and we had no guarantee of that. Even though the new term hadn't started, I had to be in work the next day for essential administrative work in preparation for the two days of teacher inset on the Thursday and Friday. I simply had to go to bed. As it turned out, a second rerun of the match was shown the following afternoon and so I released myself early from duties to go home and see the second half of the action from the previous night at Goodison Park including Leon Osman's winner after 2 minutes and 20 seconds of injury time of which there was a stated minimum of two minutes.

That result proved to be the pinnacle of our achievements that season. In the January transfer window James Beattie and Mikel Arteta arrived and Tommy Gravesen went to Real Madrid which was a great compliment to Everton and how our stock was rising. Arteta made an instant impact but Beattie never really made an impression despite raising all our hopes with a spectacular goal after just six minutes of his first League start at Southampton. Soon afterwards he was shown a red card after eight minutes of the game at home to Chelsea for a completely unexpected and unprovoked head butt on William Gallas. Beattie's inconsistency mirrored that of the team and we picked up just 18 points in the final 16 matches of the season after that late, late winner against Portsmouth. It was as much down to the stumbling of Liverpool as to Everton's sensational first half of the season, that we finished in a Champions League position in the final League table. We achieved it with the lowest points tally of any English Champions League qualifying team ever and with a negative goal difference. The joke of Evertonians from the start of the season that the Liverpool manager should be renamed Rafael Beneathus proved prophetic as the bumbling Spaniard and his team somehow contrived to approach the finish line even more leaden legged than their blue city rivals.

Indeed, Everton's position in the elite competition of Europe was already sealed with two matches to play as Liverpool went down 3–1 to Arsenal on the penultimate Sunday of the campaign. Arsenal, who themselves had nothing to play for, having confirmed their runners-up position to Chelsea, then took on the other team from Merseyside at Highbury. It was a night to be savoured. Everton, the miracle of Champions League football confirmed the Saturday before with a 2–0 win at home to Newcastle in an electric atmosphere, could go to Arsenal and enjoy themselves. It was a no lose situation. Arsenal v Everton, two teams with a proud history synonymous with sophistication and culture and tradition and, well, class, playing against each other in a spirit of celebration with both teams' achievements in the League already done and dusted and to a level of reasonable satisfaction for Arsenal and beyond all expectations in the case of Everton. And Arsenal still had an FA Cup Final to look forward to. As one Everton supporter, in euphoric mood over our entry into Europe's promised land, said when confronted by a Sky News reporter as he boarded the bus in Liverpool on Wednesday 11 May destined for north London: 'I don't care if we lose 10–0 tonight. We're in the Champions League and Liverpool are not'. Be careful what you wish for.

So on that evening approaching the middle of May 2005, I parked myself on the sofa with a couple of Clubs lined up ready to enjoy the evening irrespective of the result. I felt none of the usual pressure and felt that a defeat was likely but not to be feared. It would not hurt like a normal defeat. From the position we had been in at the start of the season when Rooney left in a cloud of acrimony leaving behind a squad that, on paper, looked like it would struggle to avoid the bottom three, the situation that we now found ourselves in as we took to the field at Highbury with two matches left was pure fairytale. The score of this particular Everton match really did not matter…or so I thought.

I mean, anyone with a single nanogram of competitiveness in their veins must feel some pain at a 7–0 defeat. Despite all the glory of our achievements for the season, receiving our heaviest Premier League defeat ever was hard to take. The predominant emotions of embarrassment and humiliation and frustration, even anger overwhelmed the consoling thought that the match was actually meaningless in the greater scheme of things. Human beings, by constitution are competitive animals; none of them can take a 7–0 mauling without some twinge of psychological discomfort. For me, who is intensely competitive, I didn't know where to look by the end of the match and, more significantly, didn't know where I would look the next day when I entered the Rainbow staff room.

Examining the match in the cold light of day, the outcome could be rationalised. Compare Lee Carsley with Patrick Vieira or James Beattie with Dennis Bergkamp. Marcus Bent with Thierry Henry, for goodness sake, and Henry was injured and not even on the pitch for this game! I rest my case. We may have finished only two places behind Arsenal that season but the chasm of 22 points was probably a more accurate reflection of the difference between the two sides. David Moyes had made up the deficit in ability of his team in so many matches throughout the season by revving his boys up in the changing room to ensure they reached their absolute potential and closed the gap in class with the strength gained from sheer dogged effort and resilience. When we had finally crossed the finishing line against Newcastle the previous weekend, there was a sub-conscious sigh of relief exhaled by the entire club and its supporters. Unintentionally, the manager and the players had not been psyched up for the match against Arsenal and, without this adrenalin rush which had made up the difference in quality on so many occasions in the previous nine months, we were left bare and exposed. On the other hand, Arsenal, when released from the shackles of needing points, simply played better; the natural ability of the likes of Bergkamp who was sublime on the night, was lubricated by the absence of a need to win. For Everton, the prop provided by the requirement of three points, was needed to prevent us showing our true level which, if Evertonians were honest with themselves, was no more than mid-table. Enormous credit is due to David Moyes for this massive over achievement and for confirming once and for all that the submission to Rooney's demands to exit the club at the start of the season had been the best decision for Everton Football Club. From fourth from bottom with him, to fourth from top without. Moyes had truly demonstrated the power of team spirit over individual flair.

Typically for Everton, though, the story of the season was not yet over. A purple patch of six second half minutes in Istanbul a fortnight after Everton's Highbury horror show, allowed Liverpool to achieve an unbelievably fortuitous win against AC Milan in the Champions League Final. All of a sudden it looked as if Liverpool might be responsible for knocking us out of Europe's premier competition without either of us playing a game just as they had done in 1985 following the nightmare of Heysel. After much procrastination from UEFA, Everton's place was finally confirmed but Liverpool were given a fifth English berth to allow them to defend their title. Just as the trouncing at Arsenal had turned our champagne flat before we had even tasted it, the fact that we had not eliminated our neighbours from the greatest club competition in the world despite pushing them below the cut-off point into fifth place meant that our success still had a hint of sourness attached. But that is life as an Evertonian; whether it's a World War that intervenes or a fluky comeback from our bitter rivals in the Champions League Final, we are destined never to have absolute gratification from the fruits of our efforts. The state of an Evertonian is one of fatalistic acceptance that we will never achieve everything that we wish for. And somehow we wouldn't have it any other way. Evertonians are happy being unhappy.

Chapter 26
Competitive spirit; you either have it or you don't

24 March 2007: Simba Telecom 5 Nina Interiors 1

I visited a friend in East Germany in 1985. I stayed in a little village near Leipzig for a week and saw at first hand what 'Big Brother' is all about. Police posts and communist propaganda everywhere you looked. It was August and quite sunny throughout my stay but all I remember is unremitting dullness. The political contours may have changed in Eastern Europe in the past two decades but it cannot stop my mind switching to black and white whenever I think of East Germany. Even though the country doesn't even exist anymore, whenever I think of the former DDR, I think of grey.

Africa is the diametric opposite. When I recall my years spent in Kenya and Uganda, the image immediately formed in my memory's eye is bright and sharp-focused. Even bad memories are framed in beautiful sunshine. I am proud of what I achieved in Rainbow International School in the space of a dozen years. The school was virtually on its knees both financially and in terms of the morale of its staff and parents when I took over as headmaster on 1 August 1999. The pupils had a serious inferiority complex believing, on the whole, that they had been dumped in a school that they regarded as a poor relation to the other two major international schools in the city probably because their parents could not afford to send them to the International School of Uganda (ISU) or Kabira (now called Kampala International School).

In my 12 years at the school I turned all that around. The school remained the cheapest (or most affordable as we liked to put it more diplomatically in the marketing literature) which enabled it to maintain its ethos of being very inclusive with the local community but it also became the most successful in terms of student intake. When I arrived the student rolls of all the three major international schools in Uganda were languishing around 300. By the time I left, Rainbow had 850 on its registers which was more than its two main rivals combined. With the increased population came the confidence. The staff became proud to work at Rainbow, even though the salaries were significantly lower than those of their competitors and the children could talk about their school with their heads held high. They could also boast about the events organised at Rainbow that became the envy of other schools. The Awards Evening introduced in 2002 was a glamorous and exciting occasion by the swimming pool at Colours Club. The Leavers' Ceremony held each June with the purpose of saying farewell to the exam students that were moving on, had an inimitable mix of formality and fun and was enjoyed by all. Then there was the spectacular Talent Show, that morphed into several different forms during my time at Rainbow but eventually became a massive media event with schools from around the city coming to perform on a big stage on our main field. I also introduced other calendar fixtures such as World Cup Fun Day featuring various five-a-side football tournaments and a Careers Fair held annually in one of the most prestigious hotels in the city.

In addition to all of these, were possibly the events that caused me most satisfaction and joy. Again, they were events that I introduced to the school in their present form. Before I left Rainbow strong forces were at play to try to change or even remove these special occasions from the Rainbow year planner so I am sure that they are no longer presented in the way that I designed them, if they continue to exist at all. I am referring to the School Sports Day and the Rainbow inter-house swimming galas. It is these events more than any that are conjured up in my head whenever I recall the essence of my days in Rainbow. Images of fun and competition and wonderful colours. Colours that are so vivid and radiant, made all the more evocative by the sunshine and smiles that are associated with each one of these magical days. The events became such an integral and essential part of the Rainbow anatomy, that the whole school would change character for the day. From the friendly but serious days of study there would be a transformation into a wild, loud and proud lava of pupils and parents and teachers and support staff all joining in the partisan but good natured competition of the day. And there was I, standing, glowing at the head of it all, giving out the announcements and the race commentaries on the booming sound system throughout the day. This style of presentation was then adopted in the inter school swimming galas hosted by Rainbow International School when we competed against mainly The International School of Uganda and Kampala International School. I would crank up the excitement with each race with my commentaries becoming ever more frantic as the scoreboard reached its climax and each race meant that little bit more. If the contest was still undecided with five races to go, I would give the instruction to not update the scoreboard again until the end and would remain silent on the exact scores so that only the very focused among the audience (and focus was seriously impaired by the mist of emotional engagement by this stage of proceedings) would know what each race meant in terms of the potential final outcome. If it turned out that the final race was still important in terms of the big picture, I would then explain exactly what was required from each swimmer in the final event for their school to achieve an overall victory.

In other words, my commentary was choreographed to ensure maximum thrill, and it always worked. Parents from other schools commented to me on several occasions that the Rainbow gala was the best of all the international school swimming galas. Rainbow became a proud school that gained a reputation for producing the most polished and exciting school sporting events in the city. I was honoured by several of the local schools in July 2011 when a special Cliff Green World Cup football competition was organised to recognise my contribution to local sports. It was a pleasing legacy to leave especially as Rainbow, by that time, had already changed unrecognisably from the one that I had created and the type of school that I had wished to leave behind.

The first seed of the changes that were starting to infiltrate the school and that would eventually overwhelm me could possibly be traced back to Friday 23 March

2007. That was the day of the Rainbow International School Sports Day for academic year 2006–07. The sunshine smiled on the day as it usually did for these events. Some people even felt that I had some influence over the weather such was my total control over the big Rainbow sports productions. Perhaps fortune favoured the committed but it was uncanny how lucky I was when it came to the one uncontrollable factor on such days. I had such a confidence in the weather that I would not even consider a plan B should it have turned inclement. Ironically the one time that this confidence proved unfounded and a rushed plan B had to be formulated due to heavy rain on the morning of Sports Day was in 2010. By then the organisation of such events had been devolved to the head teachers of primary and secondary school as I was then the overall Principal of the school. As it turned out, it was still left to me to be the one to construct an alternative programme and quickly rearrange the event over two days instead of one. It should have been the responsibility of the two head teachers but they seemed to become frozen in the headlights of a situation that necessitated thinking on their feet. It was then that I considered that perhaps God had blessed me with a special talent for such situations. Organisation of large events is not something that comes naturally to many people even to those in positions where such skills might be expected of them. Sports Day of 2010 was just an example of what I perceived as the decline in Rainbow International School particularly in terms of its ability to host grand occasions; a degeneration whose embryo was probably being formed mid-afternoon on 23 March 2007.

The Sports Day programme for that day had already been diluted somewhat by the primary school headmaster who was determined to stamp his own identity on the day having been appointed to his post a little over a year earlier. Several primary school events had been moved to the previous day thus reducing the excitement generated by the whole school involvement being concentrated on a single day which is what I had always encouraged. For me the emphasis on teamwork and inclusiveness was a crucial element of the spirit of Rainbow. A succession of primary school heads begged to differ on this approach. A health and safety and control culture exported from the UK meant that they felt much more comfortable with smaller crowds to handle. I had escaped England before such a culture had taken hold and, of course, I was not a trained primary school teacher. I never really got to grips with what the management of the primary school was trying to tell me. There may have been an element of a power struggle also at play here. When I initially took the reins at Rainbow, I had the remit to run the whole school. This was consistent with the size of the school and the size of its salaries budget. Without a training in primary education, I tended to delegate much of the management of the primary section of the school to the leaders who knew what they were doing until, in 2001, with the pupil population accelerating through the 400 barrier, I appointed a specialist headmaster of primary school. My length of service and the fact that I had appointed this person, meant that I still assumed the senior role even though on the school's organogram I was actually the headmaster of secondary school and, therefore, on a par with the headmaster of primary school. In the early days, I also had the receiver manager's title to give me added status. What it meant was that, although I did not, and have never, interfered in the affairs of primary school, I did assume the overall control of major events such as Sports Day. Having initiated and evolved these events during the period when I had total control of the whole school from 1999 to 2001, I had a great sense of ownership of them and took personal pride in how they turned out. It is easy to see how the head teachers of primary school could feel a little undermined on such occasions especially when I accessed the microphone to narrate the day's proceedings in addition to all my other input.

On this particular occasion, the headmaster had evidently taken some decisions on behalf of primary school that would affect the whole event but had either been unwilling or too scared to inform me. Thus mid-afternoon I was informed that the class dashes for the early years classes would not be taking place as the children who would be involved were still in their classrooms either too tired or indeed actually sleeping. My adrenalin was always at waterfall levels on such days and this news angered me so much that, in order to avoid an embarrassing diplomatic incident with my opinions being broadcast to the entire congregation of approximately one thousand parents, staff and pupils, I switched off the mike and the event ran for 10 minutes to a backdrop of silence from the PA system. I don't actually know what people present were concluding, but I'm sure that they didn't surmise the truth which was that I was composing myself until my anger had subsided sufficiently for me to be able to continue with my MC duties with the normal level of coherence and joyous tone.

I should elaborate on why the late, unannounced removal of the class sprints for the under fives caused me such consternation. Firstly, it was part of a tradition began by me in 2000. In an effort to ensure that every single child in the school had their moment in the spotlight on Sports Day, I had introduced the idea of class dashes throughout the school where every child in each class ran an 80 metres dash. It was intended to be fun and there were no points added to the scoreboard as a result. Many teachers understood the spirit of the event and actually participated in the races with their charges. I should give credit where credit is due and tell you that the original idea was that of Mike Matthams, a brilliant teacher and sound guy who was effectively my deputy head in my first two years at the school. I embraced this idea like several others that his innovative mind was prone to hatch and continued it well after the time that he left the school. Now this relatively new headmaster was trying to erode it with, what I considered to be a spurious excuse. Indeed, I know for sure that his rationale for cancelling a part of the day that always brought such pleasure to so many was flawed, as Clair, excited about participating in her first Sports Day especially in the kindergarten class dash in front of the entire Rainbow community, told me in the evening that all her classmates had been clamouring to go out in the afternoon sun to join in the fun of the day. They had been given orders that the headmaster was not allowing it. So much for the theory that they were all too tired or even asleep. I had been doubtful about the explanation as it had not been the case in the previous seven years. Why was Clair's year group so much more somnolent than all their predecessors?

Other factors were clearly at play, though. The fact that my own daughter had been denied her participation in a Rainbow tradition that I had been building her up for all week, obviously had some sway on my emotional state at that point as well. Indeed it was quite a roller coaster of feelings going on in my head as my microphone remained switched off and the sea of noise and excitement continued unabated all around. I weighed up the options. 1. Take the situation by the scruff of the neck and drag those little mites from their classroom so that they could participate as tradition demanded. 2. Order the primary school headmaster to carry out 1 above or 3. Bite my lip and continue as if nothing was untoward with the intention of expressing my views to the headmaster of the primary school in the sobriety of my office on Monday morning. I eventually opted for the third alternative. The headmaster of primary school, no doubt seeing my stormy face as the mike fell silent, disappeared for the remainder of the day and his deputy assumed control of primary school affairs. She was a volatile and erratic woman of British Jamaican dissent by the name of Agnes Chandiya. When I expressed my anger at the last minute change of schedule, she bluntly ordered me to grow up. The will to remain professional was hanging by the thinnest of threads but, fortunately it did not quite snap.

One aspect of all this so far overlooked, is the fact that my drive for such high standards and my obsessive need for control over such events derived from an innate competitive spirit within. Sport is an absolute essential in any school, in my opinion, and the requirement for every child to participate in physical activity from the day they start is a *sine qua non*. I am out of step with much modern educational dogma in that I don't believe that competition in sport, even at a very young age, is a bad thing as long as it is managed properly. Every child loves the feeling of winning. As long as we can handle the emotions of those that don't win, then I believe sport can enhance qualities that are very useful in all other facets of life; teamwork, leadership, maintaining perspective, winning with humility, losing with dignity. Now you can see why I was in conflict with British trained primary school managers!

You can only truly understand aspects of a certain mindset if you possess it yourself. If, in your opinion, the mindset being sought is positive, then you can try to impose it on children who are still to be guided on what is the best way to live their lives. It's not indoctrination, rather the sharing of a philosophy that you, as an adult believe to be beneficial as a life tool. I believe that the appreciation of and the participation in competitive sport can give more positive than negative support to a person in their life; I'm not talking about the pathological obsession in the football results of a particular team that much of this book is about – the jury is out on whether that does more harm than good to an individual – but the wholesome form of taking part in sport with at least a modest desire to win. I came to learn that Agnes Chandiya did not have this sporting competitiveness as part of her mental make-up. She simply did not understand why I was genuinely so upset that those three and four-year-olds had not had an opportunity to try to reach the other end of the field ahead of everyone else; she probably saw it more as some sort of public humiliation of little children served up for the gratification of the huge audience looking on. I was also acutely aware of the endearing spectacle of seeing these toddlers running along the track. I always had one eye on providing an event that was a crowd pleaser as much as an educationally rich experience. The entertainment of the masses was certainly a factor in wanting these races to happen, but I did not believe that it would be achieved at the expense of the psychological stability of these virgin minds. To my knowledge, no child had ever been traumatised by the hammer blow of not winning their particular class dash.

The next day, this argument in favour of children's competition was amplified further. Chris and Vince played in a football league called KKL (Kampala Kids League). The league was the brainchild of a man called Trevor Dudley. Seeing a void in the sporting education of many children in Uganda caused by the absence of PE in the local school curriculum and also seeing the lack of opportunities for expat children to mix with other children as they are locked in their walled and wired compounds, Trevor set up an NGO in 1998 to run KKL. Three times a year there would be a six week league run in a particular sport. Football, being the most popular, would alternate with another sport such as basketball, cricket and baseball. The registration fee was not prohibitive and sponsorship of local children to join the leagues was encouraged. For a modest entry fee, the child had a well-organised league to play in and went home at the end of it with a football kit, a team photo, a certificate and maybe a winners' trophy and medal.

At its peak in 2007 there were six leagues of six teams covering ages from six up to 14. Each squad of 15 or 16 players was computer generated equalising out the statistics of all the players in each team roster. So the aggregate body mass, age, ability level etc of each squad was roughly equal thus producing a league of fairly evenly matched teams. It made for a compelling competition. It was a massive, sophisticated organisation and resulted in six Saturdays of enormous enjoyment and excitement every two months or so. The whole operation depended on sponsors and volunteers. Local businesses would sponsor the teams and volunteers would take on the role of coaches, officials, medical people and so on.

I had volunteered my services as a coach since 1999, having the whole shebang thrust on me almost from the day I arrived at Rainbow as our grounds were used to host the league. KKL used an alternative venue from 2001 onwards. Since 2003 when Chris had reached the required minimum age, I had coached his team. Vince, being just 18 months younger soon followed and was either in Chris's team or in a team playing in one age group below which would require me to coach two different teams. In this particular league of the spring of 2007, they were both in the same league and, therefore, the same team. Each team was named after its sponsor. Chris and Vince's team was called Simba Telecom, a mobile phone company founded by a Ugandan couple who had four children attending Rainbow at that time. This was the last day of the season. As I drove the boys across the city on that Saturday lunchtime (the day after the controversial Rainbow Sports Day) for the one o'clock kick-off at Aga Khan School we knew that we would still be in contention to win the league but we didn't know the size of the task facing us in order to achieve this goal.

Our main contenders, Safi (a juice manufacturer) were playing before us. We arrived to watch the tail end of their 4–0 win. This meant that Simba Telecom had to beat bottom team Nina Interiors (a furniture store) by four clear goals to take the trophy. It was the under 10's age group so a much reduced pitch was used. Heavy rains had made some of the field unplayable so the pitch was reduced even further. This would prove advantageous. When our goalie made a howler and our lead was cut to 2–1, there remained just six minutes on the clock. On the normal sized pitch that would have represented a mission impossible. With the abridged version there was still a chance for players, even of such diminutive stature, to score three times.

From the restart from Nina's goal, we went straight up the other end and Vince made it 3–1. Then Chris put in a cross and some little guy called Matthew swept the ball home. 4–1 and still a minute left. But, hang on, the referee had blown for full time immediately after the restart. According to his watch the time was up. How cruel, how out of touch with the emotion of the moment, how inaccurate was his watch. How unlike African time when everything is usually late and never early. I couldn't take it. The crushing deflation and abject unfairness were too much to bear. All the etiquette expected of a parent and a coach, and a headmaster for God's sake, was lost in a red mist. I strode onto the pitch jabbing my finger on my watch furiously as I approached the referee, some fear now detectable in his eyes. He tried to justify his time-keeping but I wasn't listening. I bypassed him and went to the tent where the organisers sat. They agreed that there should be an extra minute of play. Whether that was simply to humour me or pacify me, or because they also wanted another 60 seconds of this heart stopping drama I don't know. No doubt they felt that one more minute was hardly likely to make a difference, anyway. How wrong they were. Pumped up with the momentum of goals and a sense of injustice, Simba Telecom went for the throat. Chris won the competitive drop-ball from a shell-shocked Nina player and fed it to our star player, Solomon. The lanky Ugandan, waltzed through three or four tackles before smashing the ball past a hapless goalie. I let out a growl of fist clenching delight. The

Simba parents jumped around, cheering. We all ran onto the field; we thought it was all over. It *was* pretty soon afterwards. I and most of the parents were as uninhibited as our offspring as we celebrated that victory. 'Are you watching, Chandiya?' I thought to myself. She would never have understood what it was all about.

Agnes Chandiya had an abrasive nature and was constantly at loggerheads with the headmaster of the primary school and soon he was on his way out after just over half of his three year contract had been completed. Agnes, in a prickly sort of way, had some leadership qualities, though. In my opinion and in view of the difficult 18 months endured with the previous head, she was the best option to take over. I strongly advised her to apply for the vacancy left by the primary headmaster's sudden exit and I strongly supported her appointment which she was duly offered. Inadvertently and metaphorically I had written the first line of my own resignation letter with the ushering in of Agnes Chandiya as headmistress of Rainbow's primary school. It was a steady downhill from here on in. But at least I had moments like that fabulous Simba Telecom win in the very last minute of the very last match of the 2007 season to ensure that my African adventure is always recalled in beautiful, stunning technicolour and not in the greyness of a world devoid of sport and the illuminating spark of a competitive spirit.

Chapter 27
Did Everton really save my life?

29 December 2007: Everton 1 Arsenal 4

Put your hand up if this has ever happened to you. You open a newspaper or hear or see the news on the radio or TV and there is a story unveiled about a place that you have very recently visited and been very familiar with and so you scrutinise the pictures and television footage carefully to try to notice any recognisable landmarks or even people that you know and, because it is a place that you are so well-acquainted with, you are inclined to tell everyone about your unique connection with it because it somehow gives you vicarious ownership of the news story and, thus, a sense of indirect fame. I wonder how many hands are up out there. You see, it has happened to me on several occasions throughout my life and I'm wondering whether the law of averages means that this is no statistical quirk but one of life's inevitabilities or whether it is that I have some Harry Potter like qualities that cause the universe in my particular vicinity to bend out of shape and compel violence, destruction or some other unforeseen phenomena to take hold. Somehow these unexpected events always happen just after I have vacated the scene that is about to turn into unpredicted havoc. Rather like that very incompetent driver who has never been in an accident but has witnessed hundreds in his rear view mirror, I seem to always end up without a scratch on me. I'm not suggesting that I am some kind of Damien figure, but the coincidences have piled up.

To stretch out my meagre student grant at university and allow me to spend a vast proportion of it on watching the Blues, I used to walk from the Halls of Residence at the end of Smithdown Road to the main campus on the edge of Liverpool's city centre every day thus saving the daily bus fare. Occasionally, I would have company for this two mile trek but, more often than not, I would walk on my own. The journey would include several hundred metres through the more deprived areas of Toxteth. I returned to Andover in Hampshire for my three month vacation to conclude my first year away from home on 3 July 1981. On 4 July Toxteth became a name on everyone's lips, a place synonymous with one of the most spectacular examples of civil disobedience in this country in living memory. For the next few days the riots of Toxteth, allegedly precipitated by the heavy-handed arrest of a man by the name of Leroy Alphonse Cooper, filled the news bulletins of television and radio. A place previously unknown to most people outside of Liverpool was now famous around the world, a place that I had walked through twice every day for a majority of the preceding nine months.

In 1986 I embarked on a cycle ride from John O'Groats to Lands End for no other reason than to say I had done it. Not for charity or protest but simply to test my own powers of endurance. It took three weeks although I did take a rather zigzagged route, stopping off in Glasgow to catch Celtic's first match of the new season, a 1–1 draw at home to Alex Ferguson's Aberdeen and then heading diagonally across the UK to the south-east to attend a party in Amersham. By the time I finished at the tip of Cornwall, it was early September and I had clocked up over a thousand miles on my faithful blue Claud Butler. Around the middle of that expedition, on the August Bank Holiday, I found myself on the west lip of the Yorkshire Dales and in two minds. A storm was forecast and I could feel the wind picking up. I had already cycled about 45 miles from Carlisle. I had just heard the football results (including Sheffield Wednesday 2 Everton 2 at the beginning of our last Championship winning season) and I was contemplating whether to call it a day and retire to a nearby hostelry or push myself for another painful 20 miles over the Dales to the youth hostel at Grinton Lodge. Looking at the date of the party in Amersham I realised that knocking off these extra 20 miles would be a major step in roughly the direction of Buckinghamshire and so I set off with body weary from the earlier exertion and mind depressed from the two dropped points at Hillsborough.

The wind and rain began to swirl around after less than five miles. At one point I got off my bike and walked into a pub in the bleakest, most windswept location of any drinking house in the land. As I squeaked away the condensation that had immediately formed on my glasses which had made the interior of the pub look something like a sauna, I felt that I had entered another world; dry, warm and full of conviviality. The whole place fell silent to see this saturated mess standing at the door. I don't really know what I went in for. Sympathy perhaps? I probably used the toilet but did little else other than walk straight back out to force myself to remount and continue my gallant battle against the elements leaving a stunned audience behind. By the time I reached Grinton, the river running through the village was a manic torrent barely keeping within its banks. I was grateful that the youth hostel was set well up on the hill on much higher ground. The next day there were pictures of Grinton in many of the national newspapers (even on the front pages of some if my memory serves me correctly). Pictures of people sitting on the roofs of their caravans waiting for a helicopter to airlift them from the flooded fields caused by the River Swale bursting its banks in devastating fashion just minutes after I had cycled past it. It was the tail end of Hurricane Charley apparently and caused the worst August storm to have struck the British mainland since records were kept and I don't believe it has been equalled since.

So there is Toxteth and Grinton. I could add to that the US embassy bombing in Nairobi of 1998 just weeks after Violet, Christopher and I had returned to England for a summer holiday having been living in the Kenyan capital for a year. Then there is the Kampala bombing of 2010 that we avoided by a matter of days having returned to Europe for our summer break. I could mention the first August frost in Ontario for 42 years that destroyed the tobacco crop that I had travelled to Canada to help harvest in 1982 or the riots in East and West Berlin in 1987 that occurred on the day I travelled from one side of the wall to the other in that very city. As I said, I am probably reading much too much into this and there were probably a forest of hands that went up when I posed the question at the start of this chapter but, if any newshound wants an exclusive, perhaps you should just trail me for a while and trace my movements.

And so I am brought to the events of Christmas 2007. My family and I had already planned to spend Christmas in the south west of Uganda at a favourite place of ours called Kichwamba where we could view the wildlife across the plains of the Queen Elizabeth Park while supping sundowners on the balcony of our bandas at the Kingfisher Camp. All was set for a week's holiday in mid-December when news broke of a severe outbreak of the highly contagious and lethal ebola virus. People were dying in their dozens in, yes, Kichwamba. Suddenly our Christmas plans were in tatters and a rearrangement was required. It was too late to book a holiday in South Africa, a destination that I was particularly keen to visit, so I visited Lets Go Travel in Kampala city centre to book a last minute deal to stay in the Tiwi Beach Resort on the south coast of Mombasa. Spaces were limited but I managed to book for the whole family for the Christmas week. We were to depart on Monday 24 December flying to Mombasa via Nairobi and returning on the evening of Friday 28 December. The timing of the return journey had been influenced by the fact that the Everton v Arsenal match was to be shown live on DSTV on the Saturday evening. I had also planned for a brand new 37in television to be delivered to our house while we were away in Kenya. This was to be a surprise for the whole family to return to. The fact that its baptism would be the showing of an Arsenal v Everton match fitted in with the whole elaborate plan. You see, by now, our second son, Vincent, had become a very keen Arsenal fan. A brave decision in a house full of Evertonians but middle children often have a greater need than others to forge their own identity.

It was a fabulous Christmas holiday in the sun. A luxurious hotel with five swimming pools and more food on offer than we could possibly consume. There was a very well organised programme of entertainment for the children during the day and vibrant live music and dance on offer every evening. On one day we strolled about a mile northwards along the beach to visit our great friend, Dave Anderson, who was staying in the Braeburn apartments. We met up with a number of our former colleagues who had purchased accommodation in the complex built by the school as another money making venture. We found Dave in the familiar surroundings of a bar but not in a familiar condition. It was sad to see a character that we had only ever known as someone full of humour and animation and tales of Africa sitting in a wheelchair, paralysed down one side from the stroke that he had suffered earlier in the year, unable to recall much detail and unable to consume alcohol. It was the last time that we were to see him. He passed away in 2009. A wonderfully joyful and generous character who had provided a home for us at a crucial time in our lives when Christopher was born. He was also godfather to Vincent.

So on the Friday morning we packed up and headed for the airport. Violet had a lengthy conversation with the taxi driver who collected us from the hotel. As a Ugandan, Violet had had much first hand experience of political instability and violent elections. She was intrigued to know what the taxi driver thought about the presidential elections that had just taken place the day before in Kenya. He was smiling, almost smug in his certainty that everything would run smoothly even though there were early signs that the vote would be close; always a dangerous scenario in an Africa election. The taxi driver did not reveal his particular allegiance; he was just confident that there would be no chaos as the Kenyans were accustomed to peace. Later in the day, Violet met a lady in the toilets at Jomo Kenyatta airport as we awaited our connection to Entebbe. By then news was filtering out that the opposition leader Raila Odinga had a substantial lead and this lady, who hailed from his powerbase in the west, was gloating at how the Kikuyus would soon be the ones using the mops that she was presently utilising to clean out the lavatories of the airport's public toilets. Africans are prone to talk in this poetically obtuse manner especially when referring to politics where, I suppose, direct talk is more risky. Kikuyu was the tribe of the incumbent Mwai Kibaki, an elderly man who had been in power for a single five year term. This lady's mop inference was that her man was about to take over and, therefore, jobs and riches were about to transfer into the possession of her and her people at the expense of the Kikuyus, dominant and arrogant in the eyes of many, who would be left with the menial jobs and low pay. The land in much of sub-Saharan Africa is still too choked with the weeds of mistrust and tribalism to be fertile for the growth of democracy. As we boarded the 6 o'clock flight from Nairobi there was still no hint of the bloodbath that was about to ensue.

The whole family were excited by the sight of a brand new TV in the living room when we finally entered our home at around 10pm. Almost the first pictures we saw on its screen were on Sky News the following morning when we turned on to see scenes of mayhem and bonfires and machete wielding gangs patrolling the streets of Nairobi. Kibaki had intimated that he had won the election; Odinga and his supporters knew that he had not; a recipe for an outpouring of anger and frustration from the supposed defeated. This violence characterised the next two months or so as Kenya virtually descended into civil war. Friends and colleagues living in the country told us of being trapped in their homes for days on end afraid to venture out. This was not a news story that would go away after a few days, this was not a news story that was being viewed from the comfort of a living room thousands of miles away; this was terrifying bloodletting on a massive scale that was going to extend for weeks becoming more frightening by the day and it was to reach the border of Uganda and very nearly spill over into the country in which my family and I resided. Many people from western Kenya share the same culture and values as tribes from the east of Uganda, including that of my wife. Colonial borders were scribed by bureaucrats in European offices a century or so before with little concern for the population on the ground divided by these whimsical pen strokes. Many Luos, Gisu and Kalenjin from western Kenya have more affinity with the people that inhabit the border area on the Ugandan side than the Kikuyus that ruled their country from Nairobi. And, of course, there was the potential humanitarian crisis unfolding of a refugee flood into Uganda as people tried to escape with their lives and little else.

So, on that final Saturday of 2007, we watched with horror as the repercussions of a rigged election wreaked havoc on our normally peaceful neighbours.

Well away from the impending Kenyan carnage there was the football match being played in Liverpool. Watching a live Everton game in our living room had become quite an unedifying spectacle; the shouting and anger of the Goodison stands replicated in our own lounge. Eleven years earlier I had married a Ugandan lady in Kampala. It seems that the heady whirl of romance and family planning caused our marriage vows to become twisted somewhere and my wife, intentionally or not, who knows, devoted herself to Everton Football Club as well as me. I had nothing to do with it, honest. OK so she might have had to traipse around Kampala from time to time during our courtship as her husband-to-be tried to locate a bar or other venue that was showing an Everton match beamed live from England, but that would surely have alienated her from my fanatical pastime not drawn her to it. I may have also dropped the occasional heavy hint that I could not possibly share my life with a follower of Man United or Liverpool, but that still left plenty of other options. Most women would surely have tried to wean their future husband off such a debilitating obsession but, whether through a manipulative determination to ensnare her man or a genuine fascination with the club that I love, the future Mrs Green developed a curious magnetism towards Everton. Her true reason for supporting Everton was more probably to do with a desire to buck the trend of the masses of her compatriots who all pinned their colours to the red of Man United, Liverpool or Arsenal (Chelsea were not really on the Ugandan football radar in the mid-'90s). If it had been a short term stratagem to capture her *muzungu* then surely her support of Everton would have dissolved as quickly as our honeymoon was over.

So, Violet's reason for supporting Everton was to go against the grain of the football mad public of Uganda and to make an independent stand. She is a feisty character and enjoys playing Devil's Advocate with such alarming authenticity some may question whether she is actually playing at all. So, in 1996 I introduced her, through my football club, to the perfect vehicle for all her contrariness using a seemingly harmless avenue. She could have pushed some minority cause or become a rebel politician but, in that part of the world, such a path rarely leads to any long term prospects beyond incarceration and torture. Choosing the world of sport and Everton in particular as her medium for protest was a much safer option. We all have our different reasons for supporting a football team and I suppose that offering the opportunity to thumb your nose at an entire population is as good as any. Over the years of our marriage, the passion has become greater and greater (and I am not talking about conjugal activities here) to the point that, during this particular festive period, I had presented my wife with a homemade anniversary card with a picture of each of the 11 most regular members of the Everton squad pasted on the front. It read 'Congratulations on our first 11…' and then, inside concluded with the words 'years of marriage'. Not many wives would have accepted such a card without offering a firm fist in the jaw of their loved one. But Violet is a committed Blue. She accepted the card in the spirit in which it was intended. When it came to activities on the pitch, she could become more fervent than most; haranguing the opposition mercilessly and expressing joy and anger at her own team with equal venom depending on how we were faring.

Let me now introduce you to another family member, Vincent. He arrived in this world 18 months after his elder brother, Christopher and five years ahead of his adorable little sister, Clair. How did Vincent come to support Arsenal? Well, it's analogous to his mother's reasons for choosing Everton but on a smaller scale. While his mum wanted to make a stand against an entire nation, Vince had a less vaunted ambition of wanting to make his indelible mark on the Green household by choosing an alternative path. It shows the mental steel of the lad given that he was showered with Everton merchandise for the first seven years or so of his life until we realised that we had 'lost' him. He was determined not to follow in the footsteps of his parents and, perhaps more significantly, his big brother.

So there we were, a divided family sitting in front of the brand new Christmas gift about to watch Everton take on Arsenal from a cold and wet Merseyside. Knowing how uncompromising Violet's passion for Everton is, I was just a little apprehensive for our younger son's prospects over the coming two hours irrespective of who won. The first half went very well. Everton gave a fairly convincing impression of Arsenal in blue with slick passing and fluid movement while Arsenal looked pretty much like an Everton away side under Walter Smith; negative and clueless. A Tim Cahill goal gave us a well deserved half time advantage. The second half was a catastrophe. Phil Jagielka gave a good impersonation of Bambi on ice, the referee missed a blatant handball for Arsenal's crucial second, Bendtner was sent off for an appalling tackle and Arteta was later dismissed when Fabregas went down theatrically after a clash between the two diminutive Spaniards. By the end Violet was incandescent. As we had seen across the border, magnanimity in defeat is not a trait often associated with the African psyche and so I found myself in the perverse situation of having to console an Arsenal fan after his team had beaten Everton 4–1! Just as passions spilled over in our house in Kampala over a result that was not to everyone's liking, so the war raged on in Kenya well into 2008. If it had not been for Everton and my insistence on returning to Kampala in time for their final home match of the year, maybe we would have ended up in the midst of the slaughter; or maybe it was, once more, my lucky knack of fleeing from the scene of disaster, just before the proverbial hit the fan.

Chapter 28
The beginning of the end

4 February 2009: Everton 1 Liverpool 0

When an era ends in history, there is always a point in time and a defining event that signals when that end began. This is particularly true when considering the fall of a leader. No doubt Hitler rued 7 December 1941 as he contemplated those cyanide capsules amidst the Berlin rubble of 1945. That was the date when those pesky Japs invaded Pearl Harbour without his permission, thus convincing Roosevelt to send the USA into the fray of World War Two. He probably sighed resignedly to himself as he lamented that that was probably the moment when his quest for world domination started to hit the buffers. Margaret Thatcher's lengthy reign as the British Prime Minister may have started to crack in 1989 but the defining moment when the exit came fully into focus was probably 31 March 1990 when the masses stood up to what they considered the iniquity of the poll tax and tried to trash Trafalgar Square. In the world of football, was it the Kanchelskis departure that saw off Joe Royle? Was it the sudden exit of Ray Wilkins that signalled the beginning of the end for Carlo Ancelotti at Chelsea? And many would suggest that it was the flying boot that struck the head of Beckham during one of Alex Ferguson's dressing room rages that convinced the England midfielder that it was time to leave Old Trafford. Historians may examine the chronology and come to different conclusions to those above, as may the subjects of the analysis, but there is always a tipping point when the momentum for an overthrow or exit of the person at the top reaches its critical velocity and cannot be reversed.

For me, my critical velocity, started by that push from Agnes Chandiya in the 2007 Rainbow International School Sports Day and inadvertently accelerated by my impetuous act of virtually appointing her as the primary school head teacher later in that year, was reached on 24 January 2009. That was the day that Mr Rufus Sabas was appointed as the new headmaster of the secondary school. Once again I was instrumental in my own downfall in a very substantial way. Approaching a full decade at the helm of Rainbow International School and, with the student roll crashing past the 800 mark and limited in many parts of the school only by the capacity of the class size, I felt that it was time to restructure the school's management. Many schools particularly on the international circuit employ a pyramidal hierarchal framework whereby an overall manager oversees the whole school with section managers directly below. The number of sections depends on the educational system being employed and the decision of the school as to the most effective and logical way to divide up the various age groups. Thus, for example, there may be a head of early years, a head of infant school, a head of junior school, a head of secondary school and a head of sixth form studies or any combination or amalgamation of these different categories. When I had first taken over as headmaster of Rainbow in 1999 such a system already existed. I was appointed as head of the whole school with a head of Key Stage 1, a head of Key Stage 2 and a head of secondary school in place below me. As the school expanded, I had decided to delegate the responsibility of running the primary school to a headmaster of primary school as it was an area of education in which I had no training. Now, eight years after that separation was made, I was proposing that the school be unified again under the umbrella of an overall head. My proposal was that this supervisor be called a Principal and that this person would be direct line manager to the two head teachers, one for primary school and one for secondary school. They could then decide on the management structure below them that best suited their needs.

So this was my grand plan and I presented it to the Indian owners of the school. They were hesitant, almost reluctant initially but I persuaded them that it would bring a robustness to the school as well as freshen things up in secondary school where the clockwork efficiency with which I now had everything running was perhaps hindering the opportunity for new ideas and initiatives. I was always open to innovation and lateral thinking but, when the administrative systems are so embedded that everyone is comfortable and confident in their role and knows what their school is trying to achieve, it can take that little bit extra motivation to move things forward. The staff handbook evolved throughout my tenure to cover each new eventuality that occurred but there was little need for major surgery. 'If it ain't broke, why fix it?' was most definitely the mantra of Rainbow International School as we entered 2009.

I eventually prised open the owners' iron grip on the status quo, and they allowed me to go ahead and search for a new Head of Secondary School to replace me as I was the obvious candidate to take over in this newly created post of Principal. A school should have an identity and an ethos. The problem with many international schools is that their transient nature in terms of staff and pupil turnover means that the institution will also develop a fluid and inconsistent personality especially if members of the senior management come and go. Parents want to have the security of knowing that the school that their children attend is not only financially stable but also reliable in terms of its values and philosophy. Rainbow had enjoyed unrivalled solidity among the international schools in Kampala. Mr Green had become synonymous with the name Rainbow International School. People knew what Mr Green stood for and, therefore, what Rainbow stood for. The 250 per cent increase in student population over the previous decade suggested that many agreed with my values and expectations. Parents in Kampala had the luxury of having an international school available to them that offered the rare combination of continuity and stability. My knowledge of the school and intrinsic association with its history as well as my track record of unremitting success in leading Rainbow from the precipice of extinction to becoming one of the largest and most well-respected international schools in East Africa had also made me a shoo-in for the post of Principal. It may sound arrogant but I had to sell myself to the owners and I believed in what I was selling.

For all my powers of leadership and persuasion, though, I was a naive and lousy politician. I had not realised that the owners' feet dragging on this new proposal of mine was down to a power battle. The idea of devolving so much power to one person to run their business (because this was still what it was first and foremost in their eyes) made them very uncomfortable indeed and I received plenty of evidence of this over the coming months. It was not so much that they did not trust me but more that they would not have trusted anyone other than a family member to be the Principal of their school from what I could see. Also, in promoting myself above Agnes Chandiya having previously been her peer, I had unconsciously been thinking that she held me in as high esteem as many others in Rainbow did and that somehow she might remember the leg-up I gave her into her present position. Suddenly seeing me as her line manager rather than her equal, also required a large dollop of humility on her part. All in all I was anticipating a reaction from the Headmistress of Primary School that could only be achieved with a complete personality transplant on her part.

So, when Mr Sabas was shortlisted by me and then appointed mainly on my recommendation after a rigorous recruitment process that I had designed and implemented, the unsuspecting, stooping and dishevelled old man who found himself Headmaster of one of the largest international school in East Africa was not aware of the political minefield that he was entering into. I also had no idea. In a teaching career spanning 30 years, Rufus Sabas's secondary school teaching CV had only reached deputy head level in a failing school in Nigeria. A weak candidate, maybe, but with the salaries on offer at Rainbow, he was the best of an average bunch and I felt that I could guide and support him just as I had naively thought the same about Mrs Chandiya. During the day of assessments that I had set up for him when he was flown over to Kampala with one other candidate for the final decision to be made, the only section of the school who did not approve of Mr Sabas, was the student body who were singularly unimpressed with his long winded, meandering assembly about chess. On this occasion it seemed that the pupils knew best. His weakness as a leader was exploited to the full by those wishing to see the end of Mr Green. After a difficult 18 months, I cracked under the strain of what I perceived as his stubborn incompetence and constant whingeing to the Board and a loose remark in an email likening his leadership skills to that of a sheep found its way into the wrong hands and I felt obliged to resign. The school fell into chaos with students scrawling unflattering comments about Mr Sabas all over the school in bold graffiti while plastering the slogan THERE'S NO RAINBOW WITHOUT GREEN on every available wall. Once again, perhaps the pupils knew best. I suppose, given the tumultuous 21½ years that I had had travelling with my teaching career, a spectacular, indeed explosive end like this was inevitable.

The end of an era is always a poignant moment and the owners seemed sad to see me depart amidst such drama. They paid me six months' salary and offered me management posts in other arms of their business empire. They had been impressed with my work; they just did not want me anywhere near their school again! I took the money but declined the job offer. They had no business ventures in the UK. Violet and I had decided some time before that the next step after Uganda for the family would be the UK. Perhaps we had not expected to take that step so soon but, with Christopher, our baby on a Barclaycard, now approaching his GCSE years, it was not such an inconvenient time. The thought of working another day with what I considered the ineptness of Sabas and the irrationality of Chandiya made this hurried exit to England quite appealing in the end. Some of this conspiracy theorising may be conjecture but two emails in particular, sent to me by the two head teachers during 2010 left me in no doubt, if any had remained, that they were not going to accept me as their boss as well as re-enforcing my descriptions above of inept and irrational. They surely would not have written such emails if they had not been emboldened by the signals being received from the Board. The content of the emails was vicious and spiteful and, in my opinion, muddled with lies and unsubstantiated opinions exposing their own shortcomings. I responded to both and in one case received a grudging apology from Agnes Chandiya. The battle lines had been drawn, though, and the school was being severely hampered by this impasse at the top. This school was not big enough for the three of us and, in the end, I was happy to oblige by falling on my sword. I am a positive person who likes to look and move forward. Our management meetings had started to feel like a walk through a vat of blancmange where personal grievances and agendas were pursued to a painful non-conclusion. I sat through these fortnightly ordeals in Sabas's office defending myself against two people who I was supposed to be overseeing, thinking to myself: 'I'm a visionary leader, get me out of here!' Months after I left the school, an entry was posted in Wikipedia giving a completely fabricated version of why I had departed the school. Some people really seemed to have a problem with my existence. Quite flattering in a perverse sort of way! Thank you, whoever conjured up that piece of fiction for Wikipedia.

So 24 January 2009 was the beginning of the end of my relationship with a country that I had come to love and a school that I had dragged up from its bootlaces and come to take enormous pride in. That was the day when I sent that email to Mr Rufus Sabas offering him the headship of the secondary school of Rainbow International School. If I had known what was about to unfold in the next few weeks, my superstitious inclinations would have told me that the issuing of that contract of employment to the guy with a strange name and an address in Abuja, was a portent of doom. He sent his acceptance of the offer on 28 January and so a chain of unfortunate events in my life appeared to be triggered. Within three days, the British based satellite television station, GTV, that had taken over a large proportion of DSTV's share of the market, closed down without warning, bankrupt. We were left with DSTV's output of just two live Premier League matches for the weekend and no FA Cup coverage. It happened to be the week that Everton were to play Manchester United away in the League and Liverpool at home in an FA Cup replay. Two of the biggest games of the season on the immediate horizon just as the African continent's live football feed was being cut. Man United v Everton was not one of DSTV's two allocated matches that weekend. Uganda's local station saved the day and, no doubt, a number of the interiors of several bars around Kampala, by stepping in at the 11th hour and appeasing the rabid Man United fans with a live broadcast of their match at home to Everton. The programme production was of *Crossroads* ilk, wobbly studio and wooden presenters but, at least we saw the action; a predictable 1–0 defeat to a Ronaldo penalty. The 'derby' four days later was not shown anywhere and I actually found out the score the following morning. Imagine that; after several years of being able to watch almost every Everton match live on TV; four years of being a 100 per cent virtual supporter of the Blues in the tropics, I was reduced to the Kenyan days of the early '90s. I couldn't even access the result anywhere until the day after the game. Perhaps the fact that even viewers in the UK were treated to adverts instead of Dan Gosling's extra-time winner as ITV cocked up their transmission at the seminal moment was a further sign that my stars were aligning themselves in a very ominous configuration. My subscription for *The Weekly Telegraph* then inexplicably became messed up in an online banking manoeuvre that went wrong and suddenly my two greatest pleasures in life that provided sanctuary from the madness of running Rainbow; live Everton matches and a weekly immersion into the news from Blighty, had been curtailed.

A fortnight later the house next door to us in Kampala converted into a mosque. Without warning a call to prayer was being broadcast into our living room at 5.45am and 7.05pm every day out of some hideous tin speakers mounted on the roof of our neighbours. Such were the contours of the landscape where we lived, one of the speakers was directed literally straight into our living room. I protested and I fought and I raged, almost to the point of having a fatwa issued against me, but there was no way that I could win this battle against the forces of Islam. After searching for alternative accommodation, my family and I finally vacated the house that we had come to feel as home five months later with our nerves in shreds.

As I said, in hindsight, I might have traced this trail of woe back to the moment that the new headmaster was recruited into Rainbow's corridors of power. I might then have concluded that my days were numbered and maybe I might then have saved myself the torture of fighting a losing battle and quit 18 months earlier. The Muslims were evidently offering a precursor to the events that lay ahead in my life, a symbolic representation of the bigger picture, our eviction from our humble abode at Allah's behest a metaphor for the bigger displacement looming not far ahead. Even Dan Gosling proved to be a harbinger of false hope and a symbol of an uncertain future. We didn't win the FA Cup, losing 2–1 to Chelsea in the Final and he himself abandoned us for Newcastle United after promising so much. From Derby Hero to Blue Zero in the space of 18 months; about the same time it took for Sabas and those pulling his strings to seal my demise.

Chapter 29
Persecution complex

7 March 2010: Everton 5 Hull City 1

(The game when 'Persecution Complex' came to the public's attention in issue no 107 of *Speke from the Harbour*)

There should be a label for it; a psychologist's syndrome to explain the phenomenon. Why is it that when something new comes into our lives, we soon become so familiar with it, so attached to it, that we simply can not do without it even when we had existed for much of our lives in blissful ignorance of whatever it is that has now invaded our everyday routines? How many people in the developed world now could survive without a mobile phone? Well, I could actually, I hate the things, but, ignoring Luddites like me, there are many people in their '40s and beyond whose mobile phone is now an appendix to their anatomy even though for a vast majority of their lives they did not have access to such an instrument. And what about the MP3 player, the microwave, the car, the light bulb? Indeed, living in Uganda, you soon come to realise how completely dependent we are on electricity and running water. In my early days in Kampala before we could afford the luxury of a generator or an inverter, our family would suffer three hours of abject inconvenience every second evening as we had to rely on gas lamps or rechargeable lights to see us through to the return of electricity at around 10pm. At approximately 7 o'clock on the scheduled evenings we would wait with a dull sense of inevitability for the lights to silently die and send the house into a depressing gloom for the duration of the power cut. After fumbling around to put our two little boys to bed, I would use the lack of electricity as an excuse to quietly wallow in my thoughts over a few beers on the balcony looking at the twinkling lights of the opposite hill where they were afforded the luxury of electricity on the nights that we weren't. For Violet, as head of boarding, she had to struggle on for the evening organising night time prep under the unreliable light of the rechargeable lamps.

I refer to 'the luxury of electricity' because, in some parts of the world it is just that. In Uganda, running water is also not always a given. In fact, dry taps, in my opinion, are a much greater hardship than having no power supply. Having learnt to live with the annoyance of frequent black-outs and water shortages, it was such a pleasure to see things improve during my decade at Rainbow but how the anguish was multiplied on the rare occasions that the infrastructure failed us in the latter years. Having become accustomed to the 'luxury' it seemed so much harder to accept its withdrawal. There were times in the early days of Rainbow when we could go two or three days at school with no electricity at all. The school still functioned and the teachers grinned and bore it. In the last five years or so, teachers, newly arrived from the UK would cause a storm of indignation and threaten industrial action if the internet connection failed for half an hour. Perhaps it should be called the 'They don't know they're born Syndrome' or 'The Law of Instantly Diminished Memory'. I have to say, though, that towards the end of my time in Uganda, I became quite afflicted by the condition myself, in particular when it came to the satellite television broadcasting of live football from the UK. After GTV had come and gone in a fleeting 18 months rush, the old faithful DSTV, shunned by the masses when GTV outbid them for a majority of the live English football, were left to clear up the mess left by these fly-by-nights as they fled from their creditors. They made a valiant effort but, as the following article submitted by me and published in the Everton fanzine *Speke from the Harbour* in March 2010 demonstrates, they did not completely succeed in my opinion. The article was called Persecution Complex and went something like this:

Note: A nomenclature of key terms unique to the fanzine and Evertonians in general is given at the end of the chapter for those not familiar with them.

'I suppose that when you support a team that has not been able to defend its League title on two occasions due to the inconvenience of World Wars and had one of its more recent League wins blighted by the Heysel tragedy and the consequent ban of British clubs from European competition, it is inevitable that you start to think that there really is something personal about the way the world treats Everton. To accentuate this feeling of injustice, our lovable Norwegian[1] friends who occupy an enclave of the good city of Liverpool not a million miles from Goodison Park, seem to have every bit of good fortune that God has on offer. Even when we finished in that hallowed fourth position five years ago, the automatic qualification for the Champions League that usually accompanies it was not quite such a foregone conclusion for a few nervous weeks as it looked like we were to be kicked out of the prestigious competition by our neighbours without us even kicking a ball just as was the case twenty years earlier. Different circumstances but the same stench of iniquity nonetheless. Even now as we chase down an improbable European place after our disastrous start to the season, the one team above us that will lose no points at all if Portsmouth go out of business while we go backwards three points is those clueless Reds who benefit simply by being so inept that they managed to lose to a team with no money, no morale and almost no points.

To add to the conspiracy theories there is Clive Thomas, Pierluigi Collina, Mark Clattenberg and don't even get me started on the way we are completely ignored by Sky when it comes to coverage of the Europa League. But am I just seeing things through blue tinted glasses? Perhaps I just need to get some perspective on the matter or just get a life!

Out here in Uganda, though, I have to say I think I have genuine cause to believe that every negative vibe is tuned to the detriment of Everton Football Club. It is not so much some supernatural signals that are conspiring against us; more like satellite signals. There is virtually a monopoly of the airwaves here on the African continent when it comes to satellite television providers. Apart from the odd rogue station emanating from India or such like, the dominant force in this market is a station based in South Africa called DSTV. Now, don't get me wrong, it does a fine job. We can switch onto BBC, Sky, CNN, Al Jazeera and a plethora of movie channels at the jab of a remote control button. There is the History Channel, National Geographic and enough food channels to feed Africa three times over. There are seemingly hundreds of kids' channels churning out hours and hours of cartoons and Hannah Montana and then there are the nerve grinding music channels that make me wonder if I ever really was a teenager. Does what they listen to now really sound the same as the Sex Pistols and the Jam sounded to me thirty years ago?

And then we come to the sports channels. Let me go through them: Channel 200 (Supersport Blitz) which shows a constant loop of updated sports action from around the world as well as the odd hour of Sky Sports News here and there. Channels 201, 202, 205 and 206 (Supersport 1, 2, 5 and 6) show live tennis, cricket, athletics, golf and any other significant sport going on around the world. Channels 203, 207 and, occasionally 205 (Supersport 3, 7 and… yes, yes, you get the picture) are dedicated to live or recorded footie including every single premiership match, FA Cup, Mickey Mouse Cup[2], Serie A, La Liga, the Portuguese League, all international matches both friendly and competitive, Champions League and, yes, even the Europa League. Channel 209 is some sort of add-on filled in with stuff no one wants to see like Liverpool FC TV. Channel 211 is another footie channel only in Portuguese which meant that I could actually see Everton v Sporting Lisbon with Portuguese commentary if I wanted to, which I didn't, so I watched it live on Supersport 7 instead. Then there is ESPN and ESPN Classic which is great for watching archives of major sporting events or oddities like the 1970s BBC Superstars presented by David Vine and Ron Pickering; do you remember that? Malcolm Macdonald taking on David Hemery at 100m; great stuff. Those of you following this closely and not distracted by the thought of MacDonald's bandy legs will wonder where Supersport 4 and 8 have gone to. Supersport 8 is actually called Maximo and is sport in Spanish, I think; I never watch it. As for Supersport 4, most of us on this continent wonder what happened to that. Even if you pay the full subscription of $65 per month, you get nothing on that channel. And maybe that is the black hole that Everton falls through.

You see, you might think that, with such an array of sports viewing options, my thirst for all things sporting would be permanently sated. But that assumption overlooks the fact that I am an ardent Evertonian; therefore, I am not just passionate about my club, I am ultra-sensitive to any suggestion that we are being discriminated against.

To get into the Fat Spanish Waiter[3] Syndrome let me continue as follows:

Fact: On 22nd February 2009 Newcastle v Everton is advertised to be live on Supersport 6. Strange because Supersport 6 doesn't usually show football.

Fact: On that fateful Sunday afternoon when Anichebe and Arteta are put out of action for a season we have Fulham v WBA and the Norwegians v Money City[4] live on DSTV. I am reduced to listening to the St James's Park bloodbath through the haze of World Service. That is until 5 minutes from the end when the BBC suddenly, inexplicably, infuriatingly ends transmission to give us some incomprehensible Swahili programme.

Fact: On 4th March 2009 Blackburn v Everton is advertised to be live on Supersport 6. Strange because Supersport 6 doesn't usually show football.

Fact: On that depressing Wednesday evening we are subjected to watching Manure[5] get a jammy win at Newcastle live on Supersport 3. Even as the ticker tape announces as it threads its way across the bottom of the St James's Park scene that Blackburn v Everton is now on Supersport 6, I switch to that channel to find something completely different and completely and utterly uninteresting being shown.

Fact: Until just before the F.A.Cup semi-finals last year not a single F.A.Cup match for 2009 had been shown in highlights form or live on our only English football TV provider here in Africa. Suddenly due to the furore caused by the local Manure fans, our semi-final is broadcast live (as is the other semi-final I should add). DSTV are clearly upset at the outcome and, although the Cup Final is briefly advertised as to be shown live on 30th May, surreptitiously it disappears from the trailers. The penny drops with me and probably many others with about 2 weeks to go to the final that our beloved South African TV station has actually decided it isn't worth transmitting a Cup Final if Manure are not part of it. Exactly why they change their minds on 29th May and decide to show the Wembley showpiece after all is a mystery. I like to think my abusive emails and phone calls have some effect but, up against arrogance like DSTV, I think I'm deluding myself. There must have been some other self-serving motive. I mean, this a station and a country that fills an hour of airtime every Monday evening with a phone-in programme that never deviates beyond the 'The Big Fat Boring Four'. I suppose DSTV would say that they are only serving their market. They are not there to educate the South African masses that there is actually a world beyond (and, yes, below) Manure, Cheatski[6], Arsenal and the Norwegians. But they don't have to reinforce it with comments like (after our 2–2 draw at the Emirates) 'I've just received excited text messages from all the Everton fans in South Africa…all three of them!' Did the white pundit realise what an insult he had just dealt to his own country by that remark? Maybe he had a point, though, in deducing that a country that locked up Nelson Mandela for 27 years for being black, hasn't the collective intelligence to understand that football is about more than just money and winning. Mind you it wasn't the blacks who locked up Mandela so we know he is actually only referring to a certain section of the South African populace. i.e. a section that would not include Steven Pienaar, if you get my meaning.

Anyway, back to the theme and onto the 2009/10 season.

Fact: On 25th October 2009 Bolton v Everton is advertised as live on Supersport 6. Strange because Supersport 6 doesn't usually show football (yawn!).

Fact: As Everton's season seems to plunge to another depth, I haven't even got the pleasure of watching us score two goals in an exciting game, as the DSTV soccer channels are jammed with The Norwegians v Manure and Money City v Fulham made worse by Lescott scoring his first goal for Money. Unlike every other premiership game of the season thus far, Bolton v Everton isn't even shown as a recorded match.

Fact: On 31st October 2009 Everton v Aston Villa is advertised as live on Supersport 7. It then mysteriously gets switched to the soccer graveyard of Supersport 6. We all know what that means. At least we all have the pleasure of watching the Norwegians lose 3–1 at Fulham on Supersport 3.

Fact: Of course, Everton v Villa is not shown live. It is then advertised to be shown recorded at 2 o'clock in the morning. I mess up my weekend by staying up to watch the uninspiring 1–1 draw.

Fact: On January 28th 2010 Everton v Sunderland is to be shown recorded at 1.00am on Supersport 3.

Fact: Having kept up to date with the scores while watching Manure reach the Mickey Mouse final, I prepare myself to watch the first half only of Everton v

Sunderland from Goodison as that's when both goals were scored. After all I have work next day. I settle down in my Everton kit ready for an enjoyable forty-five minutes but what appears? Despite the information bar actually saying Everton v Sunderland from Goodison Park, Cheatski v Birmingham unfolds before my very eyes. What makes this even more galling is that the Cheatski match has just been shown live on Supersport 7 while Manure v Money was on Supersport 3. In other words Cheatski v Birmingham is shown twice both live and recorded straight after each other while Everton v Sunderland is not shown at all.

Fact: On 31st January Wigan v Everton is advertised to be broadcast at 10.00am on the Sunday after the game is actually played.

Fact: Very sociable hour, I think. Thank you, DSTV, I think. But then, I think, actually Everton have won and DSTV hate Everton so it won't be shown. Surely they can't be this blatant, though. Oh yes they can! Despite the information bar claiming that Wigan v Everton from the DW Stadium is now showing we actually have the worst game of the weekend between West Ham and Blackburn being served up before us. A match that they had already shown a few hours earlier in the middle of the night incidentally. Wigan v Everton? That is not shown at all.

Fact: On 10th Feb 2010 Everton v Cheatski is to be shown live on Supersport 7 according to the DSTV schedules. Two days before the event it gets doomed to Supersport 6 as Villa v Manure is on Supersport 7 and Arsenal v The Norwegians is on Supersport 3.

Fact: Of course, I am reduced to getting latest scores on the ticker tape displayed in front of the beautiful match at the Emirates which also states that I can watch the game live from Goodison on Supersport 6 if I wish. Can I bollocks! At least the game is recorded at 1.00am and, obviously I'm prepared to wreck my Thursday work output by restricting myself to three hours sleep to watch The Tart[7] present us with our first win against Cheatski for nearly a decade.

Whenever I phone the people at DSTV in the local office they give the same information that is falsely advertised on the screen. When I ask why they are lying, they say it is the information they get from South Africa. Can a subscriber contact DSTV head office directly? That's about as possible as the people of Soweto rising above a dollar a day.

Communication is a problem in Africa; it has a lot to do with a lack of money and poor infrastructure but what does a multi-million pound, white dominated monopoly specialising in communication, for God's sake, have as its excuse for constantly giving the viewers garbage information and why is it always Evertonians that get the worst of it? They would not dare treat their beloved Manure following with such disdain. But they actually do not treat the fans of any other Premier League club with such utter contempt. One of the main presenters of their football programmes is that lanky, blond former Manure goalie from the eighties, Gary Bailey. In the recent Merseyside derby he suggested at half time that Fellaini might have faked injury to avoid being red carded after the Greek oaf[8] was sent off in that awful tackle. Some fake injury that puts a player out of action for 6 months! Would he have made any such comment against a Manure player or, indeed a Portsmouth or Wigan player? I am so convinced now that DSTV hates Everton that I think I know the answer to that question.

I will copy this to the DSTV head office in Randburg and give them chance to respond. If they do I will forward it to SFTH. I suspect, though, they will merely dismiss it as the anguish of some crackpot supporter of an insignificant team. They probably don't understand the hyperbole, the obsession for detail, the negative generalisation of a whole people and the nasty monikers being used; but that's because they don't understand the irrational language of truly passionate football fans. After all, most of them support Manure! As we say when the fans hurl their abuse from the terraces, I have paid my money (subscription) and I'm entitled to my opinion. It's now up to DSTV to explain the catalogue of misinformation and disregard shown to their viewers listed above.

Evertonians, a persecution complex? Nonsense. That's just a vicious rumour started by someone who hates us!'

So, there you are. What a transformation. Having suffered all those years of World Service wilderness trying to hear the Everton result through the hiss and pop of the short wave signal, I was now whipped into a violent froth by the fact that the Everton matches, even quite meaningless ones, were not being shown live and in their entirety on my 37in flat TV screen. Was it the heat or my age that was taking its toll, or was it simply the pressure being exerted on me by the nonsense going on day-to-day in the upper echelons of Rainbow International School. Or was it simply a very severe manifestation of 'The Law of Instantly Diminished Memory' that had gripped me? Whatever it was, it was probably time to leave.

Notes

1. Liverpool FC are commonly referred to as the Norwegians because of their strong support in far flung places well away from the city from which they herald.

2. Football League Cup. This derogatory term may change if we ever win the thing!

3. Rafa Benitez

4. Manchester City

5. Manchester United

6. Chelsea

7. John Terry who was having some unsuccessful times with newspaper injunctions at the time

8. Sotirios Kyrgiakos

Chapter 30
'Hum, hum, hum'

2 April 2011: Everton 2 Aston Villa 2

Following the furore caused by my leaked email with those disparaging comments about Mr Sabas, I had a period of about two months to sort out the numerous issues that need to be sorted out when one leaves a country where one has been resident for nearly 12 years; Violet was staying in Uganda until the end of the school year in July with the children, so at least the selling of our personal effects could happen over six months instead of two, but there was a bureaucratic forest that I had to negotiate before I could head for Entebbe airport for my final departure. This included the reclaim of my NSSF money, the equivalent of national insurance contributions made over the previous 11½ years, and the obtaining of my police clearance certificate to state that I had not strayed on to the wrong side of the law during my time in Uganda. Sabas tried to put me on the wrong side of the law, issuing a writ from his lawyer for defamation allegedly caused by that private email that I had sent to some friends but that one of his acolytes had intercepted and then had her mischief with. He was persuaded to drop the case by the owners of Rainbow not wishing to see their school receive more adverse publicity than it already had with the eruption caused by my leaving. I learnt at the time that I would have had a clear legal defence of 'honest opinion' but testing the technicalities of the law of a foreign country was not something that I had the stomach, time or wallet for at this time.

All this traipsing around various offices in Kampala allowed me to stay in Uganda until Christopher's 14th birthday on 13 March 2011. We celebrated it with a family night at The Golf Course Hotel. It was a very pleasant way to say goodbye to a country that I had become deeply attached to and to say farewell to my family for four months.

Around 50 people from the Rainbow staff and the local community dressed themselves up in green and came to see me off at the airport. They even hired a bus to transport the many who did not have the means to travel to Entebbe. It was emotional and incredibly flattering to see so many people waving to me as I went into the departure lounge, many in tears. Not one of those well-wishers was white. At my leaving party at Colours Club about a month earlier almost 150 attended. Among them four whites. This was most definitely a white *coup d'état*. Clearly I was not seen as white enough by many of my compatriots and, with that email, I had finally presented them with an open goal to do something about it. And up until then I had had no idea just how much the whites disliked me. How naive is that? And, in a strange way, how proud does that make me feel?

So, as Sabas continued to wrestle with the unrest in his school and the pile of death threats building up in his in-tray, I headed into a brand new world far removed from the maelstrom I had left behind. As I touched down at Heathrow on a cold March morning, I had many challenges ahead.

Priorities are priorities, though, and that first trip to Goodison Park was high on the agenda. For one reason or another, it didn't happen until 2 April. I drove up to Liverpool from Shrewsbury. With such fond memories of my two years in Shropshire I had chosen to relocate the family in the town that had launched my teaching career. I bought my ticket for the Upper Gwladys Street from the box office at around 11am and then headed for a pub near the ground. Being the third week of Lent, I drank orange juice as I watched West Ham v Man United on the big screen while a rather irritating Liverpool fan tried to strike up a conversation with me. Having had my fill of this gentleman as well as West Ham's second half capitulation, I departed the pub with 20 minutes of the match remaining to make my way to my spiritual home. In 22 years I had visited the home of Everton just 14 times, usually for one of the opening fixtures of a season during a summer break in England before I returned to Uganda. As I took my seat in the rickety, wooden stand and viewed the lush green turf, I felt as if I was truly back home and I texted Chris to that effect. For the first time since early 1989 I was going to a match at Goodison Park without the thought in the back of my head that such days were numbered. It was a highly entertaining 2–2 draw. There was a tinge of disappointment at the two lost points as

Beckford's shot crashed over the line from the underside of the crossbar but was not seen by the officials (oh, for goal line technology), but overall I felt a glow of satisfaction at the resurrection of what, for me, is the ultimate Saturday afternoon experience. As apoplectic fans raged on 6.06 on my car radio both in favour and against Rooney for his spittle laden verbal attack on a Sky camera at Upton Park earlier in the day, I drove the familiar route from Liverpool to my parents' home in Andover in the lengthening shadows of an extended sunny spring evening reflecting on how good life could be from here on in and how Wayne Rooney is so adept at polarising the opinion of the British public.

That four hour drive to surprise my mum for Mother's Day in the warmth of an English evening and the glow of bright future prospects proved to be a false dawn. No doubt much of my light-headed and light-hearted mood that day in April was borne out of the relief from having left the cauldron of Rainbow International School. Bowed by the daily pressure of having to lower my expectations and standards to meet the requirements of those around me, when I had mistakenly believed my role to be to raise the performance of the school's management, the release of this burden distorted my perspective on what lay ahead. Obviously being so far from the family did not make things easy especially knowing how Violet and the children were now being singled out by elements of the Rainbow staff for their perceived betrayal. In true African style, those seen as supporters of The Greens were threatened and marginalised. Sabas was showing that he had learnt some lessons during his 25 years or so living on the African continent; his methods were devious and quite brutal in trying to persuade others to support him. In the case of most of the white teachers coercion was not required.

And that is the paradox. I had left behind a school where the only people I was out of touch with were my own. I had gone to Africa more than two decades earlier with an open mind and little prior knowledge. I would recommend that that is the way that anyone should approach such an assignment. By having a blank page, anything can be written on it, no preconceived ideas have to be crossed out, no prejudices need a blob of Tippex to be obliterated knowing that they can be scratched open again in the future. Sadly most expatriates, particularly British, go to the developing world with their canvas already full of a clear picture and they are very reluctant to have their predetermined image altered in any way. And it is a state of mind, nothing more, nothing less. Many people think that cramming the basic grammar and vocabulary of a 'Teach yourself Swahili' book picked up in WH Smith before they board the plane will somehow bridge the cultural divide and make them accepted by the locals of the East African region. How wrong they are and not just because Swahili has all but died out from anywhere west of Nairobi. Typical of a Brit, my ability to learn foreign tongues has been stymied throughout my life by acute self-consciousness and the cop out that virtually everyone speaks English anyway (which is actually the case in East Africa). My A grade in O level French at school promised much more than I have ever delivered in the rest of my life. I'm ashamed to say that I can barely speak a word of Luganda which is the predominant tribal language of central Uganda and can speak even less Lugisu, the language of my wife. My knowledge of Swahili is non-existent. I also have to say that I do not travel well when it comes to the acceptance of different foods. My taste buds seem to have an intransigence that my mind thankfully does not share. I can categorically say that I find all the staple foods of East Africa quite unpalatable with the exception of cassava which I thoroughly enjoy and miss in England. So, I don't like the food and I don't know the language; how is it possible that so many Ugandans were willing to risk their jobs and spend their pittance to give me such a touching and spectacular send-off? It was truly humbling. Perhaps humility was the key ingredient on both sides.

And since I have been back in the UK, I have realised that humility is not in great abundance among the people of these shores. When thinking of what makes a solid society, I am left to hesitate. Hum, hum, hum. Is it the three hums? Humour, humanity and humility. By these criteria, both East Africa and the UK fall short. There is plenty of humour in both. In Uganda and Kenya it is a general disposition created from living in a warm climate where time and details are not regarded as being as important as they are in the UK. As a foreigner, the removal of rigidity, the absence of the health and safety culture, allowed me to enjoy the day-to-day living without fear and with a smile on my face. My default state of mind in East Africa was of good humour. Did it compensate for the inconvenience of a fractured infrastructure, with potholes, power cuts and, yes, the unreliability of DSTV? Towards the end, probably not. But there was usually a funny side to be found in everyday life and everyday situations. In England, the humour is more structured; the telling of jokes and the wit contained in day-to-day conversations. I have to say, referring back to my leaving speech in the Shrewsbury Sixth Form staff room all those years ago, that I am once again a great fan of *Coronation Street* simply for the repartee and underlying humour of most of the characters. A society in which I can function properly has to be oiled with humour and East Africa and the UK, in different ways, both qualify on that count.

Humanity is an essential ingredient for any society, in my opinion. Sadly much of sub-Saharan Africa fails in this respect. The brutality meted out on opposition politicians and their supporters, the beating of children, the violence towards women, the intolerance of homosexuals, the exploitation of workers earning less than a dollar a day, the list goes on. These all contribute to a dysfunctional society. It is sad that the vulnerable and oppressed in sub-Saharan Africa often have to look to the West for their salvation and protection. They cannot trust their own leaders to provide it. It's a dog eat dog society and compassion is trampled to death in the stampede for survival. As a foreigner with a conscience living in Africa, you have to turn a blind eye to much day-to-day cruelty. My way of coping was to try to introduce some humanity into the lives of those that I had contact with by, for example, improving the rights and the wages of the most downtrodden workers at Rainbow. I largely failed in that particular quest because there is virtually no employee protection from the employer in Uganda and, much as I was the line manager to most of the two hundred people that worked at Rainbow by the time I left, I was never their employer. By trying to improve their lot, though, it allowed me to sleep peacefully at night and, it seems from the emotional assembly that gathered at Entebbe airport on 14 March, my intentions and effort had been recognised.

Good education and true, untainted democracy will eventually provide this milk of human kindness that appears to be missing from large sections of the African community but they evolve over a long period of time. The UK has a substantial head start on East Africa in that respect. So, 2–1 to the UK with just the quality of humility to be tested.

During my years abroad I noted a change in the type of expatriates arriving at the gates of the various schools that I worked at. In the early days of Kenya, there were still remnants of the pioneering spirit of yore and an attitude of wanting to muck in with whatever was presented to them. They perhaps didn't all have the sticking power that I possessed as demonstrated by the fact that so many left Braeburn without honouring their contract, although they would, no doubt, cite the mass break-in of the staff apartments as mitigating circumstances for their exodus. Gradually, though, the nature of these new arrivals changed. Out of the nappies of the nanny state for the first time, they seemed much less adventurous, much more dependent on their communication gadgets. The umbilical cord stretching back home provided by their mobile phone and the internet meant that they never truly immersed themselves in their new environment; they were global villagers but not local villagers. And through that umbilical cord deep seated views and an immutable philosophy rammed into them by their parent state, was reinforced.

With each passing year, the trepidation brought on by a culture where accidents have been replaced by lawsuits, accountability usurped by a blame culture, has turned British travellers into rather timid creatures without the will or courage to adapt. Danger or the unknown were no longer to be faced with an element of fearlessness or, indeed, humour, but with a risk assessment form and a 'get out' clause. While I embraced the freedom of a culture where accidents were accepted as a regular part of life, they were frightened by it and felt it their responsibility to impose their own safer, oppressive culture on those around them. So many times, I was told by a British teacher, barely off the plane, that 'In England we…' I tended to switch off at that point to save myself having to make the patronising retort that 'You may not have noticed, but you are no longer in England'. Clearly that attitude permeates to the local population and so barriers are formed. To me it became a British disease of arrogance but I also perceived it as a lack of confidence and trust in their own ability to understand and accept their hosts. And here is the rub; we, as expatriates are all guests, foreigners, visitors. Would we go to someone's house as a guest and start rearranging the furniture or telling our hosts how to run their home? I wouldn't. Therefore, I wouldn't do the same in someone's country that they have been kind enough to let me live in. People who think that it is fine to throw their weight about as soon as they touch down in a new country clearly harbour a sense of superiority over their hosts. How else do you explain such behaviour?

These expatriates were simply reflecting the society from which they had come, though. In a succession of recent cases we have seen politicians and bankers and media executives all being forced to show contrition and remorse because they wouldn't do so of their own volition. The idea of saying sorry is regarded as weak or defeatist. Children believe that they have rights and entitlements without any concept of respect or responsibility that should be the flip side to the deal. Humility brings a softer, less hostile community. I have found England quite harsh since my return; courtesy, politeness and gentleness are seen as qualities of little value; humility is almost redundant. Politicians in Africa, of course, are not noted for their humility and, with the absence of humanity as well, they can end up being tyrannical and murderous. We do not need to list the most notorious culprits here. And because of the ruthless pursuit of limited resources, notably money, that goes on daily on the African continent, many African leaders in other walks of life also show little inclination to accept the contribution of God and others in their achievements. Among the middle and lower classes like the Ugandan teachers in Rainbow, though, there is nothing but warmth and friendship displayed. Living in that atmosphere of mutual respect, gentleness and humility on a day-to-day basis, made life so pleasant.

England, by comparison, is full of sharp edges and hessian roughness. There is no doubt that the fear imposed by authority in this country has moulded the character of its people. People are scared to say sorry because an admission of guilt may cost thousands of pounds. A school receptionist would not even recommend a local doctor for our children because she was not allowed to be seen to prejudice our decision; an estate agents will not issue a map to show you how to get to a property for sale because it will infringe the copyright of Ordnance Survey. And yet this avoiding of eggshells leads, not only to the erosion of personal initiative and original thought but also to an unfairness and the unbalancing of society in favour of the criminal. People in positions of responsibility have to weigh up every angle even in the most straightforward cases lest they overlook the rights of some individual or expose themselves to a legal loophole. Common sense becomes less common and decisions make no sense as the rights of the perpetrator are considered often to the detriment of the victim. I will give a brief personal example to illustrate this point.

Chris and Vince are keen and quite able footballers. I was, therefore, eager to involve them in a local football team in Shrewsbury as soon as I could. I wanted to start up my own team but was soon deterred by the red tape of CRBs and coaching qualifications. The boys asked around and found a team to play for, though, and it just happened that the team they found was looking for someone to coach it. I offered my services and was instantly put on a level 1 FA coaching course and had my CRB certificate updated. I paid the full fees for the two boys to play for the whole season. I subsequently learnt that Vince was too young to play in that particular team missing the cut-off date by 15 days. Initially I was angered by the intransigence of the FA but soon found out that the guy in charge of the club for which I had volunteered to coach its Under-15s had actually misled me. He had lied that special dispensation would be given to Vince by the FA as his birthday was so close to the cut-off point. On discovering that the FA had actually made no such promise and so the guy in charge of the club had taken the money for Vince's registration under false pretences, I requested a refund of the £80. He refused. We reached an impasse and he eventually 'sacked' me as the Under-15s coach after just three games in charge. I complained to the Shropshire FA. Having initially said that they were grateful to me for putting my complaint in writing because they had had many problems with this particular club manager in the past, they then had a hearing and decided that actually I was not entitled to my £80 back (nor incidentally any of the £90 that I had paid for Chris who had also been banished from the club evidently because of his recalcitrant father).

It was a convenient solution for the Shropshire FA to make because the club had paid for my coaching course. It completely ignored the morality of the case. I had been duped into paying £80 on the promise that Vince would have a season of football and then I was denied the opportunity to coach a team because I had had the temerity to object to the criminal action of an individual who the Shropshire FA admitted was a notorious problem case. In the end, though, the Shropshire FA were evidently too scared to confront this guy when push came to shove because presumably that may have involved upsetting him too much and who knows where a nasty character like that might find support? The European Convention on Human Rights possibly? I assume that this deranged character is still allowed to continue cheating and undermining referees with impunity, concerns that I also catalogued in my letter. I was not even afforded the courtesy of attending the hearing to give my evidence so who knows what the guy was allowed to get away with. No wonder the FA's respect campaign is in tatters. No wonder England will never ever win the World Cup. Without moral courage at the top, an institution can never fully succeed. In the modern British society, moral courage, like common sense, has been forfeited for the avoidance of some obscure legal eventuality that might result. The rights of innocent people are sacrificed. People are scared. The Shropshire FA were scared.

My wife's response to this little story is perhaps most revealing. She simply shrugged and accepted the blame for allowing me to be daft enough to pay the full £170 registration fees in advance. Coming from a culture where the ordinary people on the street accept the word of authority without question or dissent, she was according the Shropshire FA a similar misplaced deference. Also, she knew that in her country you do not trust a relative stranger with such a significant amount of money. In Uganda, economic conditions dictate that many people, often unintentionally, default on their debts and obligations. They mean well but simply find they run out of money. It is wise, therefore, not to offer the temptation of major upfront payments. Naively, I had believed that I had entered back into a culture where people were honest and not so financially strapped that they would defraud me of £80 on the pretence of my son being able to participate in a football match every Sunday. It seems that Violet's judgment of character was more perspicacious than mine; it seems that somewhere over the past 22 years the cultures of our two countries had become intertwined. How dare the whites of Rainbow consider themselves a superior race!

So East Africa scores on humility and the UK fails dismally. In the match between East African culture versus British culture it's another 2–2 draw. Bermuda strangely, on similar criteria, I would probably give a score of three for its adults but nil for its youth!

It has been a memorable journey since the day I left England on 1 September 1989. There is some legacy for me to look back on with fondness; the massive fundraising events in Bermuda, the numerous sports events in Africa and the very existence of Hillside High School which still survives to this day under the stewardship of Jim Park who proved me wrong all those years ago and remains an eccentric but effective leader of the school that I helped create. Well done, Jim. You've done a remarkable job. Sadly, I cannot say the same of Rainbow International School or its leaders. Any legacy that I may have left there has now been destroyed and it is already unrecognisable from the establishment I developed so painstakingly over 11 years. No doubt even its motto, shared with Everton Football Club, *Nil satis nisi optimum,* will soon also be erased from its signposts and stationery and, indeed from the front reception where I had it painted above the main entrance in 2001. Perhaps the loss of a motto that translates to 'only the best is good enough' should be considered a fitting comment on the direction the school is now taking rather than a snub to its originator. Time will tell.

Since my international teaching career began I have learnt much about myself and about the society and life that I desire. I left this land as a 27-year-old, single, unworldly and naive. I returned having completed almost half a century on this planet with a beautiful family, somewhat more knowledgeable of the world but still naive. I left England as a country where people seemed happier, lawyers were less prominent and the pursuit of celebrity status was less manic. I've returned to a country where people have less time for conversation or each other, harangued by the bombardment of advertising, social networking and competition. The intrusive and ubiquitous phenomenon of reality television, unheard of in 1989, has brought with it a generation of armchair travellers and eroded the sense of adventure. I have been round housing estates in Shrewsbury in the middle of the school holidays and found not a single child out playing. And then we come to the main focus of this entire book; football.

I left behind, in 1989, an English First Division with a fairly equitable distribution of wealth and the unpredictability of the League its most alluring characteristic. A League, where the success or failure of a club depended much more on the abilities of the manager rather than the obscene amounts of money in the bank, where Millwall had just finished above Manchester United in the First Division and Chelsea and Manchester City had just completed a season in the second tier. Even Liverpool's invincibility had been broken by that wonderful last minute win by Arsenal at Anfield immortalised in *Feverpitch*. It was also the immediate aftermath of the Hillsborough tragedy and four years after the Heysel disaster and the subsequent European ban for English clubs. I returned in 2011 to all-seater stadia, exorbitant prices and a sterility brought on by the fact that the League title is virtually decided in August rather than May, or at least the two or three only contenders can be listed then. Manchester City now have entered a new financial stratosphere and ripped out the competitive element of our cherished national game in the process. If you are a supporter of football it may be that you are happy that the quality of the product has improved but, if you are a football *fan* like me then the lake of money sloshing around in the coffers of Chelsea and Manchester City, simply make for a devalued competition. Where's the fun in entering a competition that you know you have, through no fault of your own, absolutely no chance of winning? I left with Everton having finished eighth in the League and I returned to find them seventh. So Everton made slight progress in those 22 years but there was an interesting journey in between. Once again the club's life reflects that of this particular supporter. The prices and my family commitments mean that trips to watch Everton are fewer and further apart than I had envisaged when I was an *Expat Evertonian* dreaming of my return to England but I am sure that I will rectify that over time. And, despite the unlevel playing field caused by the distortion of money, I still love the English Premier League as a spectacle. *Match of the Day* is already a fixture in my new life and my very existence still ebbs and flows with the results of Everton. Sometimes an uplifting fillip, sometimes a debilitating blow, but an Everton result, no matter where in the world I am or where my life is at, can change the whole complexion of my day. How strange is that?